Leckie×Leckie

Scotland's leading educational publishers

P4/P5 Maths
Practice workbook

Age 8-10

P4/P5 Maths

Practice workbook

Tom Hall

Contents

Starter Test 4

Number – Number and Place Value
Counting 12
Numbers Beyond 1000 14
Place Value 16
Roman Numerals 18
Representing Numbers.. 20
Rounding Numbers.. 22
Negative Numbers 24

Number – Addition and Subtraction
Addition and Subtraction Practice 26
Estimating and Checking Calculations 28
Addition and Subtraction Problems 30

Number – Multiplication and Division
Multiplication and Division Facts.. 32
Mental Multiplication and Division.. 34
Factors... 36
Multiplication Practice... 38
Multiplication Problems... 40

Progress Test 1.. 42

Fractions (including Decimals)
Hundredths.. 46
Equivalent Fractions 48
Addition and Subtraction of Fractions 50
Finding Fractions... 52
Fraction and Decimal Equivalents... 54
Rounding Decimals 56
Comparing Decimals 58
Dividing by 10 and 100.. 60
Decimal Problems 62

Progress Test 2.. 64

Contents

Measurement

Comparing Measures 68

Estimating Measures 70

Converting Measures 72

Measurement Calculations 74

12 and 24 Hour Time 76

Time Problems 78

Perimeter and Area 80

Progress Test 3 82

Geometry – Properties of Shapes

2-D Shapes 86

3-D Shapes 88

Lines of Symmetry 90

Angles 92

Geometry – Position and Direction

Translations 94

Coordinates 96

Shapes and Coordinates 98

Statistics

Bar Charts 100

Time Graphs 102

Pictograms.. 104

Tables 106

Progress Test 4 108

Answers (pull-out) 113

Progress Test Charts (pull-out) 127

Starter Test

1. Write the next numbers in these sequences.

   a)
   16   20   24   28   32   36

   b) 350   400   450   500   550   600

   2 marks

2. Write seven hundred and sixty in digits. _760_

   1 mark

3. Write < or > in the circles to make each number sentence correct.

   a) 658 ◯< 685   **b)** 804 ◯< 809

   2 marks

4. Circle the number that has a digit with the value of seven tens.

   697   742   871   37   707

   1 mark

5. Write the numbers the arrows point to.

   a) _25_ ↓   b) _70_ ↓

   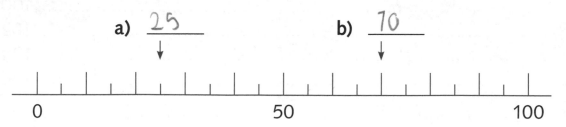

   0   50   100

   2 marks

6. Calculate:

   a)   5 2 7
      + 2 9 4
      ‾‾‾‾‾‾‾
        78 21

   b)   8 0 3
      − 2 2 7
      ‾‾‾‾‾‾‾
        5 7 6

   c)   8 3 8
      − 4 8 0
      ‾‾‾‾‾‾‾
        3 5 8

   3 marks

7. Nia has saved 389 photos on her phone. She deletes 137.

   How many photos does she have left? _252_

   1 mark

PS **8.** Ola works in a park. She plants 287 bulbs on Monday and 348 on Tuesday.

How many bulbs has she planted altogether? _635_

1 mark

9. Write the missing numbers.

a) 628 – _443_ = 185   b) 384 + _384_ = 768

2 marks

10. Harry calculates 428 + 265 = 693

Circle the inverse calculation Harry uses to check this calculation.

| 265 + 428 | | 693 + 265 | | 693 – 265 | | 428 – 265 |

1 mark

11. Work out these multiplications.

a) 18 × 3 = _____   b) 24 × 4 = _____   c) 14 × 8 = _____

3 marks

12. Work out these divisions.

a) 70 ÷ 5 = _____   b) 76 ÷ 4 = _____   c) 54 ÷ 3 = _____

3 marks

PS **13.** Carla has 4 boxes of drink cans.
Each box holds 18 cans.

How many drink cans does she have altogether? _____

1 mark

PS **14.** 69 oranges are put into packs of 3.

How many packs will there be? _____

1 mark

PS **15.** 5 sweets cost 12p.

How much would 20 sweets cost? _____p

1 mark

16. Write the fractions the arrows point to.

a) _____   b) _____

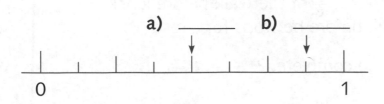

0   1

2 marks

5

PS **17.** Josef cuts a cake into ten pieces.

What fraction of the whole cake is one piece? _____

1 mark

18. Jenny buys 20 apples. $\frac{1}{5}$ of the apples are red; the rest are green.

a) How many red apples are there? _____

b) How many green apples are there? _____

c) What fraction of the apples are green? _____

3 marks

19. Write the fraction each arrow points to.

a) _____   **b)** _____

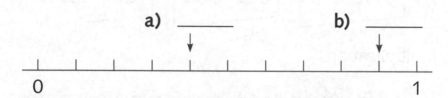

0   1

2 marks

20. Use the diagrams to find the missing numbers in these equivalent fractions.

a) [diagram] $\frac{1}{3} = \frac{\square}{6}$ **b)** [diagram] $\frac{1}{2} = \frac{\square}{8}$

2 marks

21. Write < or > in the circles to make each number sentence correct.

a) $\frac{1}{3}$ ◯ $\frac{2}{3}$ **b)** $\frac{7}{8}$ ◯ $\frac{3}{8}$

2 marks

22. Work out:

a) $\frac{1}{5} + \frac{1}{5} =$ _____   **b)** $\frac{9}{10} - \frac{6}{10} =$ _____   **c)** $\frac{1}{8} + \frac{6}{8} =$ _____

3 marks

PS **23.** A pizza is cut into ten pieces. Danny eats two of the pieces. Complete this sentence.

Danny has eaten _____-fifth of the pizza.

1 mark

PS **24.** Samir goes on a walk. He completes $\frac{3}{8}$ of the walk before lunch. He does a further $\frac{4}{8}$ of the walk before he stops for a rest.

What fraction of the walk has he completed? _____

1 mark

25. Write these lengths in order, starting with the smallest.

1 cm 1 m 1 mm

1 mark

26. Circle the longest length.

50 cm   100 mm   2 m   10 cm

1 mark

27. Write < or > in the circles to make each number sentence correct.

a) 4 kg ◯ 2000 g   **b)** 3000 g ◯ 2 kg

2 marks

PS **28.** Kate has three parcels. She writes the weights on the side of each parcel. Tick the lightest parcel.

$1\frac{1}{2}$ kg   900 g   0.5 kg

1 mark

29. Write < or > in the circles to make each number sentence correct.

a) 2 litres ◯ 400 ml   **b)** 5000 ml ◯ 1 litre

2 marks

PS **30.** Chris has three jugs. They hold 2000 ml, 4 litres and 1.5 litres.

Write the largest capacity. _____

1 mark

31. What is the mass of the parcel?

_____ kg

1 mark

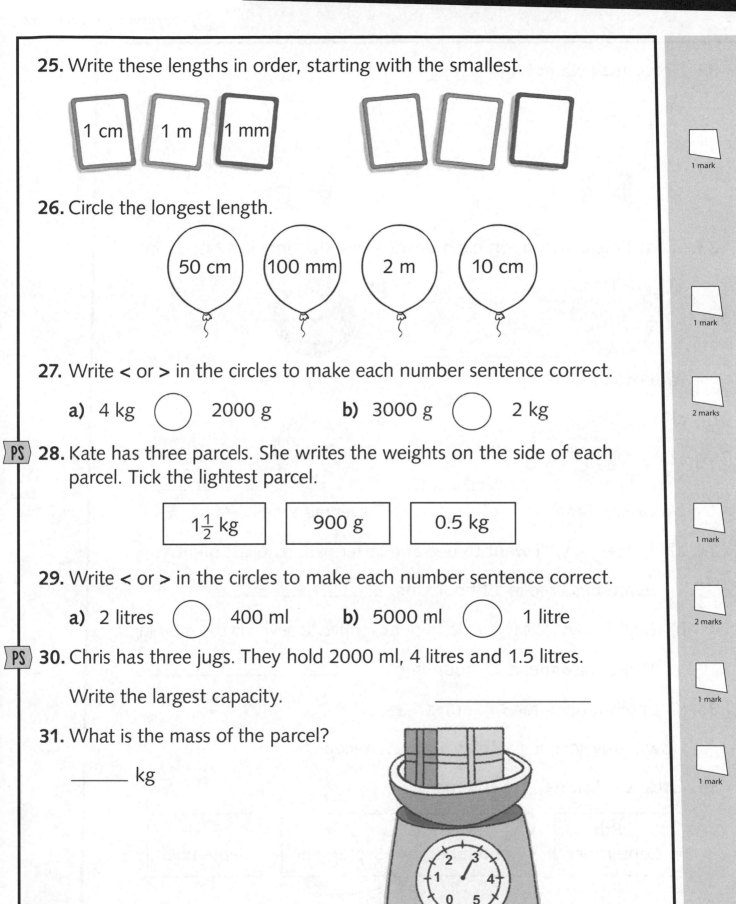

7

32. How much water is in each jug?

a)

<u>400</u> ml

b)

<u>250</u> ml

2 marks

33. What time is shown on each clock? Write the time in 12 hour time.

a)
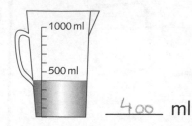
<u>2:20</u>

afternoon time

b)
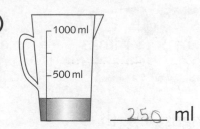
<u>9:50</u>

morning time

c)

<u>8:36</u>

morning time

d)

<u>9:45.</u>

evening time

4 marks

PS **34. a)** Kirstie says, "I went to bed at quarter past nine last night."

Write this time in 12 hour time. <u>9:15pm</u>

b) Sophie says, "I set my alarm clock for five to seven in the morning."

Write this time in 12 hour time. <u>6:55am</u>

2 marks

PS **35.** Kira boils an egg for 3 minutes.

How many seconds is this? <u>180</u> seconds

1 mark

36. Circle the last day in September.

| 28th September | 29th September | 30th September | 31st September |

1 mark

8

37. 2019 is not a leap year.

How many days will there be in 2019? _364_ days

1 mark

PS **38.** Javid's PE lesson begins at 2:20pm and finishes at 3:10pm.

How long does the PE lesson last? _50_ minutes

1 mark

39. Measure the perimeter of this rectangle.

_22 cm_

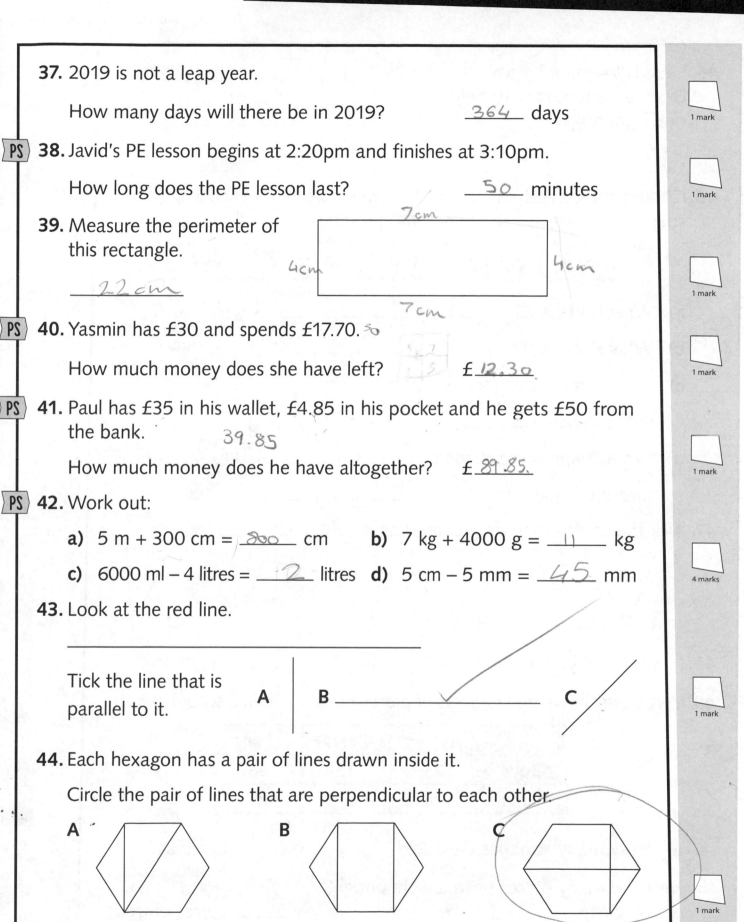

7cm

4cm   4cm

7cm

1 mark

PS **40.** Yasmin has £30 and spends £17.70. so

How much money does she have left? £ _12.30_

1 mark

PS **41.** Paul has £35 in his wallet, £4.85 in his pocket and he gets £50 from the bank.   39.85

How much money does he have altogether? £ _89.85._

1 mark

PS **42.** Work out:

a) 5 m + 300 cm = _800_ cm   b) 7 kg + 4000 g = _11_ kg

c) 6000 ml – 4 litres = _2_ litres   d) 5 cm – 5 mm = _45_ mm

4 marks

43. Look at the red line.

Tick the line that is parallel to it.

A   B _____✓   C

1 mark

44. Each hexagon has a pair of lines drawn inside it.

Circle the pair of lines that are perpendicular to each other.

A   B   C

1 mark

9

45. Here is a squared grid.
    Draw a pentagon with only
    one right angle.

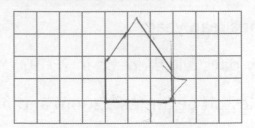

1 mark

46. Choose the correct name from the words below for each 3-D
    shape. Then answer the remaining questions.

    cylinder   cone   cube   cuboid

    a) What is shape **A**? _Cuboid_

     A

    b) What is shape **B**? _Cone_

    c) How many faces does

       shape **A** have? _6_

    B

    d) What shape is the shaded

       face on shape **B**? _Circle_

4 marks

47. Tick the angles that are greater than a right angle.

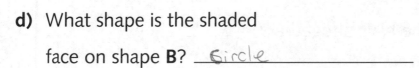

    A   B   C   D

2 marks

48. How many right angles are in a half turn? _____ right angles

1 mark

PS 49. This table shows the numbers of pieces of fruit sold in a school break.

	Apples	Pears	Bananas
Boys	23	15	28
Girls	28	9	27

    a) How many bananas were sold?   _55_ bananas

    b) How many pieces of fruit were bought
       by girls?   _63_ pieces of fruit

2 marks

PS **50.** This graph shows the number of lengths some friends swam. Altogether they swam 25 lengths.

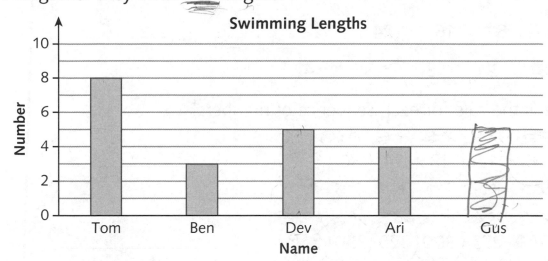

Swimming Lengths

a) Who swan 3 lengths? _ben_

b) How many more lengths did Tom swim than Dev? _3_ lengths

c) How many lengths did Gus swim? _5_ lengths

d) Complete the bar chart with the bar for Gus.

4 marks

PS **51.** This pictogram shows the number of dogs that live in four streets.

Street	Number of dogs 🐕 represents 2 dogs
Oak Street	🐕 🐕 🐕 🐕
Ivy Street	🐕 🐕 🐕
Elm Street	🐕 🐕 🐕 🐕 🐕
Ash Street	🐕 🐕 🐕 🐕

a) How many dogs live in Ash Street? _8_ dogs

b) How many more dogs live in Elm Street than in Ivy Street? _4_ dogs

c) A new street is added. 12 dogs live in Birch Street.

How many dog symbols will show 12 dogs? _6_ symbols

3 marks

Marks........./89

11

Counting

PS Problem-solving questions

Challenge 1

1 Fill in the missing terms in these sequences.

a) 0   8   16   24   32   _40_   _48_ ✓

b) 18   24   30   36   42   _48_   _54_ ✓

2 What is the rule for each sequence of numbers?

a) 6 12 18 24 30    _add 6_ ✓

b) 250 275 300 325 350    _add 25_ ✓

PS **3** Nia is counting in sevens. Will 80 be in Nia's sequence? _No_ ✓

PS **4** Poppy counts in sixes.

36   42   48   56   60

Which number is incorrect? _____

2 marks

2 marks

1 mark

1 mark

Marks.....6..... /6

Challenge 2

1 Fill in the missing terms in these sequences.

a) 18   24   30   36   _42_   _48_ ✓

b) 150   175   _200_ ✓   _225_ ✓   250   275

2 What is the rule for each sequence of numbers?

a) 70   77   84   91   98   _add 7_ ✓

b) 400   425   450   475   500   _add 25_ ✓

2 marks

2 marks

Counting

PS 3

This number grid is damaged.

What number would be in the last square?

650

275	300	325	350
375	400	425	450
475	500	525	550
575	600	625	650

1 mark

Marks........5..... /5

Challenge 3

1 Fill in the next three terms in this sequence.

 99 108 117 126 135 144 153   162 171

1 mark

2 The numbers in this sequence add the same number.
Fill in the missing terms.

| 54 | 60 | 66 | 72 | 78 |

1 mark

PS 3 Polly is counting in nines: 45   54   63   (71)   81   90

Which number is incorrect? ___71___

1 mark

4 Here is a number grid.
Moving right the numbers add 7.
Moving down the numbers add 9.
Fill in the missing numbers.

Add 7 ⟶

Add 9 ↓

21	28	35	42	49
30	37	44	51	58
39	46	53	60	67
48	55	62	69	76

1 mark

Marks.........4... /4

Total marks .....15....... /15

How am I doing?

13

Numbers Beyond 1000

PS) Problem-solving questions

Challenge 1

1 Write < or > in each circle to make these statements correct.

a) 4308 ⦵< 4380   b) 3681 ⦵> 3618   c) 5283 ⦵< 5286

3 marks

2 Tick the correct statement.

A 3670 < 3669 ☐   B 5410 < 3409 ☐   C 1872 < 2890 ☑

1 mark

3 Write these numbers in order, starting with the smallest.

3563	4645	4536	4654	3465
3465	3563	4536	4645	4654

1 mark

PS **4** Gary has these four digit cards.

What is the largest four-digit number Gary can make? 7541

1 mark

Marks.......... /6

Challenge 2

1 Write < or > in each circle to make these statements correct.

a) 5437 ⦵> 4437   b) 2718 ⦵< 2721   c) 4324 ⦵< 4342

3 marks

2 Write these numbers in order, starting with the smallest.

4831	4138	5642	5246	5264
4138	4831	5246	5264	5642

1 mark

Numbers Beyond 1000

PS **3** Tao has these five digit cards.

| 6 | 3 | 8 | 5 | 1 |

a) What is the largest three-digit number Tao can make? _865_ ✓

b) What is the smallest four-digit number Tao can make? _1356_ ✓

2 marks

Marks........ /6

Challenge 3

1 Write these numbers in order, starting with the smallest.

681 **7861** **12 612** **5891** **11 937**

681 ✓ 5891 ✓ 7861 ✓ 11937 ✓ 12612 ✓

1 mark

PS **2** Manisha writes four numbers in order, starting with the smallest.

| 6278 | 6285 | ? | 6290 |

What could the missing number be? _6289_ ✓

1 mark

PS **3** The number of people at five football matches is recorded.

Match	Number of people
Rovers vs Town	12 834
City vs Rangers	9452
United vs Albion	10 099
County vs North End	13 901
Athletic vs Wanderers	9078

Which match had the smallest number of people? ✓

Athletic vs Wanderers

1 mark

Marks........ /3

Total marks ...15..... /15   How am I doing?

Place Value

PS Problem-solving questions

Challenge 1

1 What is the value of the 4 in each of these numbers?

a) 3549 40 b) 7427 400 c) 8194 4

3 marks

2 Circle the number that has a digit with a value of 7 tens.

5752 8967 1475

1 mark

3 Circle the number that has a digit with a value of 3 hundreds.

36 341 4103

1 mark

PS **4** Arrange these numbers to make a four-digit number. 3,627

7 ones 6 hundreds 2 tens 3 thousands

1 mark

Marks...6... /6

Challenge 2

1 What is the value of the 9 in each of these numbers?

a) 7920 900 b) 6295 90 c) 9302 9000

3 marks

2 Circle the number that has a digit with a value of 8 hundreds.

8006 3890 1080

1 mark

3 Write the total of 8 + 700 + 30 + 9000. 9,738

1 mark

4 Write the total of 4 tens + 3 hundreds + 2 ones + 6 thousands. 6342

1 mark

Place Value

PS **5** Here are four digit cards.

| 4 | 3 | 5 | 6 | 2 |

a) Use any four cards to make a number larger than 5000.

6543 ✓

b) Use any four cards to make the smallest four-digit number possible.

2345 ✓

2 marks

Marks.......... /8

Challenge 3

PS **1** Jamie says, "4021 is smaller than 897 because it has smaller numbers."

Explain to Jamie why he is incorrect.

because thousends are bigger than hundreths ✓

1 mark

PS **2** Nisha is thinking of a four-digit number.
Use the clues below to work out Nisha's number. 6031

- When you add the four digits, the total is 10.
- The thousands digit is 6.
- The tens digit is half the thousands digit.
- The ones digit is 1.

1 mark

3 Work out the number that is:

a) one ten more than 9999.

9990
+100   10009 ✓

b) one hundred more than 9990 10090   10090 ✓

2 marks

Marks.......... /4

Total marks .... /18   How am I doing?

Roman Numerals

PS Problem-solving questions

Challenge 1

1 Change these Roman numerals to numbers.

a) XII __12__   b) XV __15__   c) XXVI __26__

d) VIII __8__   e) XXXIII __33__   f) XL __60__

6 marks

2 Here are some Roman calculations. Write them using numbers.

a) III + II = V   b) VI + IV = X

__3__ + __2__ = __5__   __16__ + __4__ = __10__

c) XXVI – VII = XIX

__26__ + __7__ = __19__

3 marks

PS **3** Write the time shown on each clock.

a)   b)

___04:40___   ___10:20___

2 marks

Marks.......... /11

Challenge 2

1 Change these Roman numerals to numbers.

a) LVI = __56__   b) XLVIII = __69__

c) XCVI = __106__   d) LXXXIII = __83__

4 marks

2 Write the next Roman numeral in the sequence as a number.

LXXXVI   LXXXVII   LXXXVIII   LXXXIX   _LXXXX_

88   89

1 mark

Roman Numerals

3   Here are some Roman calculations. Write them using numbers.

a)   XL + LX = C   _60_ + _40_ = _100_

         69   30

b)   LXIX – XXX = XXXIX   _69_ – _30_ = _99_

2 marks

4   Circle the Roman numeral that is equivalent to 99.

 IC   CX   XCXI   XCIX   LXLIX

1 mark

Marks.......... /8

Challenge 3

1   Write these Roman numerals in order of size, smallest first.

	XC	LXV	XXXVIII	LXIX	XLVII	

smallest						largest

1 mark

2   Complete these calculations. Write your answers as numbers.

a)   LXIV – XLVII + XXIX = _____

b)   XXIV + XIX + XCIII = _____

c)   XL + LX – L = _____

d)   XXXIX – XXI + LXVI = _____

4 marks

3   These Roman numerals are larger than 100. Write them as numbers.

a)   CXXV _____   b)   CCXXII _____

c)   CCCLIX _____

3 marks

Marks.......... /8

Total marks .... /27   How am I doing?

Representing Numbers

PS Problem-solving questions

Challenge 1

1 Estimate the numbers the arrows point to.

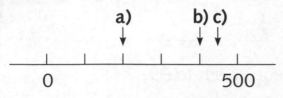
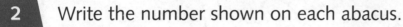

a) ↓   b) ↓ c) ↓

0   500

a) _200_

b) _480_

c) _475_

3 marks

2 Write the number shown on each abacus.

a) 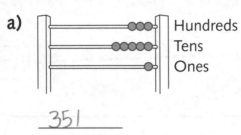 Hundreds
Tens
Ones

b) 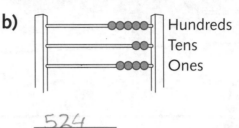 Hundreds
Tens
Ones

_351_   _524_

2 marks

3 Write these numbers using digits.

a) Five thousand, two hundred and ninety-six = _5296_

b) Seven thousand, five hundred and seventy = _7570_

c) Two thousand, eight hundred and four = _2804_

3 marks

Marks.......... /8

Challenge 2

1 Write the three-digit number represented by these blocks. _457_

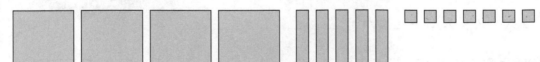

1 mark

2 Look at this calculation: 2538 = 2000 + 500 + 30 + 8

Write these numbers in a similar way.

a) 4825 = _4000_ + _800_ + _20_ + _5_

b) 6719 = _6000_ + _700_ + _10_ + _9_

2 marks

Representing Numbers

3 Estimate the numbers the arrows point to.

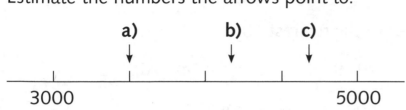

	a)	b)	c)

3000   5000

a) _4000_

b) _4045_

c) _4070_

3 marks

Marks.......... /6

Challenge 3

PS **1** 6538 can be written as 6000 + 400 + 130 + 8.

Find five ways to write 3746.

a) _3000, 700, 40, 6_   b) _____

c) _____   d) _____

e) _____

5 marks

2 Write these numbers as digits.

a) Four thousand, six hundred and nine   _4609_

b) Eight thousand and twenty   _8020_

2 marks

3 Complete the following.

a) 7000 = __7__ thousands = __0__ hundreds

= __0__ tens = __0__ ones

b) 80 tens = _800_   c) 30 hundreds = _300_

3 marks

4 Use these place value cards to write a four-digit number. _2738_

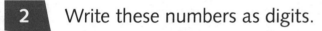

7 hundreds	8 ones	2 thousands	3 tens

1 mark

Marks.......... /11

Total marks .... /25   How am I doing?

Rounding Numbers

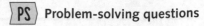 **PS** Problem-solving questions

Challenge 1

1 Round each number to the nearest 10.

a) 54 __50__   b) 99 __100__   c) 76 __80__

3 marks

2 Enrico is rounding numbers to the nearest 10.
Circle the numbers he will round to 80.

72   84   75   85   ⟨77⟩

3 marks

PS **3** Jo estimates the answer to 52 + 74 by rounding both numbers to the nearest 10 and adding.

Write Jo's estimated answer. __180__

1 mark

4 Round each number to the nearest 100.

a) 326 __300__   b) 704 __700__   c) 1477 __1500__

3 marks

Marks......... /10

Challenge 2

1 Round each number to the nearest 100.

a) 3783 __3800__   b) 6317 __6300__   c) 5078 __5100__

3 marks

2 Round 2628 to the:

a) nearest 10. __30__

b) nearest 100. __600__

c) nearest 1000. __3000__

3 marks

3 Round each number to the nearest 1000.

a) 4009 __4000__   b) 2505 __3000__   c) 8199 __8000__

3 marks

22

Rounding Numbers

4 Sean rounded a number to the nearest 100. His answer was 700.

Write three different numbers that Sean's number could have been.

_718_   _699_   _700_

3 marks

Marks.........../12

Challenge 3

1 Round each number to the nearest 1000.

a) 6043 _6000_   **b)** 789 _1000_   **c)** 3911 _4000_

3 marks

PS **2** Max has a secret number.
He rounds the number down to the nearest 1000, the answer is 7000.
He rounds the same number to the nearest 10, the answer is 7340.

Write a possible secret number.   _7342_

1 mark

3 Oliver rounds numbers to the nearest 10.
Circle the numbers Oliver has rounded.

350   4005   6000   7900   10 101

3 marks

4 Eve has four numbers cards.
She makes four-digit numbers using the cards and rounds them to the nearest 1000.

5   9   6   1

Write the 4 four-digit numbers that Eve will round to 7000.

_6_   _5_   _9_   _1_

4 marks

Marks.........../11

Total marks .... /33   How am I doing?

Negative Numbers

Challenge 1

−7 −6 −5 −4 −3 −2 −1 0 1 2 3 4 5 6

1 Use the number line.

a) Start at 3, count back 5, write the number you reach. _−2_

b) Start at 2, count back 6, write the number you reach. _−4_

c) Start at 5, count back 7, write the number you reach. _−2_

d) Start at 4, count back 9, write the number you reach. _−5_

4 marks

2 Calculate by counting backwards:

a) $4 - 6 =$ _−2_   b) $3 - 7 =$ _−4_   c) $5 - 6 =$ _−1_

3 marks

 3 Jake wants to buy a t-shirt for £7. He has £3.
He borrows the rest from his dad.
How much does Jake owe his dad? _£4.00_

1 mark

4 Start at −2, count back 3, write the number you reach. _−5_

1 mark

Marks.......... /9

Challenge 2

1 a) Start at 4, count back 8, write the number you reach. _−4_

b) Start at 2, count back 9, write the number you reach. _−6_

c) Start at 10, count back 12, write the number you reach. _−2_

d) Start at 1, count back 10, write the number you reach. _−9_

4 marks

2 Calculate by counting backwards:

a) $2 - 7 =$ _−5_   b) $12 - 17 =$ _−5_   c) $15 - 16 =$ _−1_

3 marks

3 Calculate by counting backwards:

a) $-2 - 7 =$ _−9_   b) $-5 - 12 =$ _−17_   c) $-10 - 8 =$ _−18_

3 marks

Negative Numbers

PS | **4** Look at the thermometer.

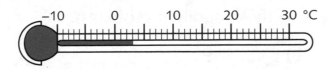

-10   0   10   20   30 °C

Write the temperature after these changes.

a) The temperature is 12°C and falls by 14°C.

b) The temperature is −4°C and falls by 5°C.

c) The temperature is −3°C and rises by 7°C.

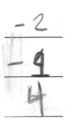
-2
-9
4

3 marks

Marks......... /13

Challenge 3

1 Arrange these numbers in order, starting with the largest.

−6   5   −1   −4   3

largest | 5 | 3 | −1 | −4 | −6 | smallest

1 mark

2 This number line runs from −10 to 10. Four arrows point to whole numbers. Write the numbers the arrows point to.

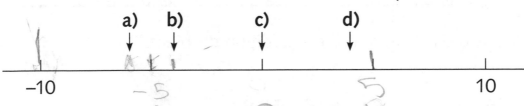

a)   b)   c)   d)

−10   −5   5   10

a) _−6_   b) _−4_   c) _0_   d) _4_

4 marks

3 Calculate:

a) 3 + 12 = _−9_   b) 5 − 20 = _−15_   c) 12 − 20 = _−8_

d) −5 − 9 = _−14_   e) −12 − 12 = _−24_   f) −8 + 4 = _−4_

6 marks

Marks.......... /11

Total marks .... /33   How am I doing?

Addition and Subtraction Practice

Challenge 1

1 Work out the answers to these addition problems.

a)
```
   3 2 7
 + 4 2 2
 _____

 _____
```

b)
```
   7 9 2
 + 2 0 5
 _____

 _____
```

c)
```
   4 9 2
 + 5 1 3
 _____

 _____
```

2 Work out the answers to these subtraction problems.

a)
```
   6 5 8
 - 2 5 7
 _____

 _____
```

b)
```
   5 8 8
 - 4 9 7
 _____

 _____
```

c)
```
   7 0 1
 - 1 7 3
 _____

 _____
```

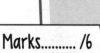 3 marks

3 marks

Marks.......... /6

Challenge 2

1 Work out the answers to these addition problems.

a)
```
   8 5 4
 + 6 7 4
 _____

 _____
```

b)
```
   8 3 9
 + 5 7 9
 _____

 _____
```

c)
```
   8 8 4 4
 + 4 8 8 4
 _____

 _____
```

 3 marks

Addition and Subtraction Practice

2 Work out the answers to these subtraction problems.

a)
```
    9 0 3
  – 2 6 0
  _____

  _____
```

b)
```
    7 9 0
  – 3 8 4
  _____

  _____
```

c)
```
    5 3 3 1
  – 1 7 3 5
  _____

  _____
```

 3 marks

Marks.......... /6

Challenge 3

1 Work out the answers to these addition problems.

a)
```
    5 9 2 1
  + 6 4 7 9
  _____

  _____
```

b)
```
    8 5 3 6
  + 2 7 7 6
  _____

  _____
```

c)
```
    6 4 3 7
  + 6 4 7 2
  _____

  _____
```

 3 marks

2 Work out the answers to these subtraction problems.

a)
```
    6 6 7 3
  – 5 4 7 7
  _____

  _____
```

b)
```
    9 0 6 3
  – 5 0 9 0
  _____

  _____
```

c)
```
    8 4 7 2
  – 3 6 7 9
  _____

  _____
```

 3 marks

Marks.......... /6

Total marks .... /18   How am I doing?

Estimating and Checking Calculations

Challenge 1

1 Round each number to the nearest 10. Then use the rounded numbers to give an estimated answer to each calculation.

a) 54 + 74 _____

b) 33 + 64 _____

c) 76 + 85 _____

3 marks

PS **2** Tara calculates 125 + 265 = 390. She wants to check her calculation by calculating the inverse.

Circle the calculation that is the inverse of Tara's calculation.

| 265 + 390 | 390 – 265 | 390 + 125 | 265 – 125 |

1 mark

3 Write the inverse of each calculation.

a) 235 + 328 = 563 b) 529 – 236 = 293 c) 525 – 214 = 311

_____   _____   _____

3 marks

PS **4** A gardener plants tulip and daffodil bulbs. Altogether, there are 486 bulbs. She plants 259 tulip bulbs.

How many are daffodil bulbs? _____

1 mark

Marks.......... /8

Challenge 2

PS **1** Joshua thinks of a number. He adds 56 to the number. Joshua's answer is 412.

What was Joshua's number? _____

1 mark

PS **2** Kia thinks of a number. She subtracts 94 from the number. Kia's answer is 536.

What was Kia's number? _____

1 mark

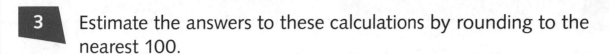

Estimating and Checking Calculations

3 Estimate the answers to these calculations by rounding to the nearest 100.

a) 418 + 629 _____

b) 907 – 798 _____

2 marks

4 Estimate the answers to these calculations by rounding to the nearest 1000.

a) 6321 – 2976 _____

b) 6602 + 3532 _____

2 marks

Marks.......... /6

Challenge 3

PS **1** Bryn estimates the price of two pens as 50p and 80p by rounding to the nearest 10p. The actual cost of the two pens is £1.35.

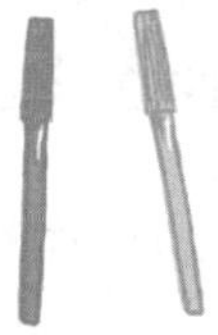

What could the price of each pen have been? _____ and _____

1 mark

PS **2** Estimate answers to these calculations by rounding to the nearest 1000.

a) 7286 + 9781 _____

b) 12 084 – 6822 _____

2 marks

PS **3** Ari completes this calculation: 6432 + 3826 = 9258

Use an inverse calculation to check Ari's calculation. If it's wrong, correct the answer.

_____

1 mark

PS **4** Dino adds a number and 732, then subtracts 218 and reaches an answer of 861.

Write the number that Dino started with. _____

1 mark

Marks.......... /5

Total marks .... /19   How am I doing?

29

Addition and Subtraction Problems

Challenge 1

PS **1** In a school, there are 286 children in Primary 4 and 139 children in Primary 3.

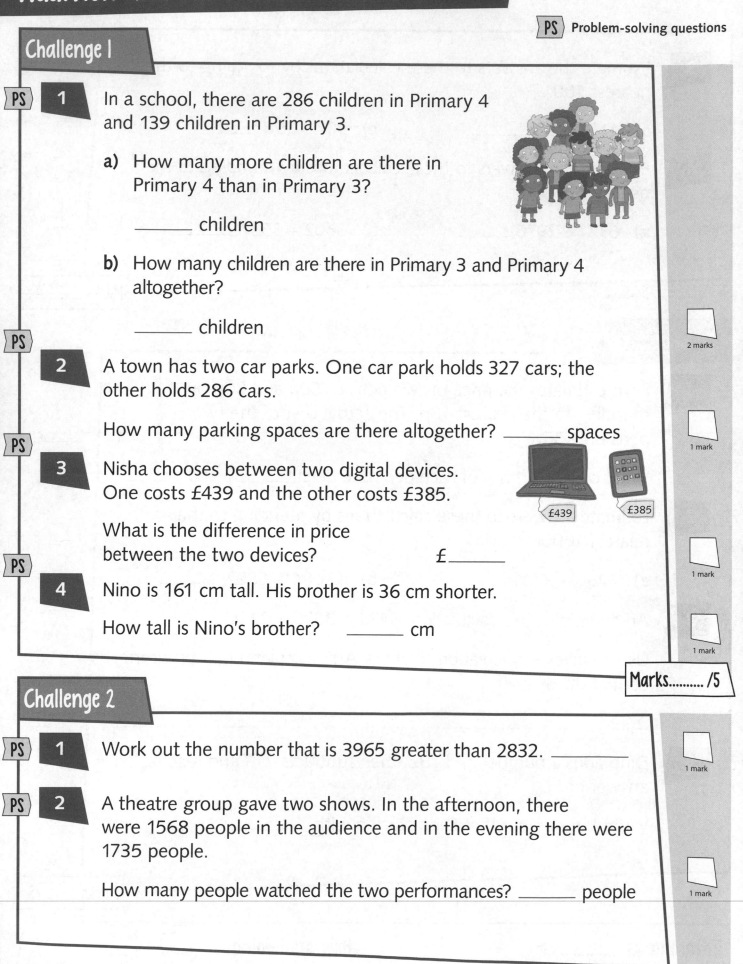

a) How many more children are there in Primary 4 than in Primary 3?

_____ children

b) How many children are there in Primary 3 and Primary 4 altogether?

_____ children

2 marks

PS **2** A town has two car parks. One car park holds 327 cars; the other holds 286 cars.

How many parking spaces are there altogether? _____ spaces

1 mark

PS **3** Nisha chooses between two digital devices. One costs £439 and the other costs £385.

£439   £385

What is the difference in price between the two devices?   £_____

1 mark

PS **4** Nino is 161 cm tall. His brother is 36 cm shorter.

How tall is Nino's brother?   _____ cm

1 mark

Marks.......... /5

Challenge 2

PS **1** Work out the number that is 3965 greater than 2832. _____

1 mark

PS **2** A theatre group gave two shows. In the afternoon, there were 1568 people in the audience and in the evening there were 1735 people.

How many people watched the two performances? _____ people

1 mark

Addition and Subtraction Problems

PS **3** Noah went on holiday. He drove 864 km from London to the south of France. He drove 365 km whilst on holiday and then he drove back to London.

How many kilometres did he drive altogether? _____ km

1 mark

PS **4** A shop has a stock of 3475 t-shirts. It sells 1294 t-shirts.

How many t-shirts does it have left? _____ t-shirts

1 mark

Marks.......... /4

Challenge 3

PS **1** Write the missing numbers in these calculations.

a)
```
  3 □ 7 □
+ □ 6 □ 3
─────────
  6 5 1 7
```

b)
```
  □ 3 □ 4
- 2 □ 5 □
─────────
  5 7 2 4
```

2 marks

PS **2** Here are six number cards:

Use the cards to complete this calculation.

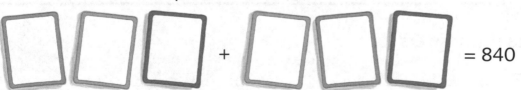 + = 840

1 mark

PS **3** Work out these calculations and circle the one with the greatest answer.

A | 5236 + 1609 = _____

B | 9343 – 2434 = _____

C | 2354 + 4567 = _____

4 marks

Marks.......... /7

Total marks .... /16   How am I doing?

31

Multiplication and Division Facts

PS Problem-solving questions

Challenge 1

1 Write the answers to:

a) 7 × 5 = _35_ ✓

b) 3 × 8 = _24_

c) 11 × 8 = _88_ ✓

d) 12 × 3 = _36_ ✓

e) 7 × 10 = _70_ ✓

f) 8 × 4 = _32_ ✓

6 marks

2 Fill in the missing numbers.

a) 4 × _7_ = 28 ✓

b) 5 × _~~12~~_ = 60 ✓

c) 3 × _7_ = 21 ✓

d) _6_ × 8 = 48 ✓

e) _10_ × 10 = 100 ✓

f) _6_ × 4 = 24 ✓

6 marks

3 Write the answers to:

a) 16 ÷ 2 = _8_ ✓

b) 45 ÷ 5 = _9_ ✓

c) 36 ÷ 4 = _9_ ✓

d) 56 ÷ 8 = _7_ ✓

e) 18 ÷ 3 = _6_ ✓

f) 48 ÷ 4 = _12_ ✓

6 marks

Marks......... /18

Challenge 2

1 Write the answers to:

a) 7 × 6 = _42_

b) 4 × 7 = _23_

c) 9 × 11 = _99_

d) 8 × 7 = _56_

e) 9 × 9 = _81_

f) 12 × 7 = _84_

6 marks

2 Fill in the missing numbers.

a) 7 × _7_ = 49

b) 9 × _8_ = 72

c) 6 × _12_ = 72

d) _12_ × 9 = 108

e) _12_ × 12 = 144

f) _9_ × 7 = 63

6 marks

32

Multiplication and Division Facts

3 Write the answers to:

a) $121 \div 11 =$ _____

b) $27 \div 9 =$ _____

c) $66 \div 6 =$ _____

d) $96 \div 8 =$ _____

e) $54 \div 9 =$ _____

f) $36 \div 9 =$ _____

6 marks

Marks......... /18

Challenge 3

PS **1** Complete the multiplication squares.

a)

×	7	9	12
7	49		
9			
12			

b)

×		8	
6	42		
		64	
		84	108

7 marks

PS **2** Use different whole numbers only to complete these multiplication facts.

a) $6 \times 8 =$ _____ $\times$ _____

b) $4 \times 9 =$ _____ $\times$ _____

c) $3 \times 8 =$ _____ $\times$ _____

d) $6 \times 12 =$ _____ $\times$ _____

4 marks

PS **3** Use whole numbers only to complete these division facts.

a) $54 \div 6 =$ _____ $\div 9$

b) $64 \div 8 =$ _____ $\div 7$

c) $96 \div 12 =$ _____ $\div 8$

d) $132 \div 11 =$ _____ $\div 10$

4 marks

Marks......... /15

Total marks .... /51

How am I doing?

Mental Multiplication and Division

Challenge 1

1 Write the answers to:

a) $5 \times 1 = $ __5__

b) $10 \times 0 = $ __0__

c) $0 \times 8 = $ __0__

d) $20 \times 3 = $ __60__

e) $40 \times 4 = $ __160__

f) $70 \times 5 = $ __350__

6 marks

2 Fill in the missing numbers.

a) __20__ $\times 5 = 100$

b) __20__ $\times 4 = 80$

c) __30__ $\times 3 = 90$

3 marks

3 Write the answers to:

a) $80 \div 2 = $ __40__

b) $150 \div 5 = $ __30__

c) $200 \div 4 = $ __50__

3 marks

4 Fill in the missing numbers.

a) $180 \div$ __3__ $= 60$

b) $250 \div$ __5__ $= 50$

c) $160 \div$ __4__ $= 40$

3 marks

Marks......... /15

Challenge 2

1 Write the answers to:

a) $15 \times 2 = $ __30__

b) $22 \times 5 = $ __110__

c) $16 \times 4 = $ __64__

d) $23 \times 3 = $ __69__

e) $32 \times 4 = $ __128__

f) $51 \times 5 = $ __255__

6 marks

2 Write the answers to:

a) $45 \div 3 = $ __15__

b) $52 \div 4 = $ __13__

c) $70 \div 5 = $ __14__

d) $68 \div 2 = $ __34__

e) $64 \div 4 = $ __16__

f) $66 \div 3 = $ __22__

6 marks

Mental Multiplication and Division

3 Write the answers to:

a) $4 \times 2 \times 6 =$ _48_

b) $5 \times 2 \times 9 =$ _90_

c) $6 \times 2 \times 6 =$ _72_

3 marks

Marks......... /15

Challenge 3

1 Fill in the missing numbers.

a) $23 \times$ _3_ $= 69$ b) $32 \times$ _4_ $= 128$

c) $51 \times$ _5_ $= 255$ d) $53 \times$ _3_ $= 159$

e) $24 \times$ _5_ $= 120$ f) $82 \times$ _3_ $= 246$

6 marks

2 Fill in the missing numbers.

a) $3 \times 5 \times$ _3_ $= 45$ b) $4 \times$ _6_ $\times 5 = 120$

c) _4_ $\times 10 \times 2 = 80$ d) $7 \times 3 \times$ ___ $= 84$

e) $2 \times$ ___ $\times 2 = 48$ f) ___ $\times 3 \times 8 = 72$

6 marks

3 Fill in the missing numbers.

a) $12 \times 6 = 6 \times 3 \times$ ___

b) $15 \times 6 = 6 \times 5 \times$ ___

c) ___ $\times 8 = 8 \times 5 \times 3$

d) ___ $\times 7 = 7 \times 8 \times 3$

4 marks

Marks......... /16

Total marks .... /46   How am I doing?

Factors

PS Problem-solving questions

Challenge 1

1 Circle the true statements.

(A) | 6 is a factor of 12   **B** | 4 is a factor of 18

(C) | 15 is a factor of 5   **(D)** | 8 is a factor of 24

E | 3 is a factor of 35   **(F)** | 9 is a factor of 72

3 marks

2 Write the missing numbers.

a) $5 \times 7 = 7 \times$ _5_

b) $12 \times 4 = 4 \times$ _12_

2 marks

3 Write the missing factor of 36.

4   36   6   2   18   3   12   1   _9_

1 mark

PS **4** Circle the factors of 30.

(1) (3) 4 (5) 8 (10) 12 (15)

1 mark

Marks.......... /7

Challenge 2

1 Write all the factors of:

a) 10 _1, 2, 5, 10_

b) 21 _1, 3, 7, 21_

c) 32 _1, 2, 4, 8, 16, 32_

d) 40 _1, 2, 4, 5, 8, 10, 20, 40_

4 marks

2 Write the missing factor pair of 42.

| 1 and 42 | 3 and 14 | 6 and 7 | _____ and _____ |

1 mark

3 Write the missing factor pair of 56.

| 1 and 56 | 2 and 28 | 4 and 14 | _____ and _____ |

1 mark

Factors

4 Circle any correct statements.

A $8 \div 9 = 9 \div 8$ B $12 \times 11 = 11 \times 12$

1 mark

PS **5** I think of a number greater than 6. It is a factor of both 28 and 49.

What is my number? _____

1 mark

Marks.......... /8

Challenge 3

1 Write these numbers in the Venn diagram.

4   5   6   8   10

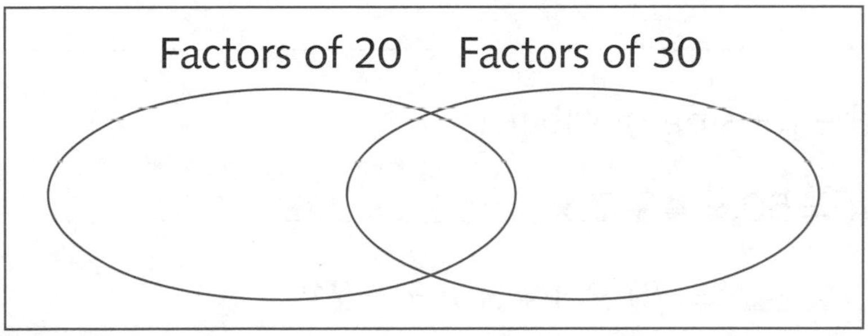

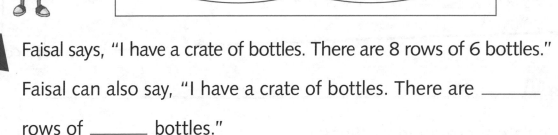

Factors of 20   Factors of 30

5 marks

PS **2** Faisal says, "I have a crate of bottles. There are 8 rows of 6 bottles."

Faisal can also say, "I have a crate of bottles. There are _____

rows of _____ bottles."

1 mark

3 List the factor pairs of:

a) 48 _____

b) 60 _____

c) 100 _____

3 marks

4 Write the factors of 56 that are not factors of 28. _____

1 mark

Marks......... /10

Total marks .... /25   How am I doing?

37

Multiplication Practice

Challenge 1

1 Calculate these multiplications.

a) $\begin{array}{r} 4\ 6 \\ \times\quad 5 \\ \hline \\ \hline \end{array}$ b) $\begin{array}{r} 5\ 3 \\ \times\quad 6 \\ \hline \\ \hline \end{array}$ c) $\begin{array}{r} 6\ 2 \\ \times\quad 4 \\ \hline \\ \hline \end{array}$ d) $\begin{array}{r} 3\ 7 \\ \times\quad 3 \\ \hline \\ \hline \end{array}$

4 marks

2 Set out these problems using column multiplication and calculate.

a) $36 \times 6 =$	b) $72 \times 5 =$	c) $84 \times 8 =$

3 marks

3 Write in the missing numbers.

a) $57 \times 4 = 50 \times 4 + 7 \times \underline{\hspace{1cm}} = 228$

b) $73 \times \underline{\hspace{1cm}} = 70 \times 3 + 3 \times 3 = 219$

2 marks

Marks......... /9

Challenge 2

1 Calculate these multiplications.

a) $\begin{array}{r} 2\ 5\ 3 \\ \times\qquad 6 \\ \hline \\ \hline \end{array}$ b) $\begin{array}{r} 6\ 0\ 7 \\ \times\qquad 5 \\ \hline \\ \hline \end{array}$ c) $\begin{array}{r} 6\ 3\ 7 \\ \times\qquad 7 \\ \hline \\ \hline \end{array}$

3 marks

2 Write in the missing numbers.

a) $725 \times 6 = 700 \times \underline{\hspace{1cm}} + 20 \times \underline{\hspace{1cm}} + 5 \times \underline{\hspace{1cm}} = 4350$

b) $321 \times 4 = 642 \times \underline{\hspace{1cm}}$

2 marks

Multiplication Practice

3 Set out these problems using column multiplication and calculate.

a) 427 × 7 =	b) 683 × 6 =	c) 427 × 9 =

3 marks

 Marks.......... /8

Challenge 3

1 Set out these problems using column multiplication and calculate.

a) 856 × 7 =	b) 967 × 8 =	c) 956 × 9 =

3 marks

 2 Fill in the missing numbers.

a)
$$\begin{array}{r} \square\,4\,\square \\ \times \qquad 7 \\ \hline 3\ 8\ 2\ 9 \end{array}$$

b)
$$\begin{array}{r} \square\,8\,\square \\ \times \qquad 9 \\ \hline 3\ 4\ 6\ 5 \end{array}$$

c)
$$\begin{array}{r} \square\,7\,\square \\ \times \qquad 8 \\ \hline 2\ 2\ 0\ 8 \end{array}$$

3 marks

 3 Nishi has four number cards. She arranges them into a multiplication.

Fill in the multiplication on the right to find the largest total Nishi can make.

1 mark

 Marks.......... /7

Total marks .... /24   How am I doing?

39

Multiplication Problems

PS Problem-solving questions

Challenge 1

PS **1** There are 48 bottles in a crate.

How many bottles will there be in 6 crates? ______ bottles

1 mark

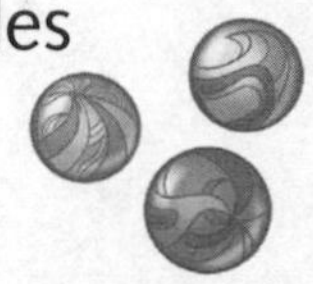

PS **2** Jack has 35 marbles in a bag. He has 8 similar bags.

How many marbles does he have altogether? ______ marbles

1 mark

PS **3** Jess buys 3 packs of apples. There are 15 apples altogether.

How many apples will there be in 12 packs? ______ apples

1 mark

PS **4** A pack of 4 tins of beans costs £1.75.

How much would you pay for 20 tins of beans? £______

1 mark

PS **5** There are 6 classes in a school. Each class has 28 children.

How many children are in the school? ______ children

1 mark

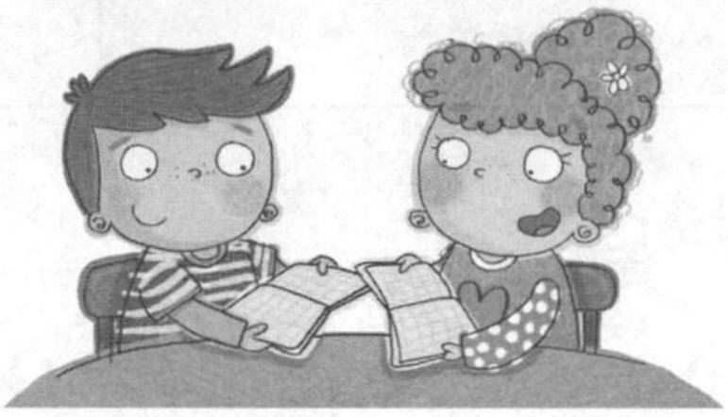

Marks........../5

Challenge 2

PS **1** A farmer keeps 186 chickens. Each chicken lays 4 eggs a week.

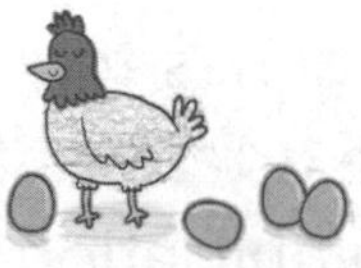

How many eggs are laid in a week? ______ eggs

1 mark

PS **2** A sack of tulip bulbs holds 256 bulbs. Dave plants 6 sacks of bulbs.

How many bulbs has Dave planted? ______ bulbs

1 mark

PS **3** A shop sells 3 televisions that cost £375 each and 7 televisions that cost £435 each.

What is the total cost of the televisions? £______

1 mark

Multiplication Problems

PS | **4** A school puts on a show in the school hall.
It sells 278 tickets for each performance.
There are 5 performances.

How many tickets are sold? _____ tickets

1 mark

PS | **5** A teacher buys 8 jars of counters. Each jar holds 475 counters.

How many counters are there altogether? _____ counters

1 mark

Marks.......... /5

Challenge 3

PS | **1** This table shows the cost of different air fares from London.

To From	New York	Los Angeles	Dubai	New Delhi	Sydney
London (One way)	£346	£465	£486	£518	£648
London (Return)	£452	£573	£549	£647	£732

What is the cost of:

a) 5 one-way tickets to Dubai? £_____

b) 4 return tickets to Sydney? £_____

c) 6 one-way tickets to Los Angeles? £_____

d) 8 return tickets to New Delhi? £_____

e) 7 one-way tickets to New York? £_____

5 marks

Marks.......... /5

Total marks .... /15 How am I doing?

Progress Test 1

PS Problem-solving questions

1. Write the next numbers in the sequences.

a)

48	54	60	66		

b)

775	800	825	850		

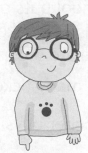

2 marks

2. Write these numbers in order, starting with the smallest.

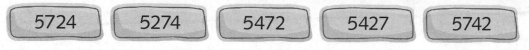

5724 5274 5472 5427 5742

_____ _____ _____ _____ _____

1 mark

3. Write < or > in the circles to make each number sentence correct.

a) 7903 ◯ 7907 b) 5634 ◯ 5833

2 marks

PS **4.** A car is for sale and costs £8799. The car dealer reduces the price by £1000.

What is the reduced price of the car? £_____

1 mark

5. Work out:

a) 6835 – 1000 = _____ b) 4008 + 1000 = _____

2 marks

6. Circle the number in which the digit 2 has a value of two thousand.

4285 **5629** **2390** **6132** **7264**

1 mark

PS **7.** Sunil has these number cards.

3 5 4 8

Use the cards to make the largest possible number with three hundreds. _____

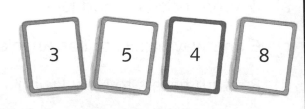

1 mark

8. Write these Roman numerals as numbers.

a) XXXVIII = _____

b) LXIV = _____

2 marks

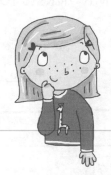

9. These Roman numerals are written as a calculation: XXXV + VII = ?
Circle the correct answer.

LXII   **XLIIIV**   **LII**   **XLII**

1 mark

10. Write the three-digit number represented by these blocks. _____

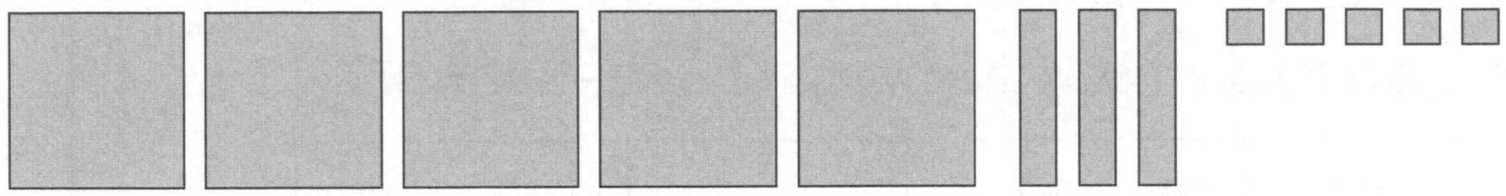

1 mark

11. Write the numbers the arrows point to.

a) _____   **b)** _____

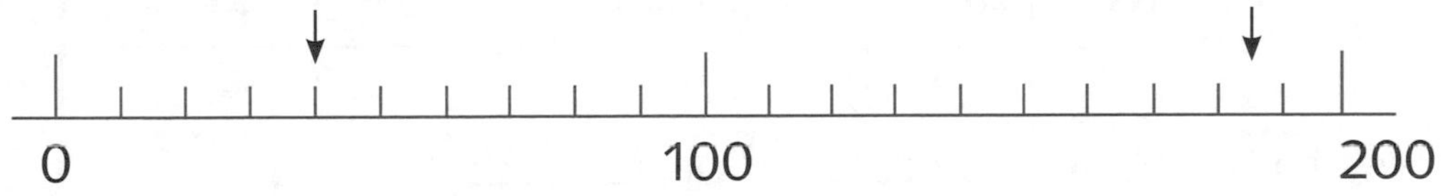

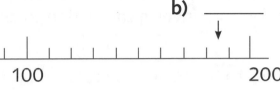

2 marks

12. Round each number to the nearest 100.

a) 528 _____   **b)** 761 _____   **c)** 89 _____

3 marks

13. Complete this table by rounding the number to the nearest 10,
100 and 1000.

	Rounded to the nearest 10 is	Rounded to the nearest 100 is	Rounded to the nearest 1000 is
5826			

3 marks

14. Write the next two numbers in this sequence.

1 mark

PS **15.** Flo counts back in fives from 20.

Write the first number below zero she counts. _____

1 mark

16. Work out:

a) 4 2 7
      − 1 8 7
      _____

b) 7 9 5
      + 2 8 5
      _____

c) 8 1 5
      − 2 7 0
      _____

3 marks

Progress Test 1

PS Problem-solving questions

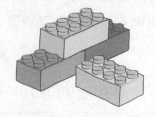

PS **17.** Write in the missing numbers.

a)
```
  5 □ 7
– □ 5 □
-------
  1 7 4
```

b)
```
  □ 5 □
+ 5 □ 1
-------
  9 0 9
```

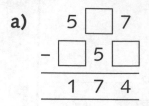

2 marks

18. Circle the calculation that is the inverse of 694 – 322 = 372

372 + 694	694 – 322	372 + 322	372 – 322

1 mark

PS **19.** Sven completes the calculation shown on the right. He then works out the inverse calculation to check his work.

```
  3 8 2
+ 4 6 5
-------
  7 4 7
```

Write the answer to Sven's inverse calculation. ______

1 mark

PS **20.** Ivete has 275 minutes talk time left on her phone. She uses up another 126 minutes and then her monthly allowance increases the talk time by 450 minutes.

How many minutes does Ivete have on her phone now? ______ minutes

1 mark

PS **21.** Tarun has to drive 356 kilometres. After 186 kilometres he stops to have lunch and then, after another 137 kilometres, he stops for a coffee.

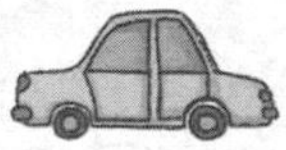

How much further does Tarun have to drive? ______ kilometres

1 mark

22. Work out:

a) 5 × 7 = ______ **b)** 3 × 9 = ______ **c)** 7 × 12 = ______

d) 48 ÷ 6 = ______ **e)** 144 ÷ 12 = ______ **f)** 54 ÷ 9 = ______

6 marks

PS **23.** Write the missing numbers in this multiplication square.

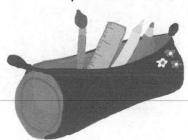

×	6	9	
4	24	36	48
		81	
7	42	63	84

2 marks

24. Work out:

a) $15 \times 5 =$ _____   b) $48 \div 3 =$ _____

c) $22 \times 4 =$ _____   d) $72 \div 4 =$ _____

e) $96 \div 8 =$ _____   f) $17 \times 6 =$ _____

6 marks

25. Write the factor pairs of:

a) 20 _____

b) 100 _____

2 marks

26. Work out:

a)
```
    6 3
  ×   6
  _____

  _____
```

b)
```
  2 6 5
  ×   4
  _____

  _____
```

c)
```
  6 0 8
  ×   7
  _____

  _____
```

3 marks

PS **27.** A school has 8 classes and each class can hold 30 children. There are 216 children in the school.

How many spare places are there?   _____ spare places

1 mark

28. Fill in the missing numbers.

$54 \times 3 = 50 \times 3 +$ _____ $\times$ _____ $= 162$

1 mark

PS **29.** A factory uses 7 metres of wood to make a wardrobe.

How much wood is needed to make 5 wardrobes? _____ metres

1 mark

30. Michael completes 3 tests worth a total of 50 marks.

How many marks are available if he completes 6 tests?

_____ marks

1 mark

Marks........ /56

Hundredths

PS Problem-solving questions

Challenge 1

1 What fraction is shown by each drawing?

a) $\frac{3}{10}$

b) $\frac{9}{10}$

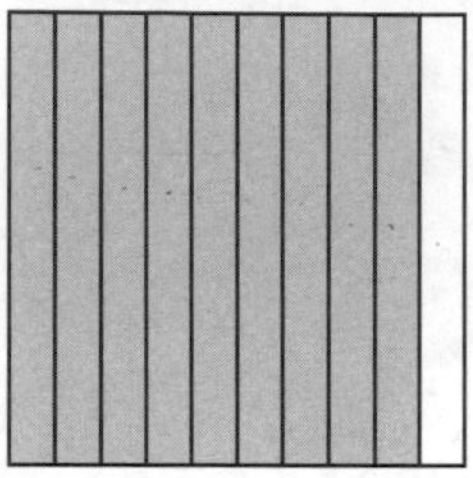

c) $\frac{7}{10}$

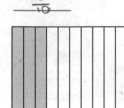

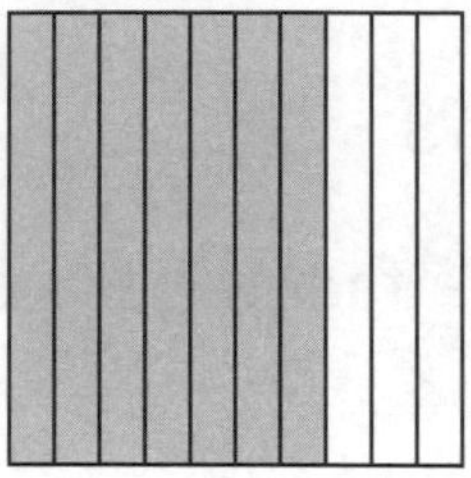

3 marks

2 Write in the missing fractions.

a) $\frac{7}{100}$ | $\frac{8}{100}$ | $\frac{9}{100}$ | $\frac{10}{100}$ | $\frac{11}{100}$ | $\frac{12}{100}$ | $\frac{13}{100}$

b) $\frac{77}{100}$ | $\frac{78}{100}$ | $\frac{79}{100}$ | $\frac{80}{100}$ | $\frac{81}{100}$ | $\frac{82}{100}$ | $\frac{83}{100}$

2 marks

3 Complete this sentence:

When 1 is divided by 100th the answer is $\frac{1}{100}$.

1 mark

Marks........../6

Challenge 2

1 What fraction is shown by each drawing?

a) $\frac{7}{100}$

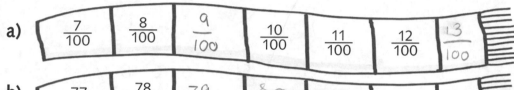

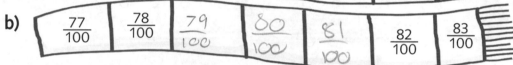

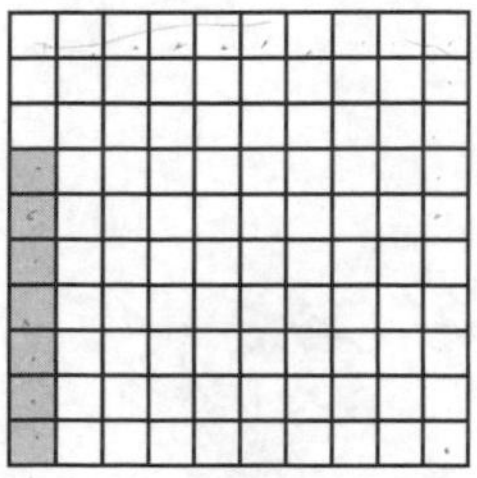

b) $\frac{43}{100}$

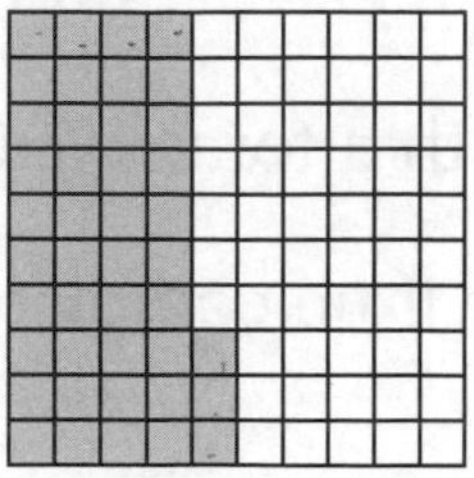

c) $\frac{89}{100}$

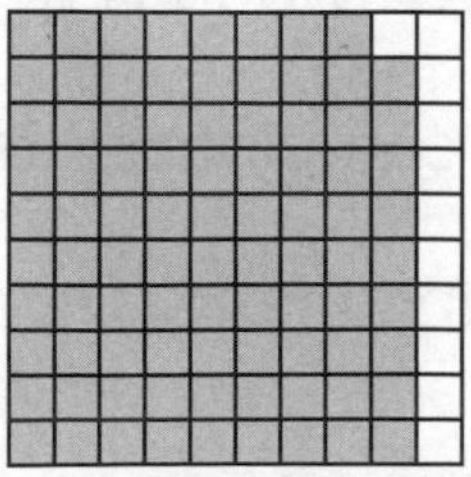

3 marks

2 Divide each number by 100. Give your answers as fractions.

a) 6 $\frac{6}{100}$ b) 9 $\frac{9}{100}$ c) 2 $\frac{2}{100}$

3 marks

PS **3** Kesha has a 5 litre bottle of juice. This is exactly enough juice to make 100 drinks.

5000 ml

How much juice is used in each drink? Give your answer as a fraction of a litre.

$\frac{1}{20}$

1 mark

PS **4** How many centimetres are in $\frac{1}{100}$ of a metre? ____1____ cm

1 mark

Marks.........../8

Challenge 3

1 Circle the calculation with the correct answer.

$50 \div 100 = \frac{5}{100}$

$5 \div 100 = \frac{5}{10}$

$500 \div 100 = \frac{5}{100}$

$5 \div 100 = \frac{5}{100}$

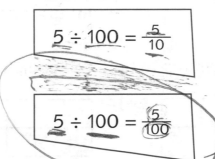

1 mark

2 Circle both calculations that have an answer of $\frac{1}{100}$.

$1 \div 10$ $1 \div 100$ $0.1 \div 10$ $0.1 \div 100$

2 marks

3 Write in the missing numbers.

a) _____ $\div 100 = \frac{7}{100}$

b) _____ $\div 100 = \frac{5}{100}$

c) _____ $\div 10 = \frac{7}{100}$

3 marks

4 Write in the missing numbers.

a) $0.6 \div 10 =$ _____ $\div 100$

b) $0.7 \div$ _____ $= 7 \div 100$

2 marks

Marks.........../8

Total marks ..../22

How am I doing?

47

Equivalent Fractions

PS Problem-solving questions

Challenge 1

1 Fill in the missing equivalent fractions shown by the drawings.

a) 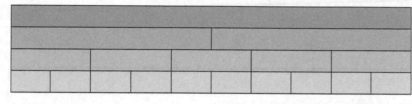 =

$\frac{3}{6}$ = $\frac{1}{2}$

b) =

$\frac{4}{8}$ = $\frac{1}{2}$

✓ 2 marks

2 Use the fraction bars to complete the equivalent fractions.

one whole
halves
fifths
tenths

a) $\frac{1}{2} = \frac{5}{10}$

b) $\frac{3}{5} = \frac{6}{10}$

c) $\frac{4}{5} = \frac{8}{10}$

✓ 3 marks

3 Use the diagrams to help you complete the equivalent fractions.

a)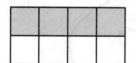

$\frac{1}{2} = \frac{4}{8}$

×4

b)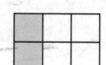

$\frac{1}{3} = \frac{2}{6}$

c)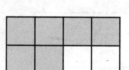

$\frac{3}{4} = \frac{6}{8}$

✓ 3 marks

Marks.......... /8

Challenge 2

1 This rectangle is divided into twentieths.

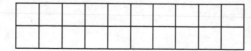

Use the diagram to help you complete the equivalent fractions.

a) $\frac{1}{2} = \frac{10}{20}$
×10

b) $\frac{3}{10} = \frac{6}{20}$
×2

c) $\frac{3}{5} = \frac{12}{20}$
×4

✓ 3 marks

Equivalent Fractions

2 This rectangle is divided into fifteenths.
Use the diagram to help you complete the
equivalent fractions.

a) $\frac{1}{3} = \frac{\boxed{5}}{15}$ ×5

b) $\frac{2}{3} = \frac{\boxed{10}}{15}$ ×5

c) $\frac{3}{5} = \frac{\boxed{9}}{15}$ ×3

3 marks

3 Here are families of equivalent fractions. Complete the fractions.

a) $\frac{1}{3} = \frac{2}{6} = \frac{3}{9} = \frac{\boxed{4}}{12} = \frac{5}{\boxed{15}} = \frac{\boxed{6}}{18} = \frac{7}{\boxed{21}} = \frac{\boxed{8}}{24}$ ×2

b) $\frac{3}{4} = \frac{6}{8} = \frac{9}{12} = \frac{\boxed{12}}{16} = \frac{15}{\boxed{20}} = \frac{\boxed{18}}{24} = \frac{21}{\boxed{28}} = \frac{\boxed{24}}{32}$

 2 marks

Marks.......... /8

Challenge 3

1 Use the fraction bars to help you complete the equivalent fractions.

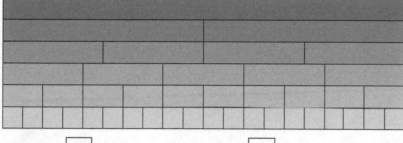

one whole
halves
quarters
fifths
tenths
twentieths

a) $\frac{1}{2} = \frac{\boxed{10}}{20}$ ×10

b) $\frac{4}{5} = \frac{\boxed{16}}{20}$ ×4

c) $\frac{3}{10} = \frac{\boxed{6}}{20}$ ×2

d) $\frac{\boxed{1}}{4} = \frac{5}{20}$ ×5

e) $\frac{\boxed{2}}{5} = \frac{8}{20}$ ÷4

f) $\frac{\boxed{9}}{10} = \frac{18}{20}$ ÷2

 6 marks

2 Circle both fractions that are **not** equivalent to $\frac{1}{4}$.

$\frac{3}{12}$ $\frac{5}{20}$ $\boxed{\frac{8}{30}}$ $\frac{12}{48}$ $\frac{15}{60}$ $\boxed{\frac{20}{100}}$

 2 marks

PS 3 There are 10 cans of paint. 4 of the cans are blue paint.

Complete this sentence: $\frac{2}{\boxed{5}}$ of the cans of paint are blue.

 1 mark

Marks...1.9... /9

Total marks .... /25   How am I doing?

Addition and Subtraction of Fractions

Challenge 1

1 Complete these calculations.

Example: ☐☐☐☐ + ☐☐☐☐ =

$\frac{1}{4}$ + $\frac{2}{4}$ = $\frac{3}{4}$

a) ☐☐☐☐☐ + ☐☐☐☐☐ =

_____ + _____ = _____

b) ☐☐☐☐☐☐ – ☐☐☐☐☐☐ =

_____ – _____ = _____

2 marks

2 Work out the answers to these calculations.

a) $\frac{2}{3} + \frac{1}{3} =$ _____   b) $\frac{7}{8} + \frac{6}{8} =$ _____   c) $\frac{8}{10} + \frac{9}{10} =$ _____

3 marks

3 Work out the answers to these calculations.

a) $\frac{4}{5} - \frac{1}{5} =$ _____   b) $\frac{9}{10} - \frac{6}{10} =$ _____   c) $\frac{7}{8} - \frac{6}{8} =$ _____

3 marks

Marks.......... /8

Challenge 2

1 Complete these calculations.

Example: ☐☐☐☐ + ☐☐☐☐ =

$\frac{3}{4}$ + $\frac{2}{4}$ = $\frac{5}{4} = 1\frac{1}{4}$

a) ☐☐☐☐☐ + ☐☐☐☐☐ =

_____ + _____ = _____ = _____

b) ☐☐☐☐☐☐☐ + ☐☐☐☐☐☐☐ =

_____ + _____ = _____ = _____

2 marks

Addition and Subtraction of Fractions

2 Work out the answers to these calculations.

a) $\frac{2}{3} + \frac{2}{3} =$ _____ = _____

b) $\frac{3}{5} + \frac{4}{5} =$ _____ = _____

c) $\frac{3}{4} + \frac{3}{4} =$ _____ = _____

3 Work out the answers to these calculations.

a) $\frac{9}{10} - \frac{6}{10} =$ _____

b) $\frac{9}{12} - \frac{4}{12} =$ _____

c) $\frac{15}{10} - \frac{6}{10} =$ _____

3 marks

3 marks

Marks.......... /8

Challenge 3

1 Write in the missing fractions.

a) 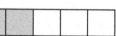 – ? =

_____ – _____ = _____

b) + ? =

_____ + _____ = _____ = _____

2 marks

2 Write the missing fractions in these calculations.

a) $\frac{2}{10} +$ _____ $= \frac{7}{10}$ b) $\frac{3}{12} +$ _____ $= \frac{9}{12}$ c) _____ $+ \frac{1}{8} = 1\frac{2}{8}$

3 marks

3 Write the missing fractions in these calculations.

a) $\frac{7}{8} -$ _____ $= \frac{2}{8}$ b) _____ $- \frac{2}{7} = \frac{4}{7}$

c) $\frac{8}{10} -$ _____ $= \frac{5}{10}$

3 marks

Marks.......... /8

Total marks .... /24   How am I doing?

Finding Fractions

Challenge 1

1 Work out:

a) $\frac{1}{3}$ of 15 = _____

b) $\frac{1}{4}$ of 24 = _____

c) $\frac{1}{6}$ of 36 m = _____ m

d) $\frac{1}{8}$ of 32 kg = _____ kg

4 marks

2 Work out:

a) $\frac{2}{3}$ of 24 = _____

b) $\frac{4}{5}$ of 20 = _____

c) $\frac{3}{4}$ of 36 ml = _____ ml

d) $\frac{2}{2}$ of 25 km = _____ km

4 marks

PS **3** Lesa is on a sponsored run. The run is 12 kilometres. Lesa has completed $\frac{1}{6}$ of the course.

How far has she run? _____ km

1 mark

PS **4** There are 28 children in a class. $\frac{1}{2}$ of the class are boys.

How many girls are in the class? _____

1 mark

Marks.........../10

Challenge 2

1 Work out:

a) $\frac{1}{10}$ of 70 = _____

b) $\frac{1}{7}$ of 28 = _____

c) $\frac{1}{12}$ of £24 = £_____

d) $\frac{1}{15}$ of 30 m = _____ m

4 marks

2 Work out:

a) $\frac{2}{5}$ of 35 = _____

b) $\frac{7}{8}$ of 32 = _____

c) $\frac{11}{12}$ of 60 cm = _____ cm

d) $\frac{3}{20}$ of 40 km = _____ km

4 marks

PS **3** Cath has a 40 kilogram bag of coal. She has used $\frac{3}{5}$ of the bag.

How much coal has she used? _____ kg

1 mark

Finding Fractions

This bar is divided into fifths, but part of the bar is hidden. The value of each fifth is shown.

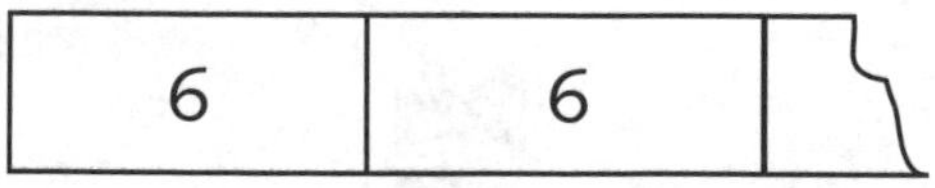

6	6	

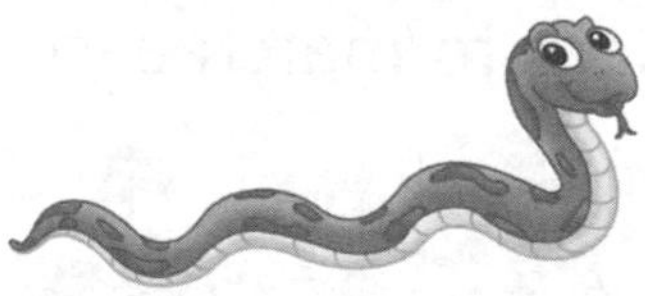

What is the value of the whole bar? _____

1 mark

Marks......... /10

Challenge 3

1 Work out: **a)** $\frac{7}{12}$ of 60 = _____   **b)** $\frac{5}{9}$ of 81 = _____

2 marks

 2 A gift shop sells 40 pens. $\frac{2}{5}$ of the pens have blue ink and $\frac{3}{8}$ of the pens have black ink. The rest have red ink.

How many pens have red ink? _____

1 mark

3 Write in the missing numbers.

a) $\frac{3}{4}$ of _____ = 15   **b)** $\frac{3}{10}$ of _____ = 9

2 marks

4 Work out $\frac{3}{2}$ of 10. _____

1 mark

5 There are 27 children in a class. Jo says, "$\frac{1}{2}$ of the class are girls and $\frac{1}{2}$ of the class are boys."

Explain why Jo must be wrong.

_____

_____

1 mark

6 Work out the missing numbers.

a) $\frac{3}{4}$ of _____ = $\frac{1}{8}$ of 24   **b)** $\frac{3}{5}$ of _____ = $\frac{3}{4}$ of 16

2 marks

Marks......... /9

Total marks ..../29   How am I doing?

53

Fraction and Decimal Equivalents

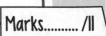 Problem-solving questions

Challenge 1

1 Draw lines to match each fraction to the equivalent decimal.

$\frac{3}{4}$ $\frac{1}{2}$ $\frac{1}{4}$

0.5   0.75   0.25

1 mark

2 Write these fractions as decimals.

a) $\frac{1}{10}$ = _____   b) $\frac{7}{10}$ = _____   c) $\frac{3}{10}$ = _____

3 marks

3 Write as decimals:

a) Nine tenths = _____   b) One and six tenths = _____

c) Two and four tenths = _____   d) Five and five tenths = _____

4 marks

4 Here is a number line.
Write the numbers that the arrows are pointing to.

a) _____   b) _____   c) _____

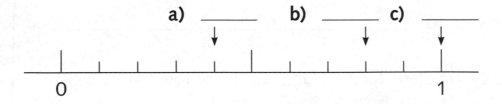

0   1

3 marks

Marks.......... /11

Challenge 2

1 Write these fractions as decimals.

a) $\frac{1}{2}$ = _____   b) $\frac{1}{4}$ = _____   c) $\frac{3}{4}$ = _____

3 marks

2 Write these fractions as decimals.

a) $\frac{9}{10}$ = _____   b) $\frac{57}{100}$ = _____   c) $\frac{3}{100}$ = _____

3 marks

Fraction and Decimal Equivalents

3 Gia says, "I have got four pounds and fifty-seven pence."

What is the usual way to write this using digits? _____

1 mark

4 Here is a number line.
Write the decimals that the arrows are pointing to.

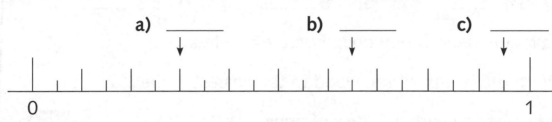

3 marks

Marks......... /10

Challenge 3

1 Write these fractions as decimals.

a) $\frac{9}{100}$ = _____   b) $\frac{20}{100}$ = _____   c) $\frac{101}{100}$ = _____

3 marks

2 Estimate the decimals that the arrows are pointing to.

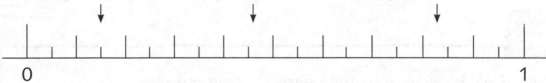

3 marks

3 Look at what James says.
Explain why he is incorrect.

_____

_____

_____

$\frac{7}{100}$ is 0.7

1 mark

4 Write in the missing numbers.

a) $\frac{3}{10}$ = 0.03 × _____   b) $\frac{70}{100}$ = 0.07 × _____

2 marks

Marks......... /9

Total marks .... /30   How am I doing?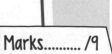

Rounding Decimals

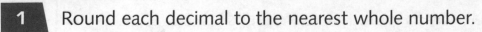

PS Problem-solving questions

Challenge 1

1 Round each decimal to the nearest whole number.

a) 5.1 _5._   b) 4.8 _5_   c) 2.9 _3_

d) 6.4 _6_   e) 7.6 _8_   f) 3.3 _3_

6 marks

PS **2** Zain cut a length of wood. It was 2.7 metres long.

Write the length of the wood to the nearest metre. _3_ m

1 mark

PS **3** A jug is filled with 1.2 litres of drink.

Write the capacity to the nearest litre. _1_ litre(s)

1 mark

PS **4** Kat thinks of a decimal number between 6 and 7. She rounds her number to the nearest whole number. The answer is 7.

Write what Kat's number could have been. _6.5_

1 mark

Marks.........9.../9

Challenge 2

1 Round each decimal to the nearest whole number.

a) 7.4 _7_   b) 6.5 _7_   c) 21.8 _22_

d) 53.7 _54_   e) 86.3 _86_   f) 105.3 _105_

6 marks

PS **2** Sam weighs 49.6 kilograms.

Write this mass to the nearest kilogram. _50_ kg

1 mark

PS **3** Tiana rounds a number to the nearest whole number. The answer is 50.

Write what Tiana's number could have been.

_49.5_

1 mark

Rounding Decimals

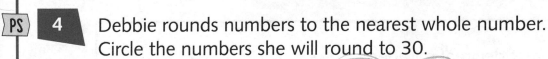

PS **4** Debbie rounds numbers to the nearest whole number.
Circle the numbers she will round to 30.

30.6   32.1   29.7   30.4   29.3

2 marks

Marks....1.0../10

Challenge 3

1 Round each decimal to the nearest whole number.

a) 116.3 __116__   b) 229.8 __230__   c) 707.0 __707__

3 marks

PS **2** Scott rounds numbers to the nearest whole number.
Circle the numbers he will round to 100.

98.9   100.3   99.6   100.9   99.1

2 marks

PS **3** Fay adds 6.2 and 7.4 together.
She estimates the answer by rounding each number to the nearest whole.

Write the total of the rounded numbers.   __13__

1 mark

PS **4** Aaron rounds numbers to the nearest whole number.
Draw lines to match the decimal numbers to the rounded numbers.

48.7   49.8   50.4   49.5   49.4

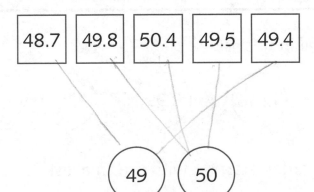

49   50

1 mark

Marks.......7../7

Total marks ....26.../26   How am I doing?

57

Comparing Decimals

PS Problem-solving questions

Challenge 1

1 Circle the largest decimal number.

0.4 0.8 0.2 0.7

1 mark

2 Circle the smallest decimal number.

2.4 2.8 3.1 2.5

1 mark

3 Write these decimal numbers in order, starting with the smallest.

5.6   6.2   5.9   4.7

_4.7_   _5.6_   _5.9_   _6.2_

1 mark

PS **4** George has £3.56, Raja has £5, Craig has £7.32 and Obe has £4.98.

Write who has the most money.   _Craig._

1 mark

PS **5** Write a decimal between 7.6 and 8.   _7.9_

1 mark

Marks.....5..... /5

Challenge 2

1 Circle the largest decimal in this list.

5.89   6.25   12.16   8.99   3.75

1 mark

2 Write these decimals in order, starting with the smallest.

34.45   45.43   45.34   35.44   43.54

_34.45_ _35.44_ _43.54_ _45.34_ _45.43_

1 mark

Comparing Decimals

PS **3** Ned puts these decimals in order, starting with the smallest.

(60.05) (60.56) (66.06) (65.66) (60.06)

Write the decimal that is third in Ned's list. _60.56_

✓ 1 mark

4 Write a decimal between 23.56 and 23.62 _23.61_

✓ 1 mark

5 Akash orders five numbers. Write what the missing numbers could be.

45.43 > _45.40_ > 45.34 > _45.30_ > 45.27

✓ 2 marks

Marks.......... /6

Challenge 3

1 Put the correct symbol < or > in each circle.

a) 5.67 $<$ 6.57   b) 23.56 $>$ 23.46

✓ 2 marks

PS **2** Jay has five pieces of wood. They are 3.25 m, 3.76 m, 2.88 m, 3.75 m and 2.98 m long.

a) Write the longest length. _3.76_ m

b) Write the shortest length. _2.88_ m

✓ 2 marks

3 5.6 and 5.7 are shown on this number line.

Mark 4.8 and 6.2 on the number line.

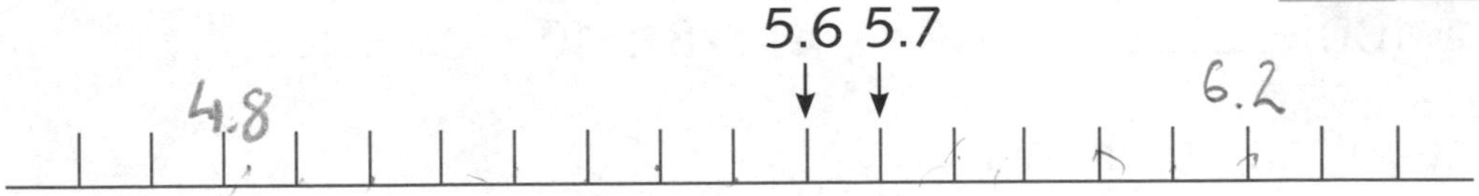

5.6 5.7
↓ ↓   6.2

4.8

✓ 2 marks

4 Write these numbers in order, smallest first.

52.5   5.25   6   50   25.5

_5.25_   _6_   _25.5_   _50_   _52.5_

✓ 1 mark

Marks.......... /7

Total marks .... /18   How am I doing?

Dividing by 10 and 100

Challenge 1

1 Complete these calculations.

a) 6 ÷ 10 = _____

b) 12 ÷ 10 = _____

c) 0.7 ÷ 10 = _____

d) 2.5 ÷ 10 = _____

4 marks

2 Fill in the missing numbers.

a) _____ ÷ 10 = 0.5

b) _____ ÷ 10 = 3.6

c) _____ ÷ 10 = 0.63

3 marks

3 Write the value of the 7 in the answer of each calculation.

a) 7 ÷ 10 = _____

b) 70 ÷ 10 = _____

c) 0.7 ÷ 10 = _____

3 marks

PS **4** A 2.5 kg bag of dog food is enough for 10 meals.

How much dog food is used for each meal? _____ kg

1 mark

Marks.......... /11

Challenge 2

1 Complete these calculations.

a) 6.7 ÷ 10 = _____

b) 54 ÷ 100 = _____

c) 15 ÷ 100 = _____

d) 78 ÷ 10 = _____

4 marks

2 Fill in the missing numbers.

a) _____ ÷ 10 = 0.57

b) _____ ÷ 10 = 3.6

c) 92 ÷ _____ = 0.92

d) 46 ÷ _____ = 0.46

4 marks

PS **3** Sunita divides a number by 100. The answer is six tenths.

Write the number Sunita divided. _____

1 mark

Dividing by 10 and 100

4 Write the value of the 4 in the answer of each calculation.

a) 34 ÷ 100 = _____

b) 6.4 ÷ 10 = _____

 2 marks

PS **5** Gus buys 100 of the same stamps and pays £64 for them.

What is the cost of each stamp? £_____

 1 mark

Marks.........../12

Challenge 3

1 Write in the missing numbers.

a) 12 ÷ _____ = 1.2

b) 27 ÷ _____ = 0.27

c) _____ ÷ 10 = 3.2

d) _____ ÷ 100 = 0.79

 4 marks

PS **2** Kagendo divides a number and works out the answer to be nine hundredths.
Sally divides the same number and works out the answer to be nine tenths.

Write what Kagendo's and Sally's calculations could have been.

Kagendo's calculation: _____

Sally's calculation: _____

 2 marks

3 Circle the calculations that have answers with 6 tenths.

| 64 ÷ 10 | 56 ÷ 100 | 6.7 ÷ 10 | 56 ÷ 10 | 36 ÷ 100 |

 2 marks

PS **4** Write division calculations dividing by 10.

a) _____ ÷ _____ = four ones and five tenths

b) _____ ÷ _____ = six ones and eight hundredths

 2 marks

Marks.........../10

Total marks ..../33   How am I doing?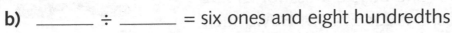

Decimal Problems

Challenge 1

PS 1 A shop sells the following items.

a) Holly buys a set of pens, a ruler and a pencil case. What was the total cost? £_____

b) Josef has a £10 note. He buys a book. How much change does he get? £_____

c) Katie spent £7.70 on two items. Which two items did she buy?

_____ _____

3 marks

PS 2 Michelle has two bottles that each hold 4 litres of water. One is half full and the other is one-quarter full. How any litres of water does Michelle have? _____ litres

1 mark

PS 3 Obi lives 2500 metres from school. He walks to and from school five days a week. How far does he walk in one week walking to and from school? Give your answer in kilometres. _____ km

1 mark

PS 4 Oranges cost £1.20 per kilogram. Jane buys 2 kilograms of oranges. How much does she pay? £_____

1 mark

Marks.......... /6

Challenge 2

PS 1 Pippa has £50. She buys a dress for £19.90 and a pair of shoes for £24.99. How much money does Pippa have left? £_____

1 mark

PS 2 Bananas cost 70p per kilogram. Tim buys $1\frac{1}{2}$ kg of bananas. How much does he pay? £_____

1 mark

Decimal Problems

PS | **3** | Sammy uses 650 grams of flour from a 2 kilogram bag. How much flour is left in the bag?

_____ kg

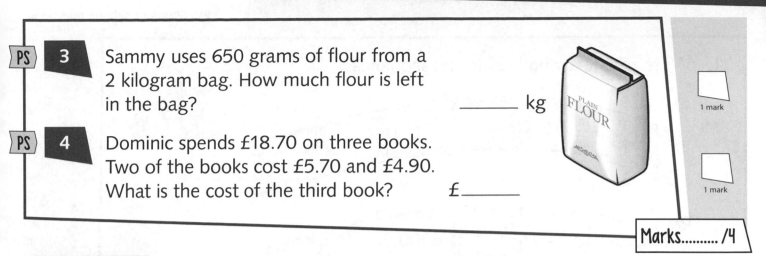

1 mark

PS | **4** | Dominic spends £18.70 on three books. Two of the books cost £5.70 and £4.90. What is the cost of the third book?

£_____

1 mark

Marks.......... /4

Challenge 3

PS | **1** | A bag of potatoes has a mass of 4.8 kilograms. What is the total mass of $2\frac{1}{2}$ bags?

_____ kg

1 mark

PS | **2** | A glass holds $\frac{1}{2}$ litre. How many times can the glass be filled from a 5 litre bottle?

_____

1 mark

PS | **3** | This is a map showing roads and some towns.

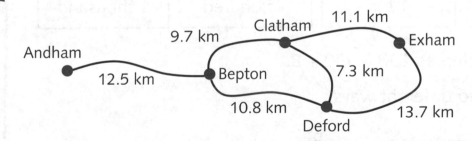

a) Jed drives from Andham to Clatham. How long is his shortest route?

_____ km

b) Dimi drives from Bepton to Exham. How long is the shortest route?

_____ km

c) Maisie drives from Deford to Exham going through Clatham. She runs out of petrol 3 kilometres from Exham. How far has she driven?

_____ km

3 marks

Marks.......... /5

Total marks .... /15

How am I doing?

1. Write the next numbers in the sequences.

   a)

   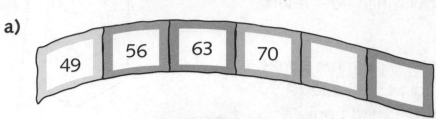

   49 | 56 | 63 | 70 | | |

   b)

   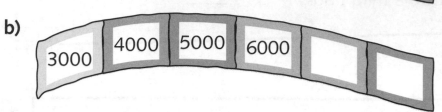

   3000 | 4000 | 5000 | 6000 | | |

   2 marks

2. Write these numbers in order, starting with the smallest.

   8314   **1834**   **1384**   **8341**   **4138**

   _____   _____   _____   _____   _____

   1 mark

3. Circle the value of the digit 1 in the number 6914.

1 one	1 ten	1 hundred	1 thousand

   1 mark

4. 538 can be written as 400 + 130 + 8.

   Write 538 in two different ways.

   a) _____   b) _____

   2 marks

5. Complete the table by rounding each number to the nearest 10.

Number	Rounded to the nearest 10
3784	
427	
79	

   3 marks

6. Write the next number in the sequence.

18	12	6	0	

   1 mark

7. Work out:

    a) 6734 + 264 = _____   **b)** 5183 − 437 = _____

2 marks

8. Estimate the answer to 568 + 357 by rounding the numbers to the nearest hundred and adding the rounded numbers.

    _____ + _____ = _____

1 mark

PS **9.** Josh buys and sells computer games. He has 387 games. He buys 56 games and sells 125 games.

    How many computer games does he have now?   _____ games

1 mark

PS **10.** Chloe has 65 metres of wood. She buys 120 more metres of wood to build a fence. She has 36 metres left over.

    How much wood did Chloe use building the fence? _____ m

1 mark

11. Work out:

    a) 6 × 4 × 3 = _____   **b)** 5 × 8 × 6 = _____

2 marks

12. A factor pair of a number is 56 and 3.

    What is the number? _____

1 mark

13. Work out:

a)		5	3	2	**b)**		9	4	0	**c)**		6	2	8
×				4	×				8	×				6

3 marks

14. Write the missing numbers in this sentence:

    2 children share 3 paint pots and 5 brushes, so 4 children share

    _____ paint pots and _____ brushes.

2 marks

15. Write in the missing number: 48 × 3 = _____ × 3 + 8 × 3 = 144

1 mark

Progress Test 2

 PS Problem-solving questions

16. Work out:

    a) $3 \div 100 =$ _____

    b) $9 \div 100 =$ _____

    c) $\frac{7}{10} \div 10 =$ _____

3 marks

17. Estimate the fraction each arrow points to.

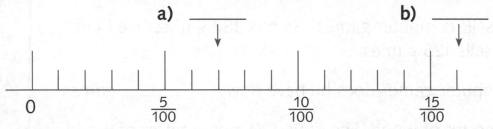

    a) _____   **b)** _____

0        $\frac{5}{100}$ $\frac{10}{100}$ $\frac{15}{100}$

2 marks

18. a) $\frac{6}{8}$ of this circle is shaded. Write in the missing number.

    $\frac{\square}{4}$ of this circle is shaded.

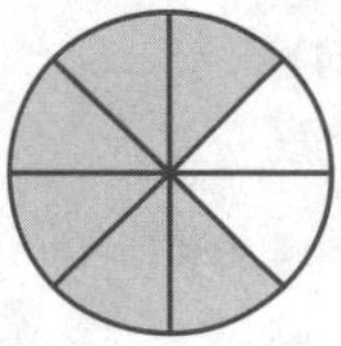

    b) $\frac{1}{2}$ of this rectangle is shaded. Write in the missing number.

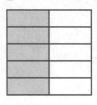

    $\frac{\square}{10}$ of this rectangle is shaded.

2 marks

19. Work out:

    a) $\frac{4}{10} + \frac{7}{10} =$ _____

    b) $\frac{7}{8} + \frac{2}{8} =$ _____

2 marks

20. Write these decimals as fractions.

    a) $0.13 =$ _____   **b)** $0.9 =$ _____   **c)** $0.09 =$ _____

3 marks

21. Write these fractions as decimals.

    a) $\frac{93}{100} =$ _____   **b)** $\frac{7}{100} =$ _____   **c)** $\frac{4}{10} =$ _____

3 marks

22. Round each decimal to the nearest whole number.

a) 4.7 _____   **b)** 15.4 _____   **c)** 29.8 _____

3 marks

 PS **23.** Billy rounds a number, less than 25, with one decimal place to the nearest whole number. The rounded number is 25.

What could Billy's number have been? _____

1 mark

24. Circle the largest number.

| 73.8 | 9.3 | 20.0 | 68.9 | 73.7 |

1 mark

25. Write these numbers in order, starting with the smallest.

31.6   **31.8**   **32.5**   **30.7**   **30.2**

_____   _____   _____   _____   _____

1 mark

26. Write in the missing numbers.

a) 5.6 ÷ _____ = 0.56   **b)** 9 ÷ _____ = 0.09

c) 16 ÷ _____ = 0.16   **d)** 0.8 ÷ _____ = 0.08

4 marks

PS **27.** Chandra divides a two-digit number by 10. The answer has 5 ones and 7 tenths.

What was the number that Chandra divided? _____

1 mark

28. Work out:

a) $\frac{2}{5}$ of 25 = _____   **b)** $\frac{3}{4}$ of 32 = _____

c) $\frac{9}{10}$ of 90 = _____

3 marks

29. Jade buys 4 t-shirts that cost £7.25 each.

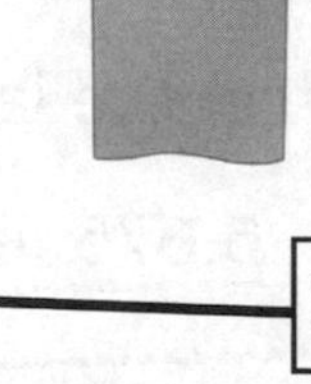

Work out the total cost of the 4 t-shirts. £ _____

1 mark

Marks.........../54

Comparing Measures

PS Problem-solving questions

Challenge 1

1 Write these lengths in order, longest first.

36.87 m **63.78 m** **83.76 m** **83.67 m** **38.76 m**

_______ _______ _______ _______ _______

1 mark

2 Write these capacities in order, smallest first.

45.78 litres **4.87 litres** **5.47 litres** **54.87 litres** **78.54 litres**

_______ _______ _______ _______ _______

1 mark

PS **3** Sonya has three different-sized jugs. The largest jug holds 4.75 litres and the smallest jug holds 4.56 litres.

What could the capacity of the third jug be? _______ litres

1 mark

4 There are three lengths of ribbon. The lengths are $1\frac{1}{2}$ metres, 1.25 metres and 1.65 metres.

Write the lengths in order, smallest first.

_______ m _______ m _______ m

1 mark

PS **5** Stan weighs 43.76 kg, Dubry weighs 46.73 kg and Tom weighs 45.87 kg.

Who is the heaviest? _______________

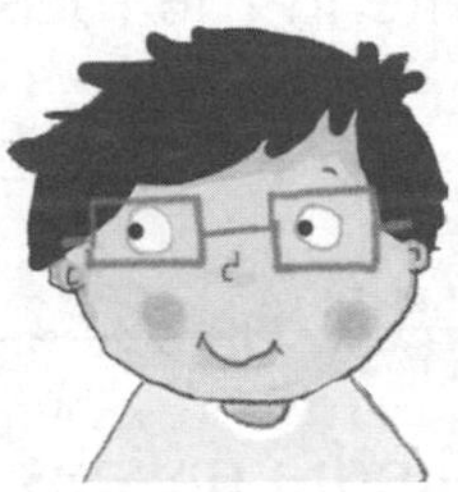

1 mark

Marks........../5

Challenge 2

1 Circle the larger mass.

a) 3.2 kg **or** 2800 g **b)** 7.8 kg **or** 8000 g

2 marks

2 Circle the shorter length.

a) 5.6 m **or** 474 cm **b)** 67 mm **or** 6 cm

2 marks

3 Circle the larger capacity.

a) 5.675 litres **or** 570 ml **b)** 8000 ml **or** 10 litres

2 marks

Comparing Measures

4 Write these lengths in order, shortest first.

475 cm   **5 m**   **4800 mm**   **4.7 m**

_____   _____   _____   _____

1 mark

PS **5** Alvin has a 5 kilogram bag of flour. He uses 255 grams. Has he used over half of the bag? _____

1 mark

Marks.......... /8

Challenge 3

1 Circle the longest length.

$4\frac{1}{2}$ m   4.6 m $4\frac{3}{4}$ m   4.8 m   4.2 m

1 mark

2 Circle the shortest length.

5.7 kilometres   4500 metres

4.85 kilometres   5000 metres

1 mark

3 Amy is offered four drinks. She wants the largest drink. Circle the drink she should choose.

300 ml can | 0.5 litre bottle | 0.25 litre glass | 1 litre bottle

1 mark

PS **4** There are three parcels. Parcel A weighs 6 kg, parcel B is $\frac{1}{2}$ kg heavier than parcel A and parcel C is 250 g lighter than parcel B.

Write the parcels in order, the heaviest mass first.

_____   _____   _____

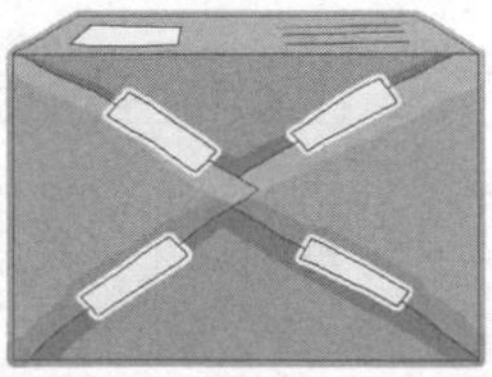

1 mark

Marks.......... /4

Total marks .... /17   How am I doing?   😊   😐   😖

Estimating Measures

Challenge 1

1 Estimate the mass of the parcel.

_____ kg

1 mark

2 Estimate the length of the line below. _____ cm

0 1 2 3 4 5 6 7 8 9 10

1 mark

3 Estimate how much liquid is in the jug. _____ litre(s)

— 1 litre

— ½ litre

1 mark

4 Phil gets £50 to go shopping. At the end he says, "I have about half of my money left."

Tick the amounts of money Phil could have.

(£45) (£24.75) (£36.50) (£26.15) (£0.50)

2 marks

Marks.......... /5

Challenge 2

1 Tick the best estimate for the length of a car.

| 40 mm | 40 cm | 4 m | 0.4 km |

1 mark

2 Tick the best estimate for the capacity of a mug.

(35 ml) (35 litres) (350 ml) (3.5 litres)

1 mark

3 Tick the best estimate for the mass of a banana.

| 120 g | 12 g | 1.2 kg | 12 kg |

1 mark

Estimating Measures

4 Melanie walks 1 kilometre to school with no stops.
Tick the best estimate for the time it will take.

| 1 minute | 12 minutes | 45 minutes | 1 hour |

1 mark

Marks.......... /4

Challenge 3

1 Adam goes for a meal. He chooses the following items.

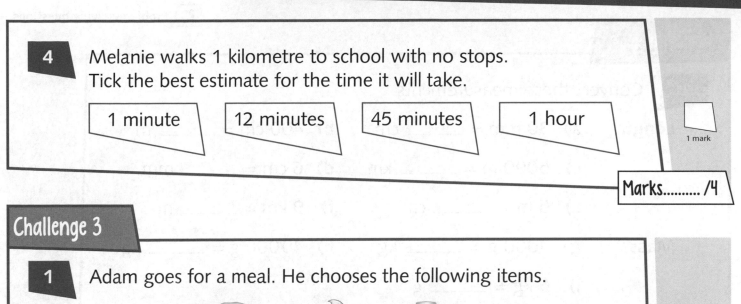

£7.60   £3.65   £2.55

Estimate the cost of the meal by rounding the prices to the nearest
pound and adding the rounded prices.   £ _____

1 mark

2 Estimate the temperature shown on the thermometer.

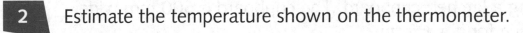

_____ °C

1 mark

3 Estimate the length of the curved line. Do not measure the line.

_____ cm

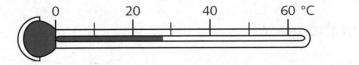

1 mark

PS **4** The same parcel is shown
on both sets of scales.
Estimate the mass of
the parcel.   _____ kg

1 mark

Marks.......... /4

Total marks .... /13   How am I doing?

Converting Measures

PS Problem-solving questions

Challenge 1

1 Convert these measurements.

Length **a)** 30 mm = ______ cm **b)** 400 cm = ______ m

c) 5000 m = ______ km **d)** 6 cm = ______ mm

e) 5 m = ______ cm **f)** 9 km = ______ m

Mass **g)** 4000 g = ______ kg **h)** 40 000 g = ______ kg

i) 5 kg = ______ g

Capacity **j)** 8 litres = ______ ml **k)** 10 000 ml = ______ litres

l) 0.5 litres = ______ ml

12 marks

PS **2** A glass holds 500 ml. How many times can the glass be filled from a 2 litre bottle of drink? ______

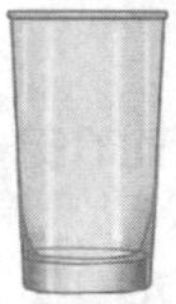

1 mark

PS **3** Tina is fitting a kitchen cupboard. The cupboard is 600 mm wide and the space for it is 65 cm.

a) Will the cupboard fit in the space? ______

b) What is the difference between the two measurements? ______

2 marks

Marks........ /15

Challenge 2

1 Convert these measurements.

a) 5.2 m = ______ cm **b)** $3\frac{1}{2}$ kg = ______ g

c) 3500 ml = ______ litres **d)** 78 mm = ______ cm

e) 250 m = ______ km **f)** $\frac{3}{4}$ m = ______ cm

g) 845 cm = ______ m **h)** 10 500 m = ______ km

8 marks

Converting Measures

PS 2 Sara buys a bag of flour that weighs 1 kilogram.
She uses some flour and there are 600 grams left.
How much flour has Sara used? _____

1 mark

PS 3 Casey has three jugs. Jug A holds 200 ml, jug B holds
250 ml and jug C holds 500 ml. Which jug will he fill
exactly four times to fill a bowl with 1 litre of water? _____

1 mark

PS 4 Ewan has a carton with 568 millilitres of milk.
He uses 0.5 litres in a recipe. How much milk
does he have left over? _____

1 mark

Marks.......... /11

Challenge 3

1 How many millimetres are there in 1 metre? _____ mm

1 mark

2 Write in the missing units.

a) 4.5 km = 4500 _____   b) 67 mm = 6.7 _____

c) 125 m = 0.125 _____   d) 6750 ml = 6.75 _____

e) 5.4 kg = 5400 _____   f) 4.5 m = 450 _____

6 marks

PS 3 Each row and each column adds up to 1 litre. Fill in the missing
capacities.

$\frac{1}{2}$ litre	300 ml	
	0.6 litres	
	$\frac{1}{4}$ litre	

1 mark

Marks.......... /8

Total marks .... /34   How am I doing?

73

Measurement Calculations

PS Problem-solving questions

Challenge 1

PS **1** Charlotte spends £3.45 on a new pen. How much change will she get from £5? £ ______ 1 mark

PS **2** Nadia buys a book for £8.49 and a magazine for £4.75. How much does she spend? £ ______ 1 mark

PS **3** Tomas buys three pens that cost £2 each. How much change will he get from £10? £ ______ 1 mark

PS **4** Subtract 5p from £5. £ ______ 1 mark

PS **5** Milly has a £10 note and a £5 note. She spends £12.33. How much money will Milly have left? £ ______ 1 mark

Marks........../5

Challenge 2

1 Calculate these measures.

a)
```
  £ 2 . 4 5
+ £ 4 . 6 5
___________

___________
```

b)
```
  1 4 . 8 5 m
- 1 1 . 0 9 m
_____________

_____________
```

c)
```
  5 6 . 7 8 kg
- 3 8 . 5 8 kg
______________

______________
```

d)
```
  3 8 . 9 5 litres
+     7 . 8 4 litres
__________________

__________________
```

4 marks

PS **2** Claire goes out for a meal. She spends £15.75 on her main course and £5.50 on dessert. She has £15.35 left. How much did Claire have when she went out? £______ 1 mark

PS **3** Rachael buys two bags of dog food. Each bag weighs 5 kg. Seven days later, she has used 3.5 kg. How much dog food does Rachael have left? ______ kg 1 mark

Measurement Calculations

PS **4** At a Sports Day, Mahmood makes three jumps of 3.15 m, 2.87 m and 3.08 m. He adds the distances together.
He is 0.15 m short of the school record.
What is the school record? _____ m

1 mark

PS **5** David buys some bottles of juice for a party.
He buys five 2 litre bottles and ten 0.5 litre bottles.
How much juice does he have altogether? _____ litres

1 mark

Marks.......... /8

Challenge 3

PS **1** Asel uses some weights to find the mass of a parcel. She uses two 1 kilogram weights, three 500 gram weights and one 50 gram weight. What is the mass of the parcel?

a) Give your answer in kilograms. _____ kg

b) Give your answer in grams. _____ g

2 marks

PS **2** Toby has £7.25 in his money box. He counts the coins; he has these coins. One coin is missing.

What is the missing coin? _____

1 mark

PS **3** Kitchen cupboards come in two sizes of width: 0.6 m and 0.4 m. Norman wants to use both sizes of cupboards to fill a 3 metre wall. How could he do this?

_____

1 mark

PS **4** A glass holds 450 ml. Yanqun has a 2 litre bottle of drink. How many times can Yanqun fill the glass? _____

1 mark

Marks.......... /5

Total marks .... /18   How am I doing?   😊   😐   😖

12 and 24 Hour Time

Challenge 1

1 These clocks show morning times.
Write the times shown on the clocks in 12 hour time.

a) _____ b) _____ c) _____

3 marks

2 These clocks show afternoon and evening times.
Write the times shown on the clocks in 24 hour time.

a) _____ b) _____ c) _____

3 marks

3 Write the time shown on these clocks in words.

a) _____ b) _____ c) _____

_____ _____ _____

3 marks

Marks.......... /9

76

12 and 24 Hour Time

Challenge 2

1 Write these digital times in 12 hour time.

  a) 15:25 _____

  b) 18:10 _____

2 Write these word times in 24 hour time.

  a) Quarter past two in the afternoon   _____

  b) Ten to twelve in the morning   _____

  c) Twenty-five to seven in the evening   _____

PS **3** The time on this clock is 40 minutes slow.

What is the correct time? _____

Marks.......... /6

Challenge 3

1 Write the missing parts of each time in this table.

	Word time		12 hour time		24 hour time
a)	Five past two in the afternoon	=	_____:05 _____	=	_____:05
b)	Twenty-five to _____ in the evening	= 8:_____ _____		=	_____:_____

PS **2** Harpreet's train leaves at 15:25.
She looks at her watch.
How many minutes is it before her
train leaves?   _____ minutes

Marks.......... /3

Total marks .... /18   How am I doing?

Time Problems

Challenge 1

1 Write in the missing numbers.

a) 2 minutes = _____ seconds b) 2 hours = _____ minutes

c) 2 days = _____ hours d) 2 weeks = _____ days

4 marks

2 Write the four months of the year that have exactly 30 days.

_____ _____

_____ _____

4 marks

3 If the year 2020 is a leap year, which year will be the next leap year? _____

1 mark

PS **4** Kim's birthday is on Tuesday, 4th May.
She has her birthday party on the first Saturday after her birthday.

What is the date of the birthday party? _____

1 mark

Marks......... /10

Challenge 2

PS **1** A film starts at 16:45 and finishes at 19:05.

How long does it last? _____ hours _____ minutes

1 mark

PS **2** Carly gets up when her alarm clock shows 07:30.
She gets washed and dressed and has her breakfast. Her watch shows the time that she leaves for school.

How long has it taken her to get ready? _____ minutes

1 mark

PS **3** It is 18:30 and Bev says, "I'll see you in three-quarters of an hour."

What will the time be? _____

1 mark

Time Problems

4 Change these units of time.

a) 4 weeks = _____ days   b) 2 years = _____ months

c) 5 minutes = _____ seconds   d) 3 days = _____ hours

4 marks

Marks.......... /7

Challenge 3

PS **1** These time periods are in order, shortest first.
Write the number of minutes that could be the missing number.

| 480 seconds | _____ minutes | $\frac{1}{6}$ of an hour |

1 mark

2 Write in the missing numbers.

a) _____ hours = _____ days = 2 weeks

b) _____ months = _____ years = 1 decade

2 marks

PS **3** Barry goes to sleep at 21:30 and he sleeps for $9\frac{1}{4}$ hours.

At what time will he wake up? _____

1 mark

PS **4** School starts at 8:50am and ends at 12:15pm. The children have
a 20-minute break. The rest of the time they are in the classroom.

For how long are they in the classroom?

_____ hours _____ minutes

1 mark

PS **5** Karen catches a train at 10:15am.
The journey lasts 3 hours 12 minutes.

At what time does the train arrive? _____

1 mark

Marks.......... /6

Total marks .... /23   How am I doing?

Perimeter and Area

Challenge 1

1 Three rectangles and squares (**A–C**) are drawn on a centimetre square grid. Find **a)** the area and **b)** the perimeter of each shape.

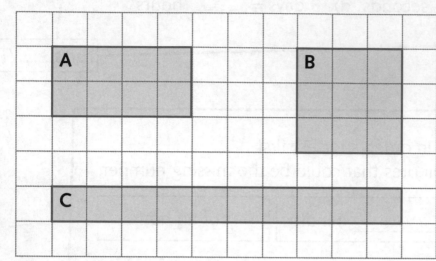

A a) _____ squares

   b) _____ cm

B a) _____ squares

   b) _____ cm

C a) _____ squares

   b) _____ cm

6 marks

Grid not to scale

Marks.......... /6

Challenge 2

1 Three shapes (**A–C**) are drawn on a centimetre square grid. Find **a)** the area and **b)** the perimeter of each shape.

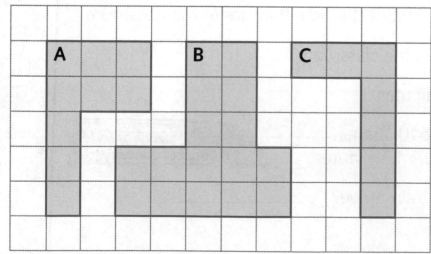

A a) _____ squares

   b) _____ cm

B a) _____ squares

   b) _____ cm

C a) _____ squares

   b) _____ cm

6 marks

Grid not to scale

Perimeter and Area

2 Work out the perimeter of this shape. Use a ruler. _____ cm

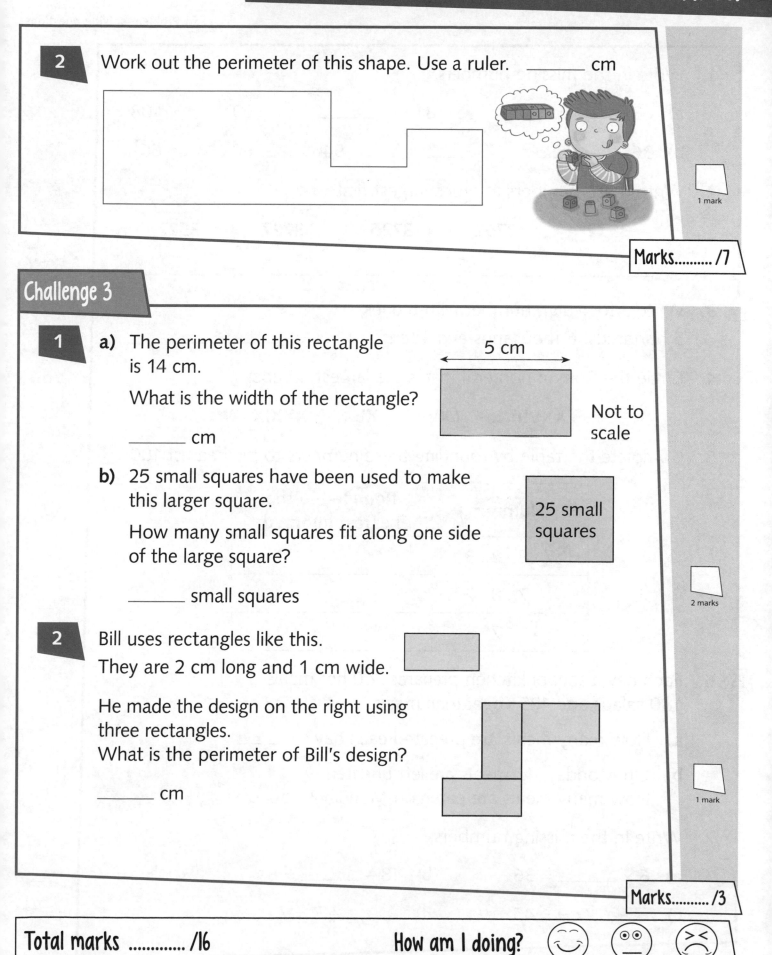

1 mark

Marks.......... /7

Challenge 3

1 **a)** The perimeter of this rectangle is 14 cm.

What is the width of the rectangle?

_____ cm

5 cm

Not to scale

b) 25 small squares have been used to make this larger square.

How many small squares fit along one side of the large square?

_____ small squares

25 small squares

2 marks

2 Bill uses rectangles like this.
They are 2 cm long and 1 cm wide.

He made the design on the right using three rectangles.
What is the perimeter of Bill's design?

_____ cm

1 mark

Marks.......... /3

Total marks .... /16   How am I doing?   😊   😐   😣

Progress Test 3

PS Problem-solving questions

1. Write in the missing numbers.

a) 63 ______ 81 ______ 99 108

b) 36 ______ ______ 54 60 66

2 marks

2. Write these numbers in order, largest first.

3572 **3752** **3725** **3727** **3527**

______ ______ ______ ______ ______

1 mark

PS 3. Write a four-digit number with 8 ones, 5 hundreds, 6 thousands and 4 tens. ______

1 mark

4. Circle the Roman numeral that is the largest number.

XXVIII **LXV** **XL** **XXXIX**

1 mark

5. Complete the table by rounding these numbers to the nearest 100.

Number	Rounded to the nearest hundred
7 8 2 3	
7 8 2	
7 8	

3 marks

PS 6. Each day a school kitchen prepares 240 hot meals, 180 salads and 125 vegetarian meals.

a) How many meals are prepared each day? ______

b) On Monday, 43 meals are left uneaten. How many meals are eaten on Monday? ______

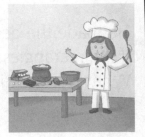

2 marks

7. Write in the missing numbers.

a) 6 × ______ = 36 b) 48 ÷ ______ = 8

c) ______ × 9 = 45 d) ______ ÷ 7 = 7

4 marks

8. Fill in the missing number. $6 \times 5 \times$ _____ $= 240$

9. Work out:

a)
```
    5  0  9
×         9
_____

_____
```

b)
```
    4  5  2
×         7
_____

_____
```

c)
```
    8  6  1
×         6
_____

_____
```

PS **10.** It takes Alice 2 hours to build 7 metres of fence.
How long will it take her to build 21 metres of fence?   _____ hours

11. Write in the missing numbers.

a) $6 \div$ _____ $= \frac{6}{100}$ **b)** $8.1 \div$ _____ $= \frac{81}{100}$

c) $0.7 \div$ _____ $= \frac{7}{100}$

12. Draw a line from $\frac{3}{5}$ to its equivalent fraction.

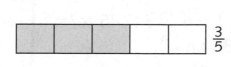 $\frac{3}{5}$

$\frac{4}{8}$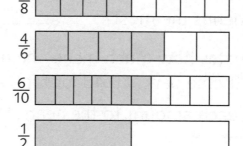

$\frac{4}{6}$

$\frac{6}{10}$

$\frac{1}{2}$

13. Fill in the missing numbers.

a) $\dfrac{\square}{8} + \dfrac{6}{8} = \dfrac{7}{8}$ **b)** $\dfrac{\square}{12} + \dfrac{5}{12} + \dfrac{3}{12} = \dfrac{11}{12}$

PS **14.** Heather has saved up £18.70.
Write this to the nearest whole pound.   £ _____

PS **15.** Mo has £20.
She spends $\frac{1}{5}$ of her money on a drink and $\frac{3}{10}$ on a sandwich.
How much money does she have left?   £ _____

PS **16.** Kate buys some things for her party.

| Balloons £1.75 | Candles £3.85 | Cake £11.85 | Plates £5.80 | Mugs £4.80 |

a) She spends exactly £17.45. Which three things did she buy?

_____   _____   _____

b) Kate pays with a £20 note.
   How much money does she have left?   £ _____

2 marks

17. Write these amounts in order, starting with the largest.

£3   90p   £0.08   £1.25   5p

_____   _____   _____   _____   _____

1 mark

PS **18.** Harvey spends £8, Tia spends 675p, Christopher spends £9.89 and Raf spends two £5 notes.

a) Who spends the least?   _____

b) Who spends the most?   _____

2 marks

PS **19.** Daryl estimates how much money he has spent. He paid £17.45 for a ticket to a theme park, £8.40 for food and £15.35 on gifts.

He rounds each amount to the nearest whole pound and adds the rounded amounts.

Write Daryl's estimate.   £ _____

1 mark

PS **20.** Katherine says, "My train leaves at quarter to 9."
The clock in the station shows 08:30.

How many minutes does Katherine need to wait?   _____ minutes

1 mark

21. The clock on the right shows an evening time.
Circle the digital clock that shows the same time.

A 20:40   B 19:40   C 21:35   D 20:50

1 mark

22. Tick the correct statement.

    A   There are 300 minutes in 5 hours. ☐

    B   There are 60 minutes in 5 hours. ☐

    C   There are 35 minutes in 5 hours. ☐

    D   There are 120 minutes in 5 hours. ☐

 **23.** Susie runs a lap of a track in 100 seconds.

Write this as minutes and seconds. _____ minutes _____ seconds

24. Change these measurements.

    a) 5 kg = _____ g   **b)** 60 mm = _____ cm

    c) 1000 cm = _____ m   **d)** 8000 ml = _____ litres

    e) 8 m = _____ cm   **f)** 2 km = _____ m

25. Measure the perimeter of each shape.

    a)   **b)**

        _____ cm   _____ cm

26. Write the area of the shaded shape.   _____ squares

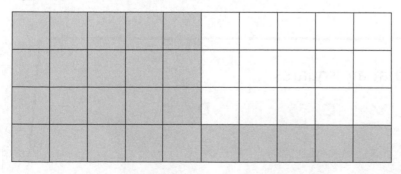

1 mark

1 mark

6 marks

2 marks

1 mark

2-D Shapes

Challenge 1

1 Tick the shapes that are rectangles.

A B C D

2 marks

2 These triangles are drawn on a squared grid.

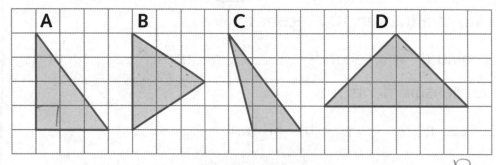

a) Write the letters of the two isosceles triangles. _B_ _D_

b) Write the letters of the two right-angled triangles. _A_ _D_

c) Write the letter of the obtuse-angled triangle. _C_

d) Write the letter of the acute-angled triangle. _B_

4 marks

3 Tick the shape that is a parallelogram.

A  B  C  D

1 mark

Marks.......... /7

Challenge 2

1 Tick the quadrilaterals that are squares.

A B C 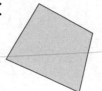 D

2 marks

2-D Shapes

2 Give a reason why this shape is not a hexagon.

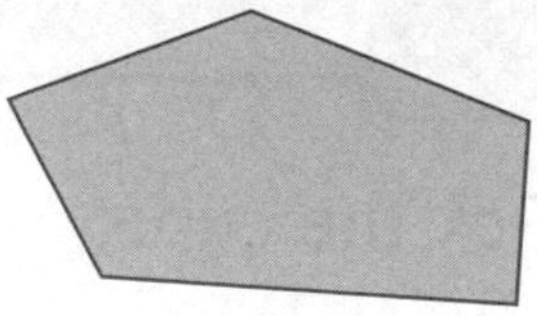

Because it, is not eqle lenths and it dosint have enuge ejes

1 mark

3 These triangles are drawn on a squared grid.
Tick the triangle that is a right-angled isosceles triangle.

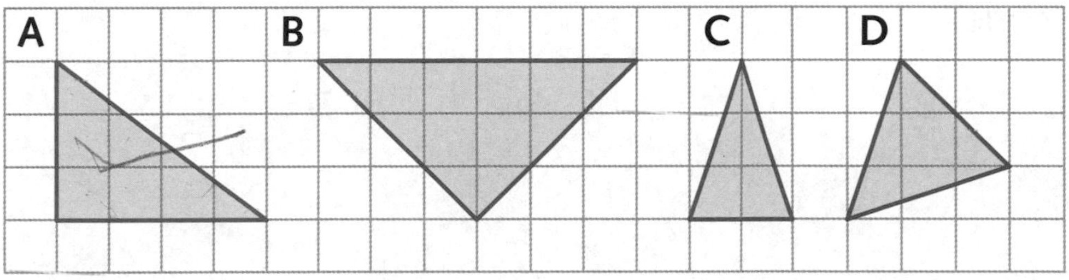

A   B   C   D

1 mark

Marks.......... /4

Challenge 3

1 Circle the shape that has the most sides.

pentagon   hexagon   parallelogram   (octagon)

1 mark

2 Tick the shapes with pairs of equal and parallel sides.

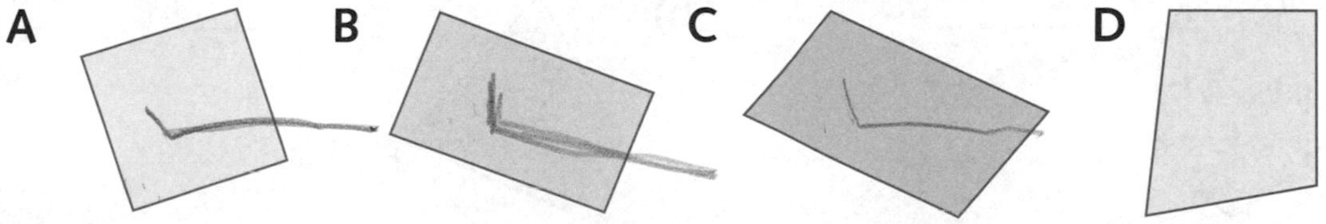

A   B   C   D

3 marks

3 Mark says, "A pentagon cannot have a right angle."
Draw a pentagon to show that Mark is incorrect.

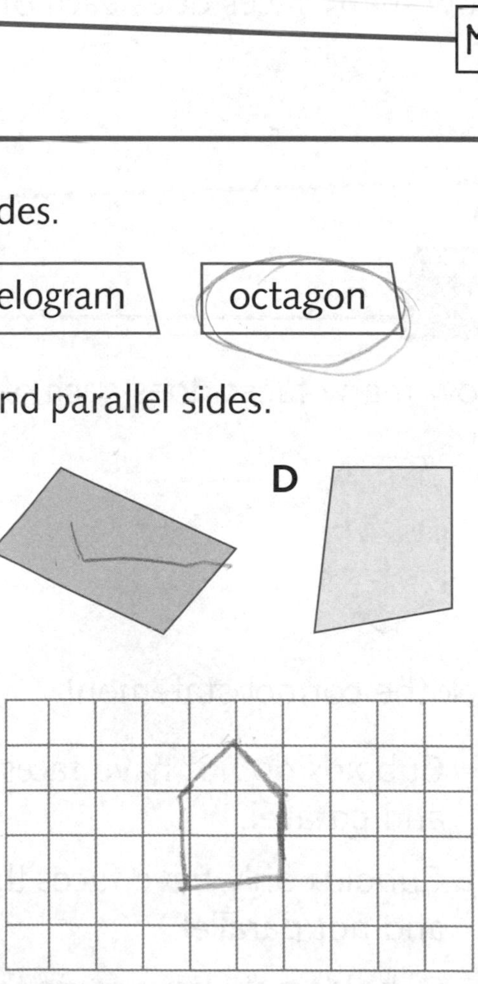

1 mark

Marks.......... /5

Total marks .... /16   How am I doing?

3-D Shapes

Challenge 1

1 Tick the cube.

A   B   C   D

1 mark

2 Tick the cone.

A   B   C   D

1 mark

3 How many faces does each of these shapes have?

a) _____   b) A cube _____

2 marks

Marks........./4

Challenge 2

1 How many faces does each of these shapes have?

a) _____   b) _____

2 marks

2 Tick the correct statement.

A Cuboids do not have faces that are perpendicular and parallel. ☐

B Cuboids only have faces that are perpendicular, and not parallel. ☐

C Cuboids only have faces that are parallel, and not perpendicular. ☐

D Cuboids have faces that are perpendicular and parallel. ☐

1 mark

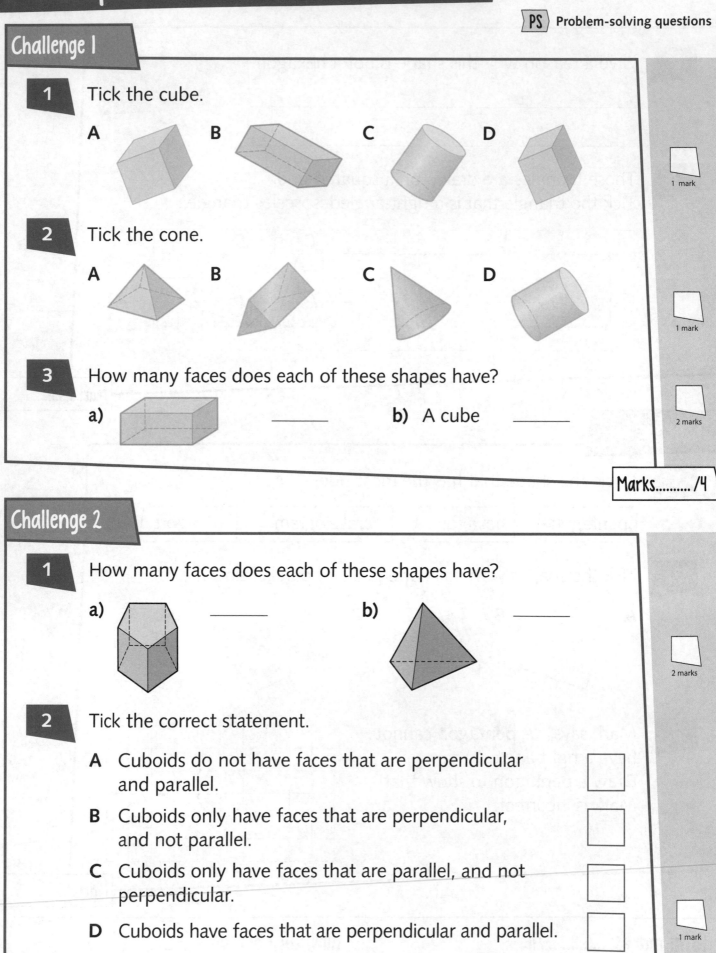

3-D Shapes

3 Complete this table.

Shape	Faces	Edges	Vertices
Cuboid			
Square-based pyramid			
Triangular prism			

3 marks

Marks.......... /6

Challenge 3

 1 Shona says, "The faces on a cuboid are always rectangles."
Is Shona correct? Explain your answer.

_____

_____

_____

1 mark

2 A prism has 15 edges. What shape is its end face?

_____

1 mark

3 **a)** How many cubes have been used to make this shape? _____

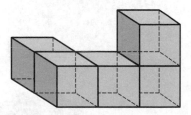

b) Rohan adds more cubes to this shape to make a cuboid. The cuboid is 3 cubes long, 2 cubes wide and 2 cubes high.

How many more cubes will Rohan need? _____

2 marks

Marks.......... /4

Total marks .... /14   **How am I doing?**

Lines of Symmetry

Challenge 1

1 Draw the lines of symmetry on these shapes.

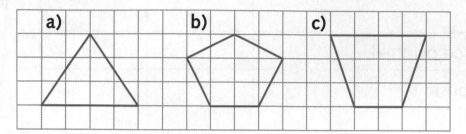

3 marks

2 The dotted lines are lines of symmetry. Complete the shapes.

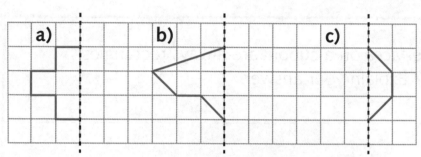

3 marks

Marks.......... /6

Challenge 2

1 How many lines of symmetry does each of these shapes have?

a)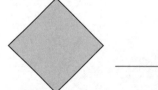

_____

b) _____

c)

_____

3 marks

Lines of Symmetry

2 The dotted lines are lines of symmetry. Complete the shapes.

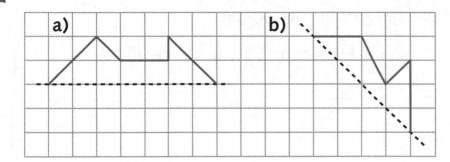

a) b)

2 marks

Marks.......... /5

1 Tick the shape that has no lines of symmetry.

A B C D E

1 mark

2 Draw three more lines on the grid to make a pentagon with one line of symmetry.

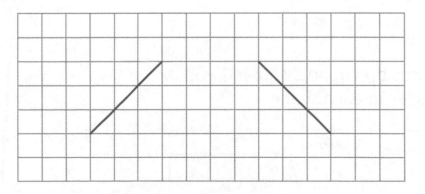

1 mark

Marks.......... /2

Total marks ..../13 How am I doing?

Angles

PS Problem-solving questions

Challenge 1

1 Write the number of angles in each shape.

a) Rectangle   b) Hexagon   c) Kite

_____   _____   _____

 3 marks

2 Tick the acute angle.

A   B   C   D

 1 mark

3 Tick the obtuse angle.

A   B   C   D

 1 mark

4 Tick the largest angle.

A   B   C   D

 1 mark

Marks.......... /6

Challenge 2

1 Here are two shapes drawn on a squared grid.
Tick the acute angles in each shape.

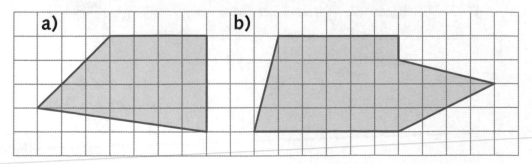

2 marks

Angles

2 Write the letters of these angles in order of size, smallest first.

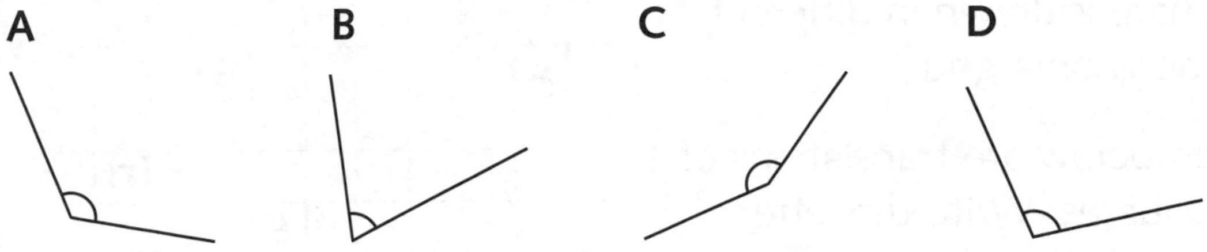

A   B   C   D

_____   _____   _____   _____

1 mark

3 Write these angles in order of size, starting with the largest.

     right   obtuse   acute

_____   _____   _____

1 mark

Marks.......... /4

Challenge 3

1 Below is a squared grid.

   a) Draw a five-sided shape with three obtuse angles.

   b) Draw a four-sided shape with three acute angles.

2 marks

PS **2** Caroline says, "Any 2-D shape can have two right angles."
Is Caroline correct? Give a reason for your answer.

_____

_____

1 mark

Marks.......... /3

Total marks .... /13   How am I doing?   😊   😐   😣

Translations

Challenge 1

1 A square is drawn in different positions on a grid.

Listed below are translations of the squares. Write the letter of the position the square moves to.

a) Square A moves 3 right and 2 down. _____

b) Square F moves 7 right and 2 up. _____

c) Square B moves 5 left and 4 down. _____

d) Square E moves 5 left and 3 up. _____

e) Square C moves 3 right and 2 up. _____

f) Write the letters of the squares that show the translation

2 right and 2 down. Square _____ to square _____.

6 marks

Marks.......... /6

Challenge 2

1 A rectangle is drawn in different positions on a grid.

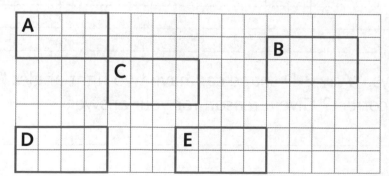

Describe these translations of the rectangle.

a) From A to B _____

94

Translations

b) From E to C _____

c) From B to C _____

d) From D to B _____

e) From A to C _____

f) From C to D _____

6 marks

Marks.......... /6

Challenge 3

1 A triangle is translated 5 units left and 7 units down.
Write the translation that moves the triangle to its original position.

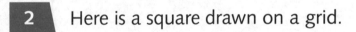

1 mark

2 Here is a square drawn on a grid.

a) Translate the square 4 right and 2 up. Draw the square.

b) Translate the square 1 left and 1 up. Draw the square.

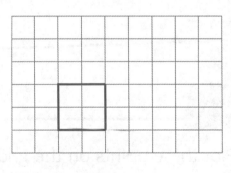

2 marks

3 Circle the correct bold word in each statement.

a) A triangle is translated 6 units left and 0 units down.

This will leave the triangle in the same **row / column**.

b) A rectangle is translated 0 units right and 5 units up.

This will leave the rectangle in the same **row / column**.

2 marks

Marks.......... /5

Total marks .... /17   How am I doing?

Coordinates

Challenge 1

1 Look at the coordinate grid.
Write the coordinates of these symbols.

a) ★ _____   b) ♥ _____

c) ⚡ _____   d) ✚ _____

e) ♠ _____   f) ☾ _____

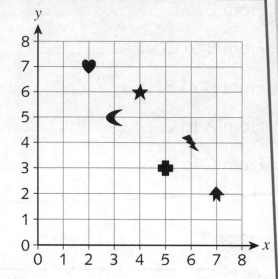

6 marks

2 Look again at the coordinate grid.

a) Plot these points on the grid: (1, 2) and (7, 8).
Join the points with a straight line.

b) What are the coordinates of the mid-point of the line? _____

2 marks

Marks.......... /8

Challenge 2

1 Plot these points on the grid.
Show each point by writing the capital letter.

a) A (6,1)   b) B (5,7)

c) C (2,6)   d) D (7,4)

e) E (1,3)   f) F (4,2)

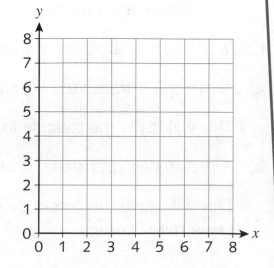

6 marks

Coordinates

2 **a)** A point is plotted at (6,4). It is then moved 1 unit left and 1 unit down.

What are the new coordinates of the point? _____

b) A point is plotted at (2,1). It is then moved 3 units right and 2 units up.

What are the new coordinates of the point? _____

2 marks

Marks.......... /8

Challenge 3

1 There are some mystery coordinates.
Work out the coordinates, write them on the lines and plot them on the coordinate grid.

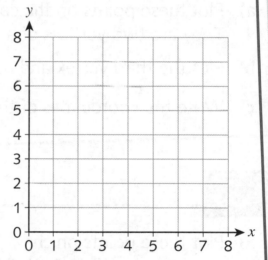

a) The x-coordinate and the y-coordinate add up to 9.
The cordinates are both multiples of 3.
The x-coordinate is the larger number. _____

b) The x-coordinate and the y-coordinate add up to 10.
The x-coordinate is 4 greater than the y-coordinate. _____

c) The difference between the coordinates is 2.
The y-coordinate is double the x-coordinate. _____

d) The x-coordinate + the y-coordinate = 13.
The x-coordinate – the y-coordinate = 1. _____

8 marks

Marks.......... /8

Total marks .... /24   How am I doing?

Shapes and Coordinates

PS Problem-solving questions

Challenge 1

1 a) Plot these points on the coordinate grid: (1,7) (1,4) (6,7). They are three vertices of a rectangle.

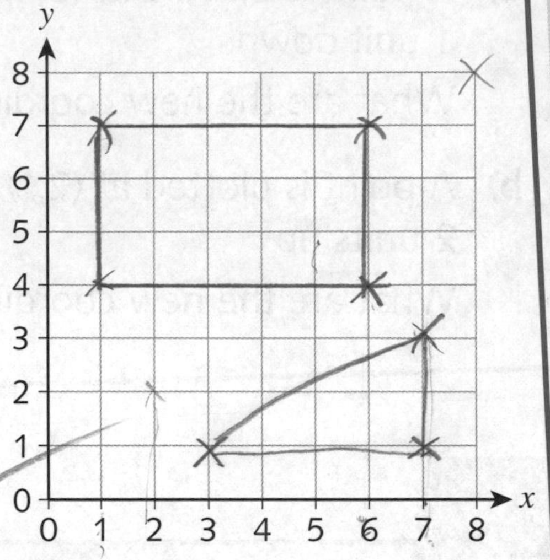

b) Plot the fourth vertex and use a ruler to complete the rectangle.

c) Write the coordinates of the fourth vertex. (4,6)

3 marks

2 a) Plot these points on the coordinate grid: (7,3) (3,1). They are two vertices of a right-angled triangle.

b) Plot the third vertex and use a ruler to complete the triangle.

c) Write the coordinates of the third vertex. (7,1)

3 marks

Marks...6..... /6

Challenge 2

1 a) Plot these points on the coordinate grid: (3,8) (1,6) (5,6). They are three vertices of a square.

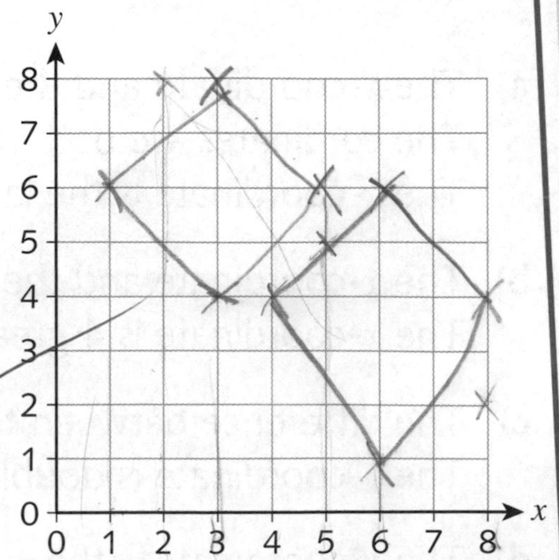

b) Plot the fourth vertex and use a ruler to complete the square.

c) Write the coordinates of the fourth vertex. (3,4)

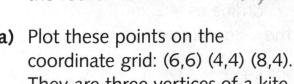

3 marks

2 a) Plot these points on the coordinate grid: (6,6) (4,4) (8,4). They are three vertices of a kite.

b) Plot a possible fourth vertex. Use a ruler to complete the kite.

c) Write possible coordinates of the fourth vertex. (6,1)

3 marks

Marks...6..... /6

Shapes and Coordinates

Challenge 3

PS **1** Three vertices of a square are: (10,15) (10,10) (15,15).

Write the coordinates of the fourth vertex. (15,10)

PS **2** Matt draws a straight line on a
coordinate grid.
He uses these coordinates:
(1,5) (3,6) (5,7) (7,8).
Matt extends the line.

Write the next pair of coordinates
in the sequence. (9,9)

3 **a)** These coordinates are the end points of a line: (2,2) (8,8).

Write the mid-point of the line. (5,5)

b) These coordinates are the end points of a line: (2,8) (8,2).

Write the mid-point of the line. (5,5)

4 Daria says, "If there is a set of coordinates and the first number
is always the same, that means the line joining them must be a
horizontal line."

Is Daria correct? Explain your answer.

that is incorrect as it is
a vertical line

1 mark

Marks.......5..../5

Bar Charts

PS Problem-solving questions

Look at the bar chart below to answer the questions on pages 100 and 101.
It shows the points scored by five teams on school sports day.

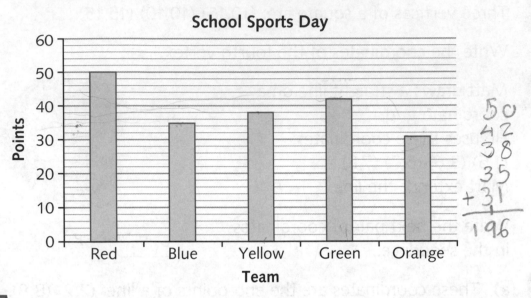

School Sports Day

50
42
38
35
+ 31

196

Challenge 1

PS **1** a) What is each small division on the
vertical axis worth?   2

b) Which team scored the most number
of points?   red

c) Which team scored the least number
of points?   orange

d) Which team scored 35 points?   blue

e) How many more points did the Red
team score than the Blue team?   15

✓
5 marks

Marks.....5.... /5

Challenge 2

PS **1** a) How many teams scored more than 35 points? 3

b) Circle the score for the Yellow team.

 35   36   37   38   39

Bar Charts

c) What was the Green team's score? _42_

d) What was the difference in the scores between the Blue and Orange teams? _4_

e) What was the difference in the scores between the Yellow and Green teams? _4_

5 marks

Marks........5... /5

Challenge 3

 1

On sports day, 1st place gained 8 points, 2nd place gained 5 points and 3rd place gained 2 points.

a) What was the points difference between the highest scoring and lowest scoring teams? _19_

b) How many points were awarded in total? _196_

c) The Green team won three races. Explain how they won the other points.

$$\begin{array}{r} ^3\!4^1\!2 \\ -\ 24 \\ \hline 18 \end{array}$$

They came 2nd 2 times and 3rd place 4 times.

d) Simon says, "The Red team won Sports Day, but never won a race."

Could Simon be correct? Explain your answer.

he is corect because they could have goton 10 2nd places

4 marks

Marks....4..... /4

Total marks ......14...... /14   **How am I doing?**

Time Graphs

PS ▷ Problem-solving questions

A class recorded the temperature in the playground throughout one day.
Look at their time graph below to answer the questions on pages 102 and 103.

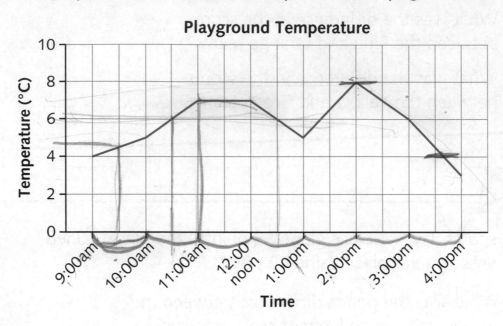

Playground Temperature

Challenge 1

PS **1**

a) Write the time the temperature was first taken.

   _9:00am_

b) Write the highest temperature.   _8_ °C

c) Write the temperature at 3:00pm.   _6_ °C

d) For how many hours did the class record the temperature?

   8 hours

e) By how many degrees did the temperature rise between 9:00am and 11:00am?

   _3_ °C

5 marks

Marks.......... /5

Time Graphs

Challenge 2

1

a) At what time did the temperature first start to go down?

_12:00pm_

b) From the first recording, how long did it take for the temperature to reach 8°C?

~~6~~ 5 hours.

c) For how long did the temperature stay at 7°C?

~~1~~ hours

d) Estimate the temperature at 10:00am.

_5_ °C

e) Estimate the time the temperature first reached 6°C.

_10:30_

5 marks

Marks.......... /5

Challenge 3

1

a) What is the difference between the temperature at 9:00am and 4:00pm?

_1_ °C

b) What was the temperature at 12:30pm?

_6_ °C

c) Estimate the temperature at 9:30am.

_5_ °C

d) Estimate the time the temperature was above 6°C.

3 hours 45

e) Estimate the time it took for the temperature to fall from 8°C to 4°C.

1 hour 40

5 marks

Marks.......... /5

Total marks .... /15   How am I doing?   😊   😐   😣

Pictograms

PS Problem-solving questions

Challenge 1

PS 1 This pictogram shows the number of rainy days from January to March in four cities.

	🌧 represents 4 rainy days
City	**Rainy days**
Carlisle	🌧🌧🌧🌧🌧🌧🌧
Birmingham	🌧🌧🌧🌧🌧
Glasgow	🌧🌧🌧🌧🌧🌧🌧🌧🌧🌧
Norwich	

a) How many rainy days are represented by a rainy cloud symbol? _4_

b) How many rainy days were there in Carlisle? _28_

c) How many more rainy days were there in Glasgow than in Birmingham? _12_

d) How many fewer rainy days were there in Carlisle than in Glasgow? _8_

e) The pictogram is not finished. There were 20 rainy days in Norwich. How many rainy day symbols will complete the pictogram for Norwich? _5_

5 marks

Marks........ /5

Challenge 2

PS 1 This pictogram shows the number of kilometres five friends cycled in one week.

	🚲 represents 10 kilometres
Name	**Number of kilometres**
Sami	🚲🚲🚲🚲🚲🚲🚲🚲🚲🚲🚲🚲🚲
Greg	🚲🚲🚲🚲🚲🚲
Ava	🚲🚲🚲🚲🚲🚲🚲🚲🚲🚲🚲🚲
Martha	🚲🚲🚲🚲🚲🚲🚲🚲🚲🚲
Ricardo	🚲🚲🚲🚲🚲🚲🚲

a) Which two friends cycled the same distance?

_____Sami_____ and _Ava_____

b) How far did Martha cycle? _100_ km

c) How much further did Sami cycle than Ricardo? _40_ km

d) How many friends cycled more than 80 km? _B 3_

4 marks

Marks.........4 /4

Challenge 3

PS | **1** | This pictogram shows the number of rooms in different hotels.

🛏 represents 20 rooms	
Hotel	**Number of rooms**
Mill Hotel	🛏🛏🛏🛏🛏🛏🛏🛏 160
Riverbank	🛏🛏🛏🛏 80
Bridge Hotel	🛏🛏🛏🛏🛏 100
Valley Hotel	🛏🛏🛏 60
Old Barn	🛏🛏 20 40

a) How many more rooms are there at the
Bridge Hotel than at the Old Barn? _60_

b) How many rooms are there at the Old
Barn and the Valley Hotel together? _100_

c) The Riverbank is only half full.
How many rooms are taken? _40_

d) 20 rooms at the Mill Hotel are empty.
How many rooms are taken? _120_

4 marks

Marks......4... /4

Total marks ....13.... /13   How am I doing?

Tables

PS Problem-solving questions

Challenge 1

PS 1   This table shows the prices of some shirts.

Design \ Size	Small	Medium	Large
Short-sleeved	£12	£14	£16
Long-sleeved	£15	£18	£21

 £12

a) What is the cost of a medium long-sleeved shirt? £ 18

£15

b) What is the cost of 2 short-sleeved large shirts? £ 32

£27

c) How much more expensive is a large long-sleeved shirt than a medium short-sleeved shirt? £ 7+

³⁴0
−27
‾‾13
£27.

d) Gordon buys a small short-sleeved shirt and a small long-sleeved shirt.
How much will he have left from £40? £ 13

4 marks

Marks.....4../4

Challenge 2

PS 1   This table shows the dinner choices of children in different classes.

Meal \ Class	A	B	C	Total
Hot meal	18	17	12	47
Vegetarian meal	5	4	9	18
Sandwich	5	8	7	20
Total	28	29	28	85

1 8
1 7
+ 1 2
‾‾4 7

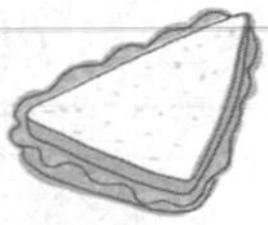

a) How many more children had a hot meal than a vegetarian meal or a sandwich in Class B? 5 4

b) How many children had a hot meal altogether?
Add this to the table.

c) The number of children who had a sandwich in Class A is missing. Calculate the missing number and add it to the table.

d) The number of children who had a vegetarian meal in Class C is missing. Calculate the missing number and add it to the table.

4 marks

Marks....4.... /4

Challenge 3

PS **1** This table gives information about visitors to a castle.

Visitor \ Day	Friday	Saturday	Sunday	Total
Men	24	18	6	48
Women	_____	38	12	76
Children	_____	_____	16	_____
Total	55	71	34	160

a) How many more men and women visited on Saturday than on Sunday? _____

b) Olivia says, "As many men visited on Friday as on Saturday and Sunday together." Is Olivia correct? Explain how you know.

_____

_____

c) How many children visited on Friday? _____

d) Which was the largest group of visitors: men, women or children? _____

4 marks

Marks.......... /4

Total marks .... /12   How am I doing?

Progress Test 4

1. Write these numbers in order, starting with the smallest.

   9018   **9801**   **9810**   **9108**   **9180**

   _____ _____ _____ _____ _____

   1 mark

2. Write the value of the 4 in each number.

   a) 7451 _____   **b)** 4925 _____   **c)** 745 _____

   3 marks

3. Write the number of tens altogether in 560.   _____

   1 mark

PS 4. Write in the missing numbers.

   a)

   ```
     7  5  □  □
   +  □  □  1  2
   _____
     9  3  1  5
   ```

   b)

   ```
     8  □  □
   -  □  6  2
   _____
     4  9  2
   ```

   2 marks

PS 5. Kerry buys some trays of plants for her garden. She buys 14 trays with 4 plants and 15 trays with 6 plants.

   How many plants does she buy altogether?   _____ plants

   1 mark

PS 6. A pizza is cut into twelfths. Jonah eats $\frac{3}{12}$ and Ken eats $\frac{4}{12}$.

   How many twelfths are left? _____

   1 mark

PS 7. Larry uses $\frac{1}{5}$ of 5 kg of potatoes on Saturday and $\frac{1}{2}$ of what is left on Sunday.

   How many kilograms are left?   _____ kg

   1 mark

8. Write these weights in order, starting with the smallest.

   5500 g   **$4\frac{1}{2}$ kg**   **4.9 kg**   **5 kg**   **4100 g**

   _____ _____ _____ _____ _____

   1 mark

PS 9. Laura spends three weeks of her summer holiday staying with her grandmother.

   How many days is this? _____ days

   1 mark

10. Draw lines to match each clock to the equivalent digital clock.

a)

b)

c)

 `20:35`   `18:50`   `19:50`   `20:45`   `19:35`

1 mark

11. Convert these measures.

a) 8000 g = _____ kg

b) 9 litres = _____ ml

c) 500 mm = _____ cm

d) 4.5 m = _____ cm

4 marks

PS **12.** Cai has two jugs that each hold 2.25 litres and a third jug that holds 3.75 litres.

How much can the three jugs hold altogether? _____ litres

1 mark

13. Work out:

a) 5 kg – 500 g = _____

b) 5 m – 500 cm = _____

2 marks

14. Below is a triangle. Circle two words, one from each column, to describe the triangle.

acute-angled   scalene

right-angled   isosceles

obtuse-angled   equilateral

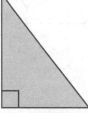

2 marks

15. Write the number of lines of symmetry in each shape.

a)

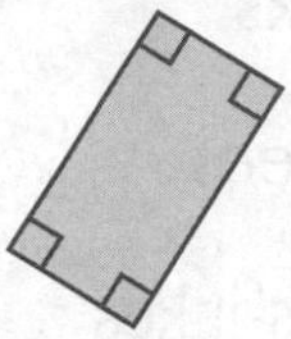

b)

_____ lines of symmetry

_____ lines of symmetry

2 marks

16. What type of angle is this?

_____

1 mark

17. A square is translated from position A to position B. Complete the sentence:

The square has moved _____ square(s)

to the left and _____ square(s) up.

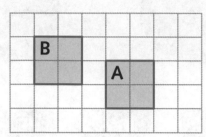

1 mark

18. Look at the coordinate grid.

a) Write the letter at the coordinates (3,6). _____

b) Carl joins the points A, B, C and D to make a straight line. He makes the line longer; write the coordinates of a point on the line.

(_____, _____)

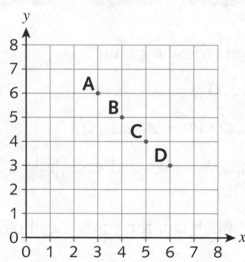

2 marks

19. This table shows the number of drinks sold in a café one weekend.

Drink Day	Teas	Coffees	Milkshakes	Juice	Total
Saturday	45	75	12	23	_____
Sunday	38	62	_____	35	150
Total	83	_____	_____	58	305

a) How many drinks were sold on Saturday? _____ drinks

b) How many coffees were sold altogether? _____ coffees

c) How many milkshakes were sold on Sunday? _____ milkshakes

3 marks

PS **20.** This time graph shows the rainfall over one week.

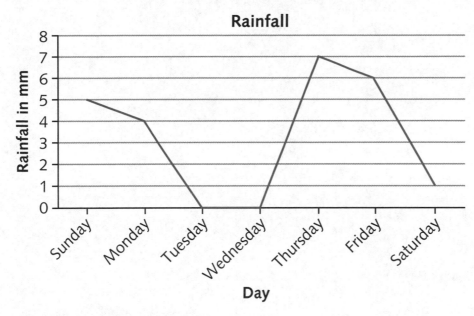

a) What was the greatest amount of rainfall
recorded that week? _____ mm

b) Which days had no rain? _____ and _____

c) On how many days was there over 5 mm of rain? _____ days

3 marks

PS **21.** This bar chart shows the marks of five children in a test.

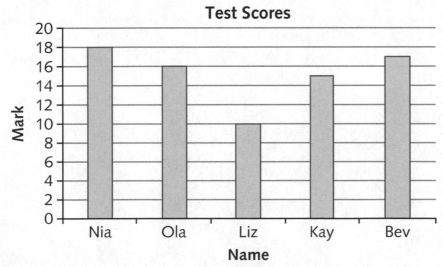

a) Write the name of the person who scored 15. _____

b) Write how many more marks Nia scored than Liz. _____

2 marks

Marks........ /36

Notes

For questions worth one mark with several answer spaces, all answers should be correct to achieve the mark, unless otherwise indicated.

Pages 4–11
Starter Test
1. a) 32, 36   b) 550, 600
2. 760
3. a) <   b) <
4. 871 circled
5. a) 25   b) 70
6. a) 821   b) 576   c) 358
7. 252
8. 635
9. a) 443   b) 384
10. 693 – 265
11. a) 54   b) 96   c) 112
12. a) 14   b) 19   c) 18
13. 72
14. 23
15. 48p
16. a) $\frac{1}{2}$ (accept equivalent fractions)

    b) $\frac{7}{8}$

17. $\frac{1}{10}$
18. a) 4   b) 16   c) $\frac{4}{5}$
19. a) $\frac{2}{5}$ (accept $\frac{4}{10}$ or 0.4)

    b) $\frac{9}{10}$ (accept 0.9)

20. a) $\frac{2}{6}$ b) $\frac{4}{8}$
21. a) <   b) >
22. a) $\frac{2}{5}$ b) $\frac{3}{10}$ c) $\frac{7}{8}$
23. one
24. $\frac{7}{8}$
25. 1 mm, 1 cm, 1 m
26. 2 m circled
27. a) >   b) >
28. 0.5 kg ticked
29. a) >   b) >
30. 4 litres
31. 3 kg (accept any weight ≥2.8 kg but ≤3.2 kg)
32. a) 400 ml (accept any capacity ≥380 ml but ≤420 ml)
    b) 250 ml (accept any capacity ≥230 ml but ≤270 ml)
33. a) 2:20pm   b) 9:50am
    c) 8:30am   d) 9:45pm
34. a) 9:15pm   b) 6:55am
35. 180 seconds
36. 30th September circled
37. 365 days
38. 50 minutes
39. 16 cm
40. £12.30
41. £89.85
42. a) 800 cm   b) 11 kg
    c) 2 litres   d) 45 mm
43. Line **B** ticked
44. Hexagon **C** circled
45. A pentagon with one right angle drawn
46. a) cuboid   b) cone   c) 6
    d) circle
47. Angles **A** and **C** ticked
48. 2
49. a) 55   b) 64
50. a) Ben   b) 3   c) 5
    d) Bar for Gus, representing 5 lengths, added to chart
51. a) 8   b) 4   c) 6

Pages 12–13
Challenge 1
1. a) 40, 48   b) 48, 54
2. a) Add 6   b) Add 25
3. No
4. 56
Challenge 2
1. a) 42, 48   b) 200, 225
2. a) Add 7   b) Add 25
3. 650
Challenge 3
1. 135, 144, 153
2. 60, 66, 72
3. 71
4.

Add 7 →

	21	28	35	42	49
Add 9 ↓	30	37	44	**51**	58
	39	**46**	53	60	67
	48	55	62	69	76

Pages 14–15
Challenge 1
1. a) <   b) >   c) <
2. Statement **C** ticked
3. 3465, 3563, 4536, 4645, 4654
4. 7541
Challenge 2
1. a) >   b) <   c) <
2. 4138, 4831, 5246, 5264, 5642
3. a) 865   b) 1356

Answers

Challenge 3
1. 681, 5891, 7861, 11 937, 12 612
2. Any number >6285 but <6290
3. Athletic vs Wanderers

Pages 16–17
Challenge 1
1. a) 40   b) 400   c) 4
2. 1475 circled
3. 341 circled
4. 3627
Challenge 2
1. a) 900   b) 90   c) 9000
2. 3890
3. 9738
4. 6342
5. a) Any combination of four digits with 5 or 6 as the first digit.
   b) 2345
Challenge 3
1. Jamie is incorrect because 4021 has four digits (thousands), which is more than 897 which only has three digits (hundreds).
2. 6031
3. a) 10 009   b) 10 090

Pages 18–19
Challenge 1
1. a) 12   b) 15   c) 26
   d) 8   e) 33   f) 40
2. a) 3 + 2 = 5   b) 6 + 4 = 10
   c) 26 − 7 = 19
3. a) 4:40 **or** twenty to five
   b) 10:20 **or** twenty past ten
Challenge 2
1. a) 56   b) 48   c) 96   d) 83
2. 90
3. a) 40 + 60 = 100   b) 69 − 30 = 39
4. XCIX circled
Challenge 3
1. XXXVIII, XLVII, LXV, LXIX, XC
2. a) 46   b) 136   c) 50   d) 84
3. a) 125   b) 222   c) 359

Pages 20–21
Challenge 1
1. a) 200   b) 400
   c) Any number >420 but <480
2. a) 351   b) 524
3. a) 5296   b) 7570   c) 2804
Challenge 2
1. 457
2. a) 4000 + 800 + 20 + 5 (accept alternatives such as 3000 + 1800 + 20 + 5)
   b) 6000 + 700 + 10 + 9 (accept alternatives such as 3000 + 3700 + 10 + 9)
3. a) Any number >3450 but <3550
   b) Any number >4100 but <4400
   c) Any number >4600 but <4900
Challenge 3
1. a)–e) Accept any five different additions that total 3746
2. a) 4609   b) 8020
3. a) 7 thousands = **70** hundreds = **700** tens = **7000** ones
   b) 800   c) 3000
4. 2738

Pages 22–23
Challenge 1
1. a) 50   b) 100   c) 80
2. 84, 75 and 77 circled
3. 120
4. a) 300   b) 700   c) 1500
Challenge 2
1. a) 3800   b) 6300   c) 5100
2. a) 2630   b) 2600   c) 3000
3. a) 4000   b) 3000   c) 8000
4. Any three numbers ≥650 but <750
Challenge 3
1. a) 6000   b) 1000   c) 4000
2. Any number ≥7335 but <7345
3. 350, 6000 and 7900 circled
4. 6951, 6915, 6591, 6519

Pages 24–25
Challenge 1
1. a) −2   b) −4   c) −2   d) −5
2. a) −2   b) −4   c) −1
3. £4
4. −5
Challenge 2
1. a) −4   b) −7   c) −2   d) −9
2. a) −5   b) −5   c) −1
3. a) −9   b) −17   c) −18
4. a) −2°C   b) −9°C   c) 4°C
Challenge 3
1. 5, 3, −1, −4, −6
2. a) −6   b) −4   c) 0   d) 4
3. a) −9   b) −15   c) −8
   d) −14   e) −24   f) −4

Pages 26–27
Challenge 1
1. a) 749   b) 997   c) 1005
2. a) 401   b) 91   c) 528

Challenge 2
1. a) 1528   b) 1418   c) 13 728
2. a) 643   b) 406   c) 3596
Challenge 3
1. a) 12 400   b) 11 312   c) 12 909
2. a) 1196   b) 3973   c) 4793

Pages 28–29
Challenge 1
1. a) 120   b) 90   c) 170
2. 390 – 265 circled
3. a) 563 – 328 or 563 – 235
    b) 293 + 236   c) 311 + 214
4. 227
Challenge 2
1. 356
2. 630
3. a) 1000   b) 100
4. a) 3000   b) 11 000
Challenge 3
1. Possible answers are: 84p + 51p, 83p + 52p,
    82p + 53p, 81p + 54p
2. a) 17 000   b) 5000
3. 9258 – 3826 = 5432
    Correct answer = 10 258
4. 347

Pages 30–31
Challenge 1
1. a) 147   b) 425
2. 613
3. £54
4. 125 cm
Challenge 2
1. 6797
2. 3303
3. 2093 km
4. 2181
Challenge 3
1. a) **3**874 + 2643   b) **8**374 – 2650
2. Accept different possible answers: 5 and 3 are
    hundreds, 1 and 2 are tens, and 6 and 4 are
    ones, e.g. 526 + 314
3. A 5236 + 1609 = **6845**
    B 9343 – 2434 = **6909**
    C 2354 + 4567 = **6921** circled
    (1 mark for each calculation worked out
    correctly; 1 mark for circling calculation C)

Pages 32–33
Challenge 1
1. a) 35   b) 24   c) 88
    d) 36   e) 70   f) 32

2. a) 7   b) 12   c) 7
    d) 6   e) 10   f) 6
3. a) 8   b) 9   c) 9
    d) 7   e) 6   f) 12
Challenge 2
1. a) 42   b) 28   c) 99
    d) 56   e) 81   f) 84
2. a) 7   b) 8   c) 12
    d) 12   e) 12   f) 9
3. a) 11   b) 3   c) 11
    d) 12   e) 6   f) 4
Challenge 3
1. a)

×	7	9	12
7	49	**63**	**84**
9	**63**	**81**	**108**
12	**84**	**108**	144

b)

×	7	8	9
6	42	**48**	**54**
8	**56**	64	**72**
12	84	**96**	108

(1 mark for each correct row)
2. a) Possible answers are: 48 × 1, 24 × 2,
       16 × 3, 12 × 4
    b) Possible answers are: 36 × 1, 18 × 2,
       12 × 3, 6 × 6
    c) Possible answers are: 24 × 1, 12 × 2, 6 × 4
    d) Possible answers are: 72 × 1, 36 × 2,
       24 × 3, 18 × 4, 9 × 8
3. a) 81   b) 56   c) 64   d) 120

Pages 34–35
Challenge 1
1. a) 5   b) 0   c) 0
    d) 60   e) 160   f) 350
2. a) 20   b) 20   c) 30
3. a) 40   b) 30   c) 50
4. a) 3   b) 5   c) 4
Challenge 2
1. a) 30   b) 110   c) 64
    d) 69   e) 128   f) 255
2. a) 15   b) 13   c) 14
    d) 34   e) 16   f) 22
3. a) 48   b) 90   c) 72

Answers

Challenge 3
1. a) 3   b) 4   c) 5
   d) 3   e) 5   f) 3
2. a) 3   b) 6   c) 4
   d) 4   e) 12   f) 3
3. a) 4   b) 3   c) 15   d) 24

Pages 36–37
Challenge 1
1. A, D and F circled
2. a) 5   b) 12
3. 9
4. 1, 3, 5, 10 and 15 circled
Challenge 2
1. a) 1, 2, 5, 10
   b) 1, 3, 7, 21
   c) 1, 2, 4, 8, 16, 32
   d) 1, 2, 4, 5, 8, 10, 20, 40
2. 2 and 21
3. 7 and 8
4. Statement B circled
5. 7
Challenge 3
1.
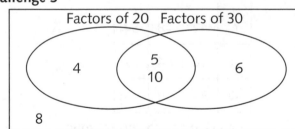
2. 6 rows of 8 bottles
3. a) 48 × 1, 24 × 2, 16 × 3, 12 × 4, 8 × 6
   b) 60 × 1, 30 × 2, 20 × 3, 15 × 4, 12 × 5, 10 × 6
   c) 1 × 100, 2 × 50, 4 × 25, 5 × 20, 10 × 10
4. 8, 56

Pages 38–39
Challenge 1
1. a) 230   b) 318   c) 248   d) 111
2. a) 216 (calculation set out as a column multiplication)
   b) 360 (calculation set out as a column multiplication)
   c) 672 (calculation set out as a column multiplication)
3. a) 4   b) 3
Challenge 2
1. a) 1518   b) 3035   c) 4459
2. a) 725 × 6 = 700 × **6** + 20 × **6** + 5 × **6**
       = 4350
   b) 2

3. a) 2989 (calculation set out as a column multiplication)
   b) 4098 (calculation set out as a column multiplication)
   c) 3843 (calculation set out as a column multiplication)
Challenge 3
1. a) 5992 (calculation set out as a column multiplication)
   b) 7736 (calculation set out as a column multiplication)
   c) 8604 (calculation set out as a column multiplication)
2. a) **547** × 7 = 3829   b) **385** × 9 = 3465
   c) **276** × 8 = 2208
3. 643 × 6 = 3858

Pages 40–41
Challenge 1
1. 288
2. 280
3. 60
4. £8.75
5. 168
Challenge 2
1. 744
2. 1536
3. £4170
4. 1390
5. 3800
Challenge 3
1. a) £2430   b) £2928   c) £2790
   d) £5176   e) £2422

Pages 42–45
Progress Test 1
1. a) 72, 78   b) 875, 900
2. 5274, 5427, 5472, 5724, 5742
3. a) <   b) <
4. £7799
5. a) 5835   b) 5008
6. 2390 circled
7. 8354
8. a) 38   b) 64
9. XLII circled
10. 535
11. a) 40
   b) Any number ≥184 but ≤186
12. a) 500   b) 800   c) 100

Answers

13.

	Rounded to the nearest 10 is	Rounded to the nearest 100 is	Rounded to the nearest 1000 is
5826	5830	5800	6000

14. −10, −20

15. −5

16. a) 240 b) 1080 c) 545

17. a) 527 − 353 = 174 b) 358 + 551 = 909

18. 372 + 322 circled

19. 282 (accept 365)

20. 599 minutes

21. 33 kilometres

22. a) 35 b) 27 c) 84
d) 8 e) 12 f) 6

23.

×	6	9	12
4	24	36	48
9	54	81	108
7	42	63	84

(1 mark for each correct row)

24. a) 75 b) 16 c) 88
d) 18 e) 12 f) 102

25. a) 1 and 20, 2 and 10, 4 and 5
b) 1 and 100, 2 and 50, 4 and 25, 5 and 20, 10 and 10

26. a) 378 b) 1060 c) 4256

27. 24

28. 54 × 3 = 50 × 3 + 4 × 3 = 162 (accept 4 and 3 in either order)

29. 35 metres

30. 100

Pages 46–47
Challenge 1

1. a) $\frac{3}{10}$ b) $\frac{9}{10}$ c) $\frac{7}{10}$

2. a) $\frac{9}{100}, \frac{13}{100}$ b) $\frac{79}{100}, \frac{80}{100}$ (accept $\frac{8}{10}$), $\frac{81}{100}$

3. 100

Challenge 2

1. a) $\frac{7}{100}$ b) $\frac{43}{100}$ c) $\frac{89}{100}$

2. a) $\frac{6}{100}$ (accept $\frac{3}{50}$) b) $\frac{9}{100}$
c) $\frac{2}{100}$ (accept $\frac{1}{50}$)

3. $\frac{1}{20}$ of a litre (accept $\frac{5}{100}$ or equivalent)

4. 1 cm

Challenge 3

1. 5 ÷ 100 = $\frac{5}{100}$ circled

2. 1 ÷ 100 and 0.1 ÷ 10 circled

3. a) 7 b) 5 c) 0.7

4. a) 6 b) 10

Pages 48–49
Challenge 1

1. a) $\frac{3}{6} = \frac{1}{2}$ b) $\frac{4}{8} = \frac{1}{2}$

2. a) $\frac{5}{10}$ b) $\frac{6}{10}$ c) $\frac{8}{10}$

3. a) $\frac{4}{8}$ b) $\frac{2}{6}$ c) $\frac{3}{4}$

Challenge 2

1. a) $\frac{10}{20}$ b) $\frac{6}{20}$ c) $\frac{12}{20}$

2. a) $\frac{5}{15}$ b) $\frac{10}{15}$ c) $\frac{9}{15}$

3. a) $\frac{4}{12}, \frac{5}{15}, \frac{6}{18}, \frac{7}{21}, \frac{8}{24}$ b) $\frac{12}{16}, \frac{15}{20}, \frac{18}{24}, \frac{21}{28}, \frac{24}{32}$

Challenge 3

1. a) $\frac{10}{20}$ b) $\frac{16}{20}$ c) $\frac{6}{20}$
d) $\frac{1}{4}$ e) $\frac{2}{5}$ f) $\frac{9}{10}$

2. $\frac{8}{30}$ and $\frac{20}{100}$ circled

3. $\frac{2}{5}$

Pages 50–51
Challenge 1

1. a) $\frac{3}{5} + \frac{1}{5} = \frac{4}{5}$ b) $\frac{5}{6} - \frac{4}{6} = \frac{1}{6}$

2. a) $\frac{3}{3}$ or 1 b) $\frac{13}{8}$ or $1\frac{5}{8}$
c) $\frac{17}{10}$ or $1\frac{7}{10}$

3. a) $\frac{3}{5}$ b) $\frac{3}{10}$ c) $\frac{1}{8}$

Challenge 2

1. a) $\frac{4}{5} + \frac{2}{5} = \frac{6}{5} = 1\frac{1}{5}$
b) $\frac{4}{6} + \frac{4}{6} = \frac{8}{6} = 1\frac{2}{6}$ or $1\frac{1}{3}$

2. a) $\frac{4}{3} = 1\frac{1}{3}$ b) $\frac{7}{5} = 1\frac{2}{5}$
c) $\frac{6}{4} = 1\frac{2}{4}$ or $1\frac{1}{2}$

3. a) $\frac{3}{10}$ b) $\frac{5}{12}$ c) $\frac{9}{10}$

Challenge 3

1. a) $\frac{5}{5} - \frac{3}{5} = \frac{2}{5}$ (accept $1 - \frac{3}{5} = \frac{2}{5}$)
b) $\frac{3}{4} + \frac{3}{4} = \frac{6}{4}$ or $1\frac{2}{4}$ or $1\frac{1}{2}$

Answers

2. a) $\frac{5}{10}$ (accept $\frac{1}{2}$)   b) $\frac{6}{12}$ (accept $\frac{1}{2}$)

    c) $\frac{9}{8}$ (accept $1\frac{1}{8}$)

3. a) $\frac{5}{8}$ b) $\frac{6}{7}$ c) $\frac{3}{10}$

Pages 52–53
Challenge 1
1. a) 5   b) 6
    c) 6 m   d) 4 kg
2. a) 16   b) 16
    c) 27 ml   d) 25 km
3. 2 km
4. 14
Challenge 2
1. a) 7   b) 4
    c) £2   d) 2 m
2. a) 14   b) 28
    c) 55 cm   d) 6 km
3. 24 kg
4. 30
Challenge 3
1. a) 35   b) 45
2. 9
3. a) 20   b) 30
4. 15
5. Explanation that shows half of 27 is not a whole number or that $13\frac{1}{2}$ boys or girls cannot be possible.
6. a) 4   b) 20

Pages 54–55
Challenge 1
1. $\frac{3}{4} = 0.75$, $\frac{1}{2} = 0.5$, $\frac{1}{4} = 0.25$
2. a) 0.1   b) 0.7   c) 0.3
3. a) 0.9   b) 1.6   c) 2.4   d) 5.5
4. a) 0.4   b) 0.8   c) 1
Challenge 2
1. a) 0.5   b) 0.25   c) 0.75
2. a) 0.9   b) 0.57   c) 0.03
3. £4.57
4. a) 0.3   b) 0.65   c) 0.95
Challenge 3
1. a) 0.09   b) 0.2   c) 1.01
2. a) 0.15
    b) Any number >0.45, <0.5
    c) Any number >0.8, <0.85
3. James is incorrect because 0.7 as a fraction is $\frac{7}{10}$, whereas $\frac{7}{100}$ is 0.07.
4. a) 10   b) 10

Pages 56–57
Challenge 1
1. a) 5   b) 5   c) 3
    d) 6   e) 8   f) 3
2. 3 m
3. 1 litre
4. Any number ≥6.5 but <7
Challenge 2
1. a) 7   b) 7   c) 22
    d) 54   e) 86   f) 105
2 50 kg
3. Any number ≥49.5 but <50.5
4. 29.7 and 30.4 circled
Challenge 3
1. a) 116   b) 230   c) 707
2. 100.3 and 99.6 circled
3. 13
4. 48.7 and 49.4 → 49
    49.8, 50.4 and 49.5 → 50

Pages 58–59
Challenge 1
1. 0.8 circled
2. 2.4 circled
3. 4.7, 5.6, 5.9, 6.2
4. Craig
5. Any number >7.6 but <8
Challenge 2
1. 12.16 circled
2. 34.45, 35.44, 43.54, 45.34, 45.43
3. 60.56
4. Any number >23.56 but <23.62
5. Any number >45.34 but <45.43 in the first space and any number >45.27 but <45.34 in the second space
Challenge 3
1. a) <   b) >
2. a) 3.76 m   b) 2.88 m
3.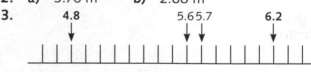
4. 5.25, 6, 25.5, 50, 52.5

Pages 60–61
Challenge 1
1. a) 0.6   b) 1.2   c) 0.07
    d) 0.25
2. a) 5   b) 36   c) 6.3
3. a) 0.7 (accept seven tenths)
    b) 7 (accept seven ones)
    c) 0.07 (accept seven hundredths)
4. 0.25 kg

Challenge 2
1. a) 0.67   b) 0.54
    c) 0.15   d) 7.8
2. a) 5.7   b) 36
    c) 100   d) 100
3. 60
4. a) 0.04 (accept four hundredths)
    b) 0.04 (accept four hundredths)
5. £0.64 (accept 64p if £ sign is crossed out)

Challenge 3
1. a) 10   b) 100
    c) 32   d) 79
2. Many possible solutions:
    Kagendo's calculation, e.g. 9 ÷ 100 = 0.09
    Sally's calculation, e.g. 9 ÷ 10 = 0.9
3. 6.7 ÷ 10 and 56 ÷ 10 circled
4. a) 45 ÷ 10
    b) 60.8 ÷ 10

Pages 62–63
Challenge 1
1. a) £9.25   b) £5.05
    c) A set of pens and a book
2. 3 litres
3. 25 km
4. £2.40

Challenge 2
1. £5.11
2. £1.05
3. 1.35 kg
4. £8.10

Challenge 3
1. 12 kg
2. 10
3. a) 22.2 km   b) 20.8 km   c) 15.4 km

Pages 64–67
Progress Test 2
1. a) 77, 84
    b) 7000, 8000
2. 1384, 1834, 4138, 8314, 8341
3. 1 ten circled
4. a) and b) Accept any two different
    combinations of numbers that total 538,
    e.g. 300 + 200 + 38
5.

Number	Rounded to the nearest 10
3784	3780
427	430
79	80

6. −6

7. a) 6998   b) 4746
8. 600 + 400 = 1000
9. 318
10. 149 m
11. a) 72   b) 240
12. 168
13. a) 2128   b) 7520   c) 3768
14. 4 children share **6** paint pots and **10** brushes.
15. 48 × 3 = **40** × 3 + 8 × 3 = 144
16. a) $\frac{3}{100}$ (accept 0.03)
    b) $\frac{9}{100}$ (accept 0.09)
    c) $\frac{7}{100}$ (accept 0.07)
17. a) $\frac{7}{100}$ b) $\frac{16}{100}$
18. a) $\frac{3}{4}$ b) $\frac{5}{10}$
19. a) $\frac{11}{10}$ or $1\frac{1}{10}$ b) $\frac{9}{8}$ or $1\frac{1}{8}$
20. a) $\frac{13}{100}$ b) $\frac{9}{10}$ (accept $\frac{90}{100}$)   c) $\frac{9}{100}$
21. a) 0.93   b) 0.07   c) 0.4
22. a) 5   b) 15   c) 30
23. Accept any of the following: 24.5, 24.6, 24.7,
    24.8, 24.9
24. 73.8 circled
25. 30.2, 30.7, 31.6, 31.8, 32.5
26. a) 10   b) 100   c) 100   d) 10
27. 57
28. a) 10   b) 24   c) 81
29. £29 (accept £29.00; do not accept £29.0)

Pages 68–69
Challenge 1
1. 83.76 m, 83.67 m, 63.78 m, 38.76 m, 36.87 m
2. 4.87 litres, 5.47 litres, 45.78 litres, 54.87 litres,
    78.54 litres
3. Accept any capacity >4.56 litres but <4.75
    litres
4. 1.25 m, $1\frac{1}{2}$ m, 1.65 m
5. Dubry

Challenge 2
1. a) 3.2 kg circled   b) 8000 g circled
2. a) 474 cm circled   b) 6 cm circled
3. a) 5.675 litres circled b) 10 litres circled
4. 4.7 m, 475 cm, 4800 mm, 5 m
5. No

Challenge 3
1. 4.8 m circled
2. 4500 metres circled
3. 1 litre bottle circled
4. B, C, A

Answers

Pages 70–71
Challenge 1
1. Accept any mass >3.4 kg but <3.9 kg
2. Accept any length >7.25 cm but <7.75 cm
3. 0.75 litre
4. £24.75 and £26.15 ticked

Challenge 2
1. 4 m ticked
2. 350 ml ticked
3. 120 g ticked
4. 12 minutes ticked

Challenge 3
1. £15
2. Accept any temperature >26°C but <30°C
3. Accept any length >8 cm but <10 cm
4. Accept any mass >2 kg but <2.5 kg

Pages 72–73
Challenge 1
1. a) 3 cm   b) 4 m   c) 5 km
   d) 60 mm   e) 500 cm   f) 9000 m
   g) 4 kg   h) 40 kg   i) 5000 g
   j) 8000 ml   k) 10 litres   l) 500 ml
2. 4
3. a) Yes   b) 5 cm or 50 mm

Challenge 2
1. a) 520 cm   b) 3500 g   c) 3.5 litres
   d) 7.8 cm   e) 0.25 km   f) 75 cm
   g) 8.45 m   h) 10.5 km
2. 400 g or 0.4 kg
3. Jug B
4. 68 ml

Challenge 3
1. 1000 mm
2. a) m   b) cm   c) km
   d) litres   e) g   f) cm
3.

$\frac{1}{2}$ litre	300 ml	200 ml

0.6 litres

$\frac{1}{4}$ litre	200 ml	550 ml

(accept equivalent measures, e.g. $\frac{1}{5}$ litre)

Pages 74–75
Challenge 1
1. £1.55
2. £13.24
3. £4 (accept £4.00; do not accept £4.0)
4. £4.95
5. £2.67

Challenge 2
1. a) £7.10   b) 3.76 m
   c) 18.20 kg   d) 46.79 litres
2. £36.60
3. 6.5 kg
4. 9.25 m
5. 15 litres

Challenge 3
1. a) 3.55 kg   b) 3550 g
2. 50p
3. Accept three 0.6 m cupboards and three 0.4 m cupboards **or** six 0.4 m cupboards and one 0.6 m cupboard.
4. 4

Pages 76–77
Challenge 1
1. a) 4:10am   b) 7:25am   c) 4:55am
2. a) 18:45   b) 17:05   c) 21:35
3. a) Twenty past eight **or** 20 past 8
   b) Five past eight **or** 5 past 8
   c) Twenty to eleven **or** 20 to 11

Challenge 2
1. a) 3:25pm   b) 6:10pm
2. a) 14:15   b) 11:50   c) 18:35
3. 12:15 **or** quarter past 12 **or** $\frac{1}{4}$ past 12

Challenge 3
1.

	Word time	12 hour time	24 hour time
a)	Five past two in the afternoon	= **2:05pm**	= **14:05**
b)	Twenty-five to **9** in the evening	= **8:35pm**	= **20:35**

2. 40 minutes

Pages 78–79
Challenge 1
1. a) 120 seconds   b) 120 minutes
   c) 48 hours   d) 14 days
2. April, June, September and November
3. 2024
4. 8th May

Challenge 2
1. Accept 2 hours 20 minutes **or** 140 minutes
2. 40 minutes
3. Accept 19:15, 7:15, 7:15pm **or** quarter past 7
4. a) 28 days   b) 24 months
   c) 300 seconds   d) 72 hours

Challenge 3
1. Accept any time >8 minutes but <10 minutes
2. a) **336** hours = **14** days = 2 weeks
   b) **120** months = **10** years = 1 decade
3. Accept 06:45, 6:45, 6:45am **or** quarter to 7

4. Accept 3 hours 5 minutes **or** 185 minutes
5. Accept 13:27, 1:27, 1:27pm **or** 27 past 1

Pages 80–81
Challenge 1
1. A a) 8 squares   b) 12 cm
   B a) 9 squares   b) 12 cm
   C a) 10 squares   b) 22 cm
Challenge 2
1. A a) 9 squares   b) 16 cm
   B a) 16 squares   b) 20 cm
   C a) 7 squares   b) 16 cm
2. 28 cm
Challenge 3
1. a) 2 cm   b) 5 small squares
2. 14 cm

Pages 82–85
Progress Test 3
1. a) 63, **72**, 81, **90**, 99, 108
   b) 36, **42**, **48**, 54, 60, 66
2. 3752, 3727, 3725, 3572, 3527
3. 6548
4. LXV circled
5.

Number	Rounded to the nearest hundred
7 8 2 3	**7800**
7 8 2	**800**
7 8	**100**

6. a) 545   b) 502
7. a) 6   b) 6
   c) 5   d) 49
8. 8
9. a) 4581   b) 3164   c) 5166
10. 6 hours
11. a) 100   b) 10   c) 10
12. A line drawn from $\frac{3}{5}$ to $\frac{6}{10}$
13. a) $\frac{1}{8}$ b) $\frac{3}{12}$
14. £19
15. £10
16. a) Balloons, candles and a cake
    b) £2.55
17. £3, £1.25, 90p, £0.08, 5p
18. a) Tia   b) Raf
19. £40
20. 15 minutes
21. Clock **B** circled
22. Statement **A** ticked
23. 1 minute 40 seconds

24. a) 5000 g   b) 6 cm   c) 10 m
    d) 8 litres   e) 800 cm   f) 2000 m
25. a) 13 cm   b) 12 cm
26. 25 squares

Pages 86–87
Challenge 1
1. Shapes **A** and **C** ticked
2. a) **B** and **D**   b) **A** and **D**
   c) **C**   d) **B**
3. Shape **B** ticked
Challenge 2
1. Shapes **B** and **D** ticked
2. A hexagon has six sides. This is a pentagon as it has five sides.
3. Triangle **B** ticked
Challenge 3
1. Octagon circled
2. Shapes **A**, **B** and **C** ticked
3. Any pentagon drawn with a right angle.

Pages 88–89
Challenge 1
1. Shape **A** ticked
2. Shape **C** ticked
3. a) 6   b) 6
Challenge 2
1. a) 7   b) 4
2. Statement **D** ticked
3.

Shape	Faces	Edges	Vertices
Cuboid	6	12	8
Square-based pyramid	5	8	5
Triangular prism	5	9	6

(1 mark for each correct row)
Challenge 3
1. Yes, Shona is correct. On each face, the angles at the vertices are right angles and the opposite edges are equal and parallel. These are the properties of a rectangle.
2. Pentagon
3. a) 5   b) 7

Pages 90–91
Challenge 1
1.

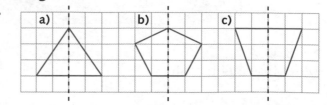

Answers

2.

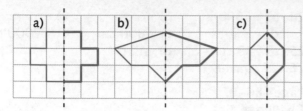

Challenge 2

1. a) 4 **b)** 2 **c)** 2

2.

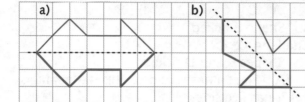

Challenge 3

1. Shape **D** ticked

2. Different answers are possible, e.g.:

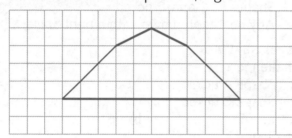

or

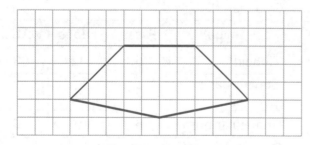

Pages 92–93
Challenge 1

1. a) 4 **b)** 6 **c)** 4

2. Angle **B** ticked

3. Angle **A** ticked

4. Angle **D** ticked

Challenge 2

1.

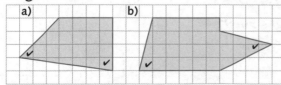

2. B, D, A, C

3. obtuse, right, acute

Challenge 3

1. a) Any five-sided shape with three obtuse angles drawn, e.g.

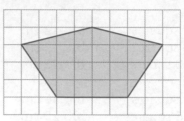

b) Any four-sided shape with three acute angles drawn, e.g.

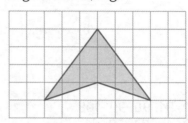

2. No, Caroline isn't correct. Triangles cannot have two right angles.

Pages 94–95
Challenge 1

1. a) C **b)** D **c)** F
  d) A **e)** B
  f) Square **B** to square **D**

Challenge 2

1. a) 11 right, 1 down **b)** 3 left, 3 up
  c) 7 left, 1 down **d)** 11 right, 4 up
  e) 4 right, 2 down **f)** 4 left, 3 down

Challenge 3

1. 5 (units) right, 7 (units) up

2.

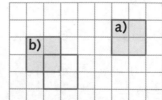

3. a) row circled **b)** column circled

Pages 96–97
Challenge 1

1. a) (4,6) **b)** (2,7) **c)** (6,4)
  d) (5,3) **e)** (7,2) **f)** (3,5)

2. a) Points (1,2) and (7,8) plotted and joined with a straight line.
  b) (4,5)

Challenge 2

1. a) A plotted at (6,1) **b)** B plotted at (5,7)
  c) C plotted at (2,6) **d)** D plotted at (7,4)
  e) E plotted at (1,3) **f)** F plotted at (4,2)

2. **a)** (5,3)   **b)** (5,3)
Challenge 3
1. **a)** (6,3) written and plotted on the grid
    b) (7,3) written and plotted on the grid
    c) (2,4) written and plotted on the grid
    d) (7,6) written and plotted on the grid
    (1 mark for each pair of coordinates written correctly; 1 mark for each pair of coordinates plotted correctly)

Pages 98–99
Challenge 1
1. **a) and b)** Rectangle plotted with vertices at (1,7), (1,4), (6,7) and (6,4)
    c) (6,4)
2. **a)** (7,3) and (3,1) plotted
    b) A right-angled triangle drawn
    c) The third vertex could be: (0,7), (1,5), (2,3), (3,3), (4,4), (5,7), (6,0), (6,5), (7,1) **or** (8,1)
Challenge 2
1. **a) and b)** Square plotted with vertices at (3,8), (1,6), (5,6) and (3,4)
    c) (3,4)
2. **a) and b)** Kite plotted with vertices at (6,6), (4,4), (8,4) and (6,3) **or** (6,6), (4,4), (8,4) and (6,2) **or** (6,6), (4,4), (8,4) and (6,1) **or** (6,6), (4,4), (8,4) and (6,0)
    c) (6,3) **or** (6,2) **or** (6,1) **or** (6,0)
Challenge 3
1. (15,10)
2. (9,9) (accept (–1,4))
3. **a)** (5,5)   **b)** (5,5)
4. No, Daria is not correct. The x-axis displays lines that are vertical. If they are all the same the line would be vertical.

Pages 100–101
Challenge 1
1. **a)** 2   **b)** Red   **c)** Orange
    d) Blue   **e)** 15
Challenge 2
1. **a)** 3   **b)** 38 circled   **c)** 42
    d) 4   **e)** 4
Challenge 3
1. **a)** 19   **b)** 196
    c) 2 second places = 10 points
        4 third places = 8 points
        or
        9 third places = 18 points
    d) Yes, Simon could be correct. Many possible explanations, e.g. 10 second places = 50 points.

Pages 102–103
Challenge 1
1. **a)** 9:00am   **b)** 8°C   **c)** 6°C
    d) 7 hours
    e) 3
Challenge 2
1. **a)** 12:00   **b)** 5 hours
    c) 1 hour
    d) 5°C
    e) Any time between 10:20 and 10:40
Challenge 3
1. **a)** 1°C
    b) Any temperature >5.5°C but <6.5°C
    c) Any temperature >4°C but <5°C
    d) Any time between 3 hours 30 minutes and 3 hours 50 minutes
    e) Any time between 1 hour 35 minutes and 1 hour 50 minutes

Pages 104–105
Challenge 1
1. **a)** 4   **b)** 28   **c)** 12
    d) 8   **e)** 5
Challenge 2
1. **a)** Sami and Ava   **b)** 100 km
    c) 40 km   **d)** 3
Challenge 3
1. **a)** 60   **b)** 100
    c) 40   **d)** 120

Pages 106–107
Challenge 1
1. **a)** £18   **b)** £32   **c)** £7   **d)** £13
Challenge 2
1. **a)** 5
    b) Hot meal total = 47, added to table
    c) Class A children who had a sandwich = 5, added to table
    d) Class C children who had a vegetarian meal = 9, added to table
Challenge 3
1. **a)** 38
    b) Yes, Olivia is correct. The Friday column shows 24 men visiting. Saturday (18) and Sunday (6) total 24.
    c) 5
    d) Women (accept 76)

Pages 108–111
Progress Test 4
1. 9018, 9108, 9180, 9801, 9810
2. **a)** four hundreds **or** 400
    b) four thousands **or** 4000
    c) four tens **or** 40

Answers

3. 56
4. a) 7503 + 1812 = 9315
   b) 854 − 362 = 492
5. 146
6. $\frac{5}{12}$
7. 2 kg
8. 4100 g, $4\frac{1}{2}$ kg, 4.9 kg, 5 kg, 5500 g
9. 21
10. a) 19:35   b) 20:45   c) 18:50
    (1 mark for all three parts correct)
11. a) 8 kg   b) 9000 ml
    c) 50 cm   d) 450 cm
12. 8.25 litres
13. a) 4.5 kg **or** 4500 g
    b) 4.5 m **or** 450 cm

14. right-angled and scalene circled
15. a) 2   b) 0
16. Obtuse
17. The square has moved **3** squares to the left and **1** square up.
18. a) A
    b) Accept any of the following coordinates: (1,8), (2,7), (7,2), (8,1)
19. a) 155   b) 137   c) 15
20. a) 7 mm
    b) Tuesday and Wednesday
    c) 2
21. a) Kay   b) 8

Notes

Progress Test 1

Q	Topic	✓ or ✗	See page
1	Counting		12
2	Numbers Beyond 1000		14
3	Numbers Beyond 1000		14
4	Numbers Beyond 1000		14
5	Numbers Beyond 1000		14
6	Place Value		16
7	Place Value		16
8	Roman Numerals		18
9	Roman Numerals		18
10	Representing Numbers		20
11	Representing Numbers		20
12	Rounding Numbers		22
13	Rounding Numbers		22
14	Negative Numbers		24
15	Negative Numbers		24
16	Addition and Subtraction Practice		26
17	Addition and Subtraction Practice		26
18	Estimating and Checking Calculations		28
19	Estimating and Checking Calculations		28
20	Addition and Subtraction Problems		30
21	Addition and Subtraction Problems		30
22	Multiplication and Division Facts		32
23	Multiplication and Division Facts		32
24	Factors		36
25	Factors		36
26	Multiplication Practice		38
27	Multiplication Problems		40
28	Multiplication Problems		40
29	Multiplication Problems		40
30	Multiplication Problems		40

Progress Test 2

Q	Topic	✓ or ✗	See page
1	Counting		12
2	Numbers Beyond 1000		14
3	Place Value		16
4	Representing Numbers		20
5	Rounding Numbers		22
6	Negative Numbers		24
7	Addition and Subtraction Practice		26
8	Estimating and Checking Calculations		28
9	Addition and Subtraction Problems		30
10	Addition and Subtraction Problems		30
11	Factors		36
12	Factors		36
13	Multiplication Practice		38
14	Multiplication Problems		40
15	Multiplication Problems		40
16	Hundredths		46
17	Hundredths		46
18	Equivalent Fractions		48
19	Addition and Subtraction of Fractions		50
20	Fraction and Decimal Equivalents		54
21	Fraction and Decimal Equivalents		54
22	Rounding Decimals		56
23	Rounding Decimals		56
24	Comparing Decimals		58
25	Comparing Decimals		58
26	Dividing by 10 and 100		60
27	Dividing by 10 and 100		60
28	Finding Fractions		52
29	Decimal Problems		62

Progress Test Charts

Progress Test 3

Q	Topic	✓ or ✗	See page
1	Counting		12
2	Numbers Beyond 1000		14
3	Place Value		16
4	Roman Numerals		18
5	Rounding Numbers		22
6	Addition and Subtraction Problems		30
7	Multiplication and Division Facts		32
8	Factors		36
9	Multiplication Practice		38
10	Multiplication Problems		40
11	Hundredths		46
12	Equivalent Fractions		48
13	Addition and Subtraction of Fractions		50
14	Rounding Decimals		56
15	Finding Fractions		52
16	Decimal Problems		62
17	Comparing Measures		68
18	Comparing Measures		68
19	Estimating Measures		70
20	12 and 24 Hour Time		76
21	12 and 24 Hour Time		76
22	Time Problems		78
23	Time Problems		78
24	Converting Measures		72
25	Perimeter and Area		80
26	Perimeter and Area		80

Progress Test 4

Q	Topic	✓ or ✗	See page
1	Numbers Beyond 1000		14
2	Place Value		16
3	Representing Numbers		20
4	Addition and Subtraction Practice		26
5	Multiplication Problems		40
6	Addition and Subtraction of Fractions		50
7	Finding Fractions		52
8	Comparing Measures		68
9	Time Problems		78
10	12 and 24 Hour Time		76
11	Converting Measures		72
12	Measurement Calculations		74
13	Measurement Calculations		74
14	2-D Shapes		86
15	Lines of Symmetry		90
16	Angles		92
17	Translations		94
18	Coordinates Shapes and Coordinates		96 98
19	Tables		106
20	Time Graphs		102
21	Bar Charts		100

What am I doing well in? _____

_____

What do I need to improve? _____

_____

This revision guide is matched to the new single award **AQA GCSE Science specifications (A and B)**, which cover the whole programme of study for KS4 science. It provides full coverage of the three units of **substantive content** (scientific explanations and evidence relating to Biology, Chemistry and Physics) and the **procedural content**, How Science Works, which is explained thoroughly on pages 6–13.

Clear explanations of all the essential material on which you may be assessed are provided, and colour diagrams are used to help clarify key concepts. In certain places we have included slightly more information than the specification suggests you need to know in order to aid understanding.

For each sub-section of substantive content, the AQA GCSE Science specification identifies **activities** you should be able to complete using your skills, knowledge and understanding of how science works. Many of these activities focus on issues that highlight the role of science in society and the impact it has on our lives, and require you to evaluate information, develop arguments and draw conclusions. These activities are dealt with in this guide on the **How Science Works** pages (picked out with shaded backgrounds), which are integrated into the three main units.

This guide is suitable for use by **Foundation and Higher Tier** students. The content on the AQA GCSE Science specifications (A and B) is not tiered, so there is no additional material which needs to be revised if you are preparing for the Higher Tier test/ exam questions.

How to Use this Revision Guide

AQA GCSE Science Specifications A and B are identical in content; they differ only in the style of **assessment:**

If you are studying Specification A, you will have to complete a 30-minute objective test under exam conditions for each separate section of content – Biology 1a, Biology 1b, Chemistry 1a, Chemistry 1b,

Physics 1a and Physics 1b (6 in total).

Each objective test features matching and multiple choice style questions and represents 12.5% of your total mark.

If you are studying Specification B, you will have to complete a 45-minute written exam for each unit – Biology 1 (a & b), Chemistry 1 (a & b) and Physics 1 (a & b).

Each written exam paper features structured questions and represents 25% of your total mark.

The **contents list and page headers** in this revision guide clearly identify the separate sections, to help you revise for the individual test/exam papers.

All of the test/exam papers will include questions on **How Science Works**, so make sure you work through the How Science Works section at the front of this guide and the dedicated pages in the relevant section.

The points identified on the **How Science Works** pages are designed to provide a starting point, from which you can begin to develop your own conclusions. They are not meant to be definitive or prescriptive.

You will find **exam-style questions**, along with model answers and handy hints at the end of each unit to help you understand what is expected of you in the tests/exams.

At the end of each unit there is a page of **key words and definitions**. These pages can be used as checklists to help you with your revision. Make sure you are familiar with all the words listed and understand their meanings and relevance - they are central to your understanding of the material in that unit!

Don't just read the information in this guide - learn actively! Jot down anything you think will help you to remember, no matter how trivial it may seem and constantly test yourself by looking away from the text.

Acknowledgements

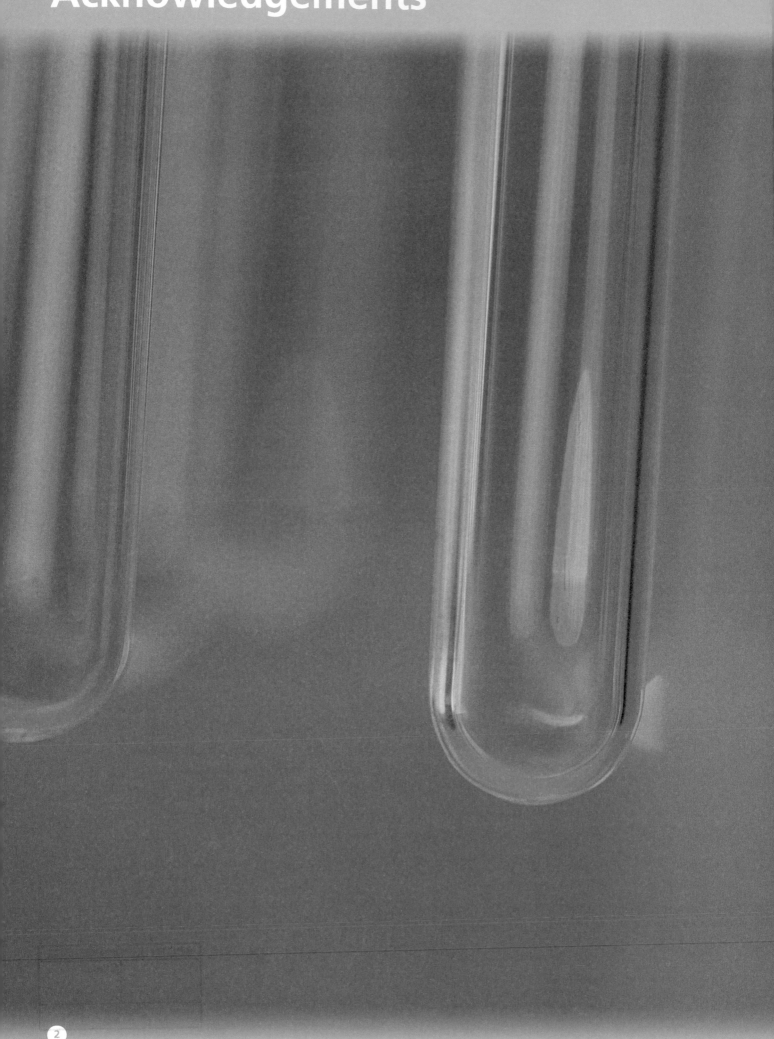

Acknowledgements

Author Information

Andrew Catterall (Physics), Lynn Henfield (Biology) and Christine Horbury (Chemistry) are all science consultants for LEAs. They work closely with the exam boards and have an excellent understanding of the new science specifications, which they are helping to implement in local schools.

As former science teachers, with over 70 years experience between them, their main objective in writing this book was to produce a user-friendly revision guide for students, which would also act as a useful reference for teachers. As such, this guide provides full coverage of all the essential material, cross-referenced to the specification for ease of use and presented in a clear and interesting manner that is accessible to everyone.

Published by Lonsdale, a division of Huveaux PLC

Lonsdale make every effort to ensure that all paper used in our books is made from wood pulp obtained from well-managed forests, controlled sources and recycled wood or fibre.

The authors and publisher would like to thank everyone who contributed images to this book:

IFC	©iStockphoto.com / Andrei Tchernov
p.3	©iStockphoto.com / Dane Wirtzfeld
p.5	©iStockphoto.com / Andrei Tchernov
p.7	©iStockphoto.com / Audrey Roorda
p.8	©iStockphoto.com / Todd Smith
p.9	©iStockphoto.com / James Antrim
p.18	©iStockphoto.com / Gary Caviness
p.18	©iStockphoto.com / Elena Korenbaum
p.25	©iStockphoto.com / Rob Gentile
p.25	©iStockphoto.com / Richard Scherzinger
p.28	©iStockphoto.com / Leah-Anne Thompson
p.31	©iStockphoto.com / Ben Phillips
p.33	©iStockphoto.com / Mikhail Tolstoy
p.43	©iStockphoto.com / Mike Morley
p.43	©iStockphoto.com / Alex Bramwell
p.56	©iStockphoto.com / Don Wilkie
p.61	©iStockphoto.com / Duncan Walker
p.64	©iStockphoto.com / Laurin Rinder
p.68	©iStockphoto.com / Jim Parkin
p.69	©iStockphoto.com / Sean Fishlock
p.69	©iStockphoto.com / Stephan Kohler
p.85	©iStockphoto.com / Michael Finch
p.93	©iStockphoto.com / Larry Manire
p.98	©iStockphoto.com / Marc Dietrich
p.98	©iStockphoto.com / Vallentin Vassileff
p.103	©iStockphoto.com / Mack Reed
p.107	NASA

Artwork supplied by HL Studios.

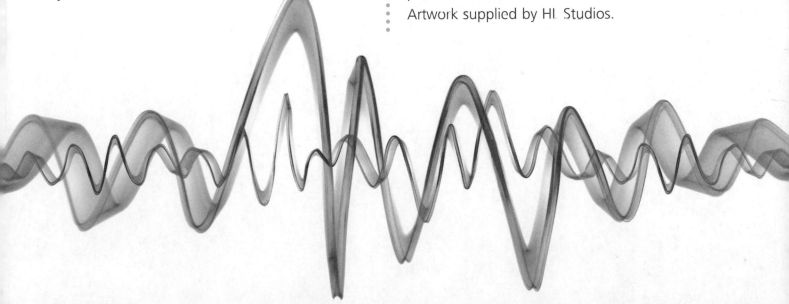

Contents

Contents

6 How Science Works (10.1–10.9)

Biology Unit 1a – Human Biology

14 How do human bodies respond to changes inside them and to their environment? (11.1)

19 What can we do to keep our bodies healthy? (11.2)

23 How do we use / abuse medical and recreational drugs? (11.3)

30 What causes infectious diseases and how can our bodies defend themselves against them? (11.4)

Biology Unit 1b – Evolution and Environment

34 What determines where particular species live and how many of them there are? (11.5)

37 Why are individuals of the same species different from each other? What new methods do we have for producing plants and animals with the characteristics we prefer? (11.6)

41 Why have some species of plants and animals died out? How do new species of plants and animals develop? (11.7)

44 How do humans affect the environment? (11.8)

50 Biology Unit 1 - Example Questions

51 Biology Unit 1 - Key Words

Chemistry Unit 1a – Products from Rocks

52 How do rocks provide building materials? (12.1)

57 How do rocks provide metals and how are metals used? (12.2)

62 How do we get fuels from crude oil? (12.3)

Chemistry Unit 1b – Oils, Earth and Atmosphere

65 How are polymers and ethanol made from oil? (12.4)

70 How can plant oils be used? (12.5)

73 What are the changes in the Earth and its atmosphere? (12.6)

80 Chemistry Unit 1 – Example Questions

81 Chemistry Unit 1 – Key Words

Physics Unit 1a – Energy and Electricity

82 How is heat (thermal energy) transferred and what factors affect the rate at which it is transferred? (13.1)

84 What is meant by the efficient use of energy? (13.2)

86 Why are electrical devices so useful? (13.3)

89 How should we generate the electricity that we need? (13.4)

Physics Unit 1b – Radiation and the Universe

94 What are the uses and hazards of the waves that form the electromagnetic spectrum? (13.5)

99 What are the uses and dangers of emissions from radioactive substances? (13.6)

105 What do we know about the origins of the Universe and how it continues to change (13.7)

108 Physics Unit 1 – Example Questions

109 Physics Unit 1 – Key Words

110 How Science Works Key Words

111 Index

112 Periodic Table

The numbers in brackets correspond to the reference numbers on the AQA GCSE Science specifications.

How Science Works

The new AQA GCSE Science specifications incorporate two types of content:

- **Science Content** (example shown opposite)
  This is all the scientific explanations and evidence that you need to be able to recall in your exams (objective tests or written exams). It is covered on pages 14–109 of the revision guide.

- **How Science Works** (example shown opposite)
  This is a set of key concepts, relevant to all areas of science. It is concerned with how scientific evidence is obtained and the effect it has on society. More specifically, it covers…

  - the relationship between scientific evidence and scientific explanations and theories
  - the practices and procedures used to collect scientific evidence
  - the reliability and validity of scientific evidence
  - the role of science in society and the impact it has on our lives
  - how decisions are made about the use of science and technology in different situations, and the factors affecting these decisions.

Because they are interlinked, your teacher will have taught the two types of content together in your science lessons. Likewise, the questions on your exam papers are likely to combine elements from both types of content, i.e. to answer them, you will need to recall the relevant scientific facts *and* draw upon your knowledge of how science works.

The key concepts from How Science Works are summarised in this section of the revision guide. You should be familiar with all of them, especially the practices and procedures used to collect scientific data (from all your practical investigations). But make sure you work through them all. Make a note if there is anything you are unsure about and then ask your teacher for clarification.

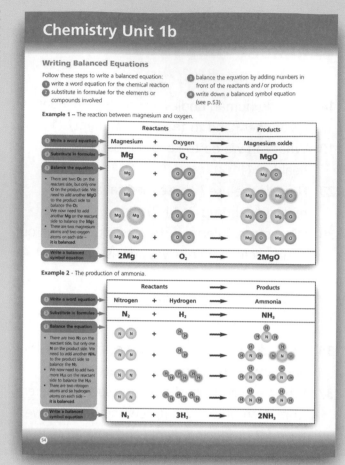

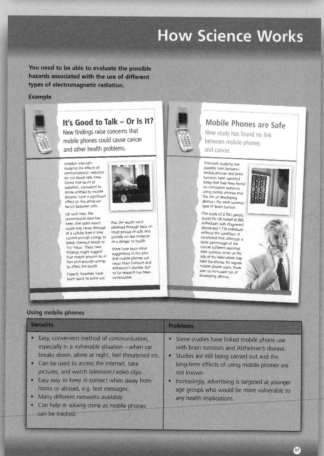

How to Use this Revision Guide

The AQA GCSE Science specifications include activities for each sub-section of science content, which require you to apply your knowledge of how science works, to help develop your skills when it comes to evaluating information, developing arguments and drawing conclusions.

These activities are dealt with on the How Science Works pages (on a tinted background) throughout the revision guide. Make sure you work through them all, as questions relating to the skills, ideas and issues covered on these pages could easily come up in the exam. Bear in mind that these pages are designed to provide a starting point from which you can begin to develop your own ideas and conclusions. They are not meant to be definitive or prescriptive.

Practical tips on how to evaluate information are included in this section, on page 13.

What is the Purpose of Science?

Science attempts to explain the world we live in. The role of a scientist is to collect evidence through investigations to...

- explain phenomena (e.g. explain how and why something happens)
- solve problems.

Scientific knowledge and understanding can lead to the development of new technologies (e.g. in medicine and industry) which have a huge impact on society and the environment.

Scientific Evidence

The purpose of evidence is to provide facts which answer a specific question, and therefore support or disprove an idea or theory. In science, evidence is often based on data that has been collected by making observations and measurements.

To allow scientists to reach appropriate conclusions, evidence must be...

- **reliable**, i.e. it must be reproducible by others and therefore be trustworthy
- **valid**, i.e. it must be reliable and it must answer the question.

N.B. If data is not reliable, it cannot be valid.

To ensure scientific evidence is reliable and valid, scientists employ a range of ideas and practices which relate to...

1. **observations** – how we observe the world
2. **investigations** – designing investigations so that patterns and relationships can be identified
3. **measurements** – making measurements by selecting and using instruments effectively
4. **presenting data** – presenting and representing data
5. **conclusions** – identifying patterns and relationships and making suitable conclusions.

These five key ideas are covered in more detail on the following pages.

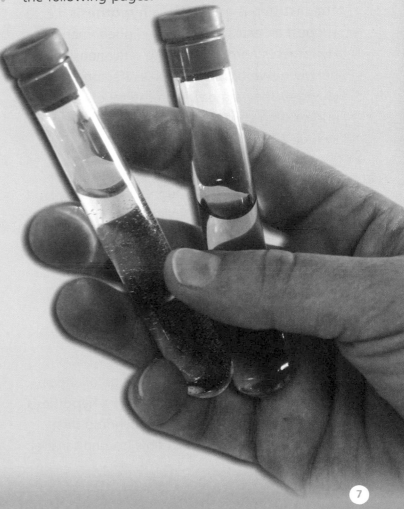

How Science Works

❶ Observations

Most scientific investigations begin with an observation, i.e. a scientist observes an event or phenomenon and decides to find out more about how and why it happens.

The first step is to develop a **hypothesis**, i.e. to *suggest* an explanation for the phenomenon. Hypotheses normally propose a relationship between two or more variables (factors that change). They are based on careful observations and existing scientific knowledge, and often include a bit of creative thinking.

The hypothesis is used to make a prediction, which can be tested through scientific investigation. The data collected during the investigation might support the hypothesis, show it to be untrue, or lead to the development of a new hypothesis.

Example

A biologist **observes** that freshwater shrimp are only found in certain parts of a stream.

He uses current scientific knowledge of shrimp behaviour and water flow to develop a **hypothesis**, which relates the distribution of shrimp (first variable) to the rate of water flow (second variable).

Based on this hypothesis, the biologist **predicts** that shrimp can only be found in areas of the stream where the flow rate is beneath a certain value.

The prediction is **investigated** through a survey, which looks for the presence of shrimp in different parts of the stream, representing a range of different flow rates.

The **data** shows that shrimp are only present in parts of the stream where the flow rate is below a certain value (i.e. it supports the hypothesis). However, it also shows that shrimp are not *always* present in parts of the stream where the flow rate is below this value.

As a result, the biologist realises there must be another factor affecting the distribution of shrimp. So, he **refines his hypothesis**, to relate the distribution of shrimp (first variable) to the concentration of oxygen in the water (second variable) in parts of the stream where there is a slow flow rate.

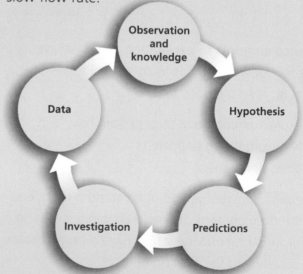

If new observations or data do not match existing explanations or theories, e.g. if unexpected behaviour is displayed, they need to be checked for reliability and validity.

In some cases it turns out that the new observations and data are valid, so existing theories and explanations have to be revised or amended. This is how scientific knowledge gradually grows and develops.

② Investigations

An investigation involves collecting data to try to determine whether there is a relationship between two variables. A variable is any factor that can take different values (i.e. change). In an investigation you have two variables:

- **independent variable**, which is controlled or known by the person carrying out the investigation. In the shrimp example on page 8, the independent variable is the flow rate of the water.

- **dependent variable**, which is measured each time a change is made to the independent variable, to see if it also changes. In the shrimp example on page 8, the dependent variable is the distribution of shrimp (i.e. whether shrimp are present or not).

Variables can have different types of values...

- **continuous variables** – can take any numerical values. These are usually measurements, e.g. temperature or height.

- **discrete variables** – can only take whole-number values. These are usually quantities, e.g. the number of shrimp in a population.

- **ordered variables** – have relative values, e.g. small, medium or large.

- **categoric variables** – have a limited number of specific values, e.g. the different breeds of dog: dalmatian, cocker spaniel, labrador etc.

Numerical values tend to be more powerful and informative than ordered variables and categoric variables.

An investigation tries to establish whether an observed link between two variables is...

- **causal** – a change in one variable causes a change in the other, e.g. in a chemical reaction the rate of reaction (dependent variable) increases when the temperature of the reactants (independent variable) is increased

- **due to association** – the changes in the two variables are linked by a third variable, e.g. a link between the change in pH of a stream (first variable) and a change in the number of different species found in the stream (second variable), may be the effect of a change in the concentration of atmospheric pollutants (third variable)

- **due to chance** – the change in the two variables is unrelated; it is coincidental, e.g. in the 1940s the number of deaths due to lung cancer increased as did the amount of tar being used in road construction, however, one *did not* cause the other.

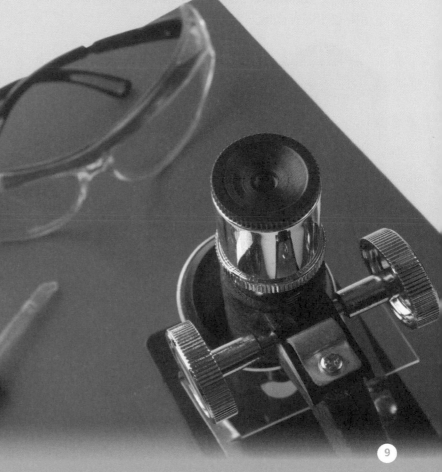

How Science Works

Fair Test

A fair test is one in which the only factor that can affect the dependent variable is the independent variable. Any other variables (outside variables) that could influence the results are kept the same.

This is a lot easier in the laboratory than in the field, where conditions (e.g. weather) cannot always be physically controlled. The impact of outside variables, like the weather, has to be reduced by ensuring all measurements are affected by the variable in the same way. For example, if you were investigating the effect of different fertilisers on the growth of tomato plants, all the plants would need to be grown in a place where they were subject to the same weather conditions.

If a survey is used to collect data, the impact of outside variables can be reduced by ensuring that the individuals in the sample are closely matched. For example, if you were investigating the effect of smoking on life expectancy, the individuals in the sample would all need to have a similar diet and lifestyle to ensure that those variables do not affect the results.

Control groups are often used in biological research. For example, in some drugs trials, a placebo (a dummy pill containing no medicine) is given to one group of volunteers – the control group – and the drug is given to another. By comparing the two groups, scientists can establish whether the drug (the independent variable) is the only variable affecting the volunteers and, therefore, whether it is a fair test.

Accuracy and Precision

In an investigation, the mean (average) of a set of repeated measurements is often calculated to overcome small variations and get a best estimate of the true value. Increasing the number of measurements taken will improve the accuracy and the reliability of their mean.

$$\text{Mean} = \frac{\text{Sum of all measurements}}{\text{Number of measurements}}$$

The purpose of an investigation will determine how accurate the data collected needs to be. For example, measures of blood alcohol levels must be accurate enough to determine whether a person is legally fit to drive.

The data collected must also be precise enough to form a valid conclusion, i.e. it should provide clear evidence for or against the hypothesis.

Fertiliser 1

Fertiliser 2

Fertiliser 3

③ Measurements

Even if all outside variables have been controlled, there are certain factors that could still affect the reliability and validity of any measurements made:

- **the accuracy of the instruments used** – The accuracy of a measuring instrument will depend on how accurately it has been calibrated. Expensive equipment is likely to be more accurately calibrated.
- **the sensitivity of the instruments used** – The sensitivity of an instrument is determined by the smallest change in value it can detect. For example, bathroom scales are not sensitive enough to detect the changes in weight of a small baby, whereas the scales used by a midwife to monitor growth are.
- **human error** – When making measurements, random errors can occur due to a lapse in concentration, and systematic (repeated) errors can occur if the instrument has not been calibrated properly or is repeatedly misused.

Any anomalous (irregular) values, e.g. values that fall well outside the range (the spread) of the other measurements, need to be examined to try to determine the cause. If they have been caused by an equipment failure or human error, it is common practice to ignore such values and discount them from any following calculations.

| Range | = | Maximum value | – | Minimum value |

④ Presenting Data

Data is often presented in a format that makes the patterns more evident. This makes it easier to see the relationship between two variables. The relationship between variables can be linear (positive or negative) or directly proportional.

Clear presentation of data also makes it easier to identify any anomalous values.

The type of chart or graph used to present data will depend on the type of variable involved.

Tables organise data (patterns and anomalies in the data are not always obvious).

Height (cm)	127	165	149	147	155	161	154	138	145
Shoe size	5	8	5	6	5	5	6	4	5

Bar charts are used to display data when the independent variable is categoric or discrete and the dependent variable is continuous.

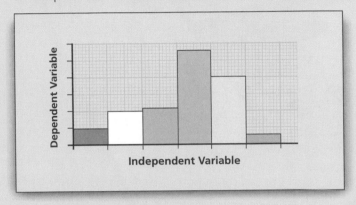

Line graphs are used to display data when both variables are continuous.

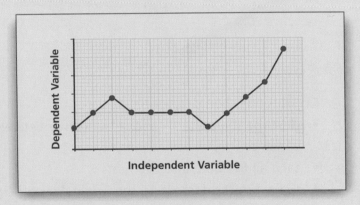

Scattergrams (or scatter diagrams) are used to show the underlying relationship between two variables. This can be made clearer by including a line of best fit.

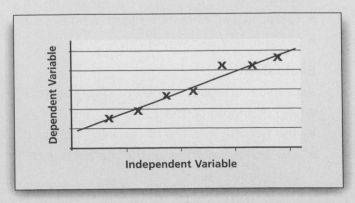

How Science Works

⑤ Conclusions

Conclusions should...
- describe the patterns and relationships between variables
- take all the data into account
- make direct reference to the original hypothesis / prediction.

Conclusions should not...
- be influenced by anything other than the data collected
- disregard any data (other than anomalous values)
- include any speculation.

Evaluation

An evaluation looks at the investigation as a whole. It should consider...
- the original purpose of the investigation
- the appropriateness of the methods and techniques used

- the reliability and validity of the data
- the validity of the conclusions (e.g. whether the original purpose was achieved).

The reliability of an investigation can be increased by...
- looking at relevant data from secondary sources
- using an alternative method to check results
- ensuring that the results can be reproduced by others.

Science and Society

Scientific understanding can lead to technological developments, which can be exploited by different groups of people for different reasons. For example, the successful development of a new drug benefits the drugs company financially and improves the quality of life for patients.

The applications of scientific and technological developments can raise certain issues. An issue is an important question that is in dispute and needs to be settled. Decisions made by individuals and society about these issues may not be based on scientific evidence alone.

Social issues are concerned with the impact on the human population of a community, city, country, or even the world.

Economic issues are concerned with money and related factors like employment and the distribution of resources. There is often an overlap between social and economic issues.

Environmental issues are concerned with the impact on the planet; its natural ecosystems and resources.

Ethical issues are concerned with what is morally right and wrong, i.e. they require a value judgement to be made about what is acceptable. As society is underpinned by a common belief system, there are certain actions that can never be justified. However, because the views of individuals are influenced by lots of different factors (e.g. faith and personal experience) there are also lots of grey areas.

How Science Works

Evaluating Information

It is important that you can evaluate information relating to social-scientific issues. You could be asked to do this in the exam, but it will also help you make informed decisions in life (e.g. decide whether or not to have a particular vaccination or become involved in a local recycling campaign).

When you are asked to **evaluate** information, start by making a list of the pluses and the minuses. Then work through the two lists, and for each point consider how this might impact on society. Remember, **PMI** – pluses, minuses, impact on society.

You also need to be sure that the source of information is reliable and credible. Here are some important factors to consider:

- **opinion**

  Opinions are personal viewpoints. Opinions which are backed up by valid and reliable evidence carry far more weight than those based on non-scientific ideas (e.g. hearsay or urban myths).

- **bias**

  Information is biased if it does not provide a balanced account; it favours a particular viewpoint. Biased information might include incomplete evidence or try to influence how you interpret the evidence. For example, a drugs company might highlight the benefits of their drugs but downplay the side effects in order to increase sales.

- **weight of evidence**

  Scientific evidence can be given undue weight or dismissed too lightly due to...

  - political significance, e.g. evidence that is likely to provoke an extreme and negative reaction from the public might be downplayed

  - status (academic or professional status, experience, authority and reputation), e.g. evidence is likely to be given more weight if it comes from someone who is a recognised expert in that particular field.

Limitations of Science

Science can help us in lots of ways but it cannot supply all the answers. We are still finding out about things and developing our scientific knowledge. There are some questions that we cannot answer, maybe because we do not have enough reliable and valid evidence.

There are some questions that science cannot answer at all. These tend to be questions relating to ethical issues, where beliefs and opinions are important, or to situations where we cannot collect reliable and valid scientific evidence. In other words, science can often tell us whether something *can* be done and *how* it can be done, but it cannot tell us whether it *should* be done.

Biology Unit 1a

How do human bodies respond to changes inside them and to their environment?

The nervous system and hormones allow the human body to respond to changes. To understand this, you need to know…

- what the nervous system and hormones are
- how the brain coordinates a response
- how hormones regulate functions and how they are involved in controlling fertility.

Parts of the Nervous System

The nervous system consists of the **brain**, the **spinal cord**, the **spinal nerves** and **receptors**. It allows organisms to react to their surroundings and to coordinate their behaviour. Information from **receptors** passes along **neurones** (nerve cells) to the brain, which coordinates the response produced by the **effectors** (e.g. muscles or glands).

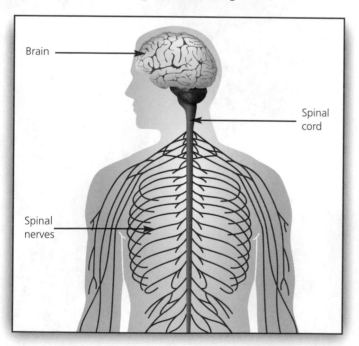

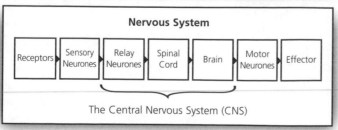

The Three Types of Neurone

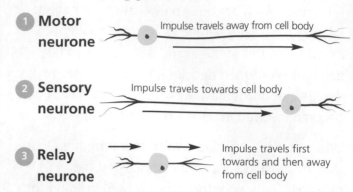

1 **Motor neurone** — Impulse travels away from cell body

2 **Sensory neurone** — Impulse travels towards cell body

3 **Relay neurone** — Impulse travels first towards and then away from cell body

Neurones are specially adapted cells that can carry an electrical signal, e.g. a nerve impulse.

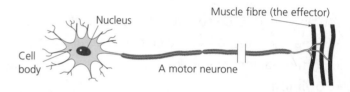

They are elongated (stretched out) to make connections between parts of the body. They have branched endings which allow a single neurone to act on many muscle fibres. The cell body has many connections to allow communication with other neurones.

Connections Between Neurones

Neurones do not touch each other; there is a very small gap between them called a **synapse** (see diagram below). When an electrical impulse reaches the gap via Neurone A, a chemical transmitter is released, which activates receptors on Neurone B and causes an electrical impulse to be generated in Neurone B. The chemical transmitter is then destroyed.

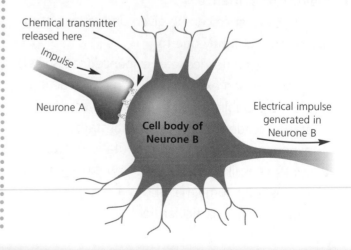

Types of Receptor

Receptors detect (respond to) stimuli which include light, sound, change in position, taste, smell, touch, pressure, pain and temperature.

- **Light** – receptors in the eyes.
- **Sound** – receptors in the ears.
- **Change of position** – receptors in the ears (balance).
- **Taste** – receptors on the tongue.
- **Smell** – receptors in the nose.
- **Touch, pressure, pain and temperature** – receptors in the skin.

Conscious Action

The pathway for receiving information and then acting upon it is as follows:

Stimulus	Receptors	Coordinator	Effectors	Response
Loud music	Sound-sensitive receptors in the ear	**Sensory Neurones** ▼ **Central Nervous System** ▼ **Motor Neurones** ▶	Muscles in arms and fingers	Turn music down

The coordinator is the central nervous system, to which impulses are transmitted via the spinal nerves.

Reflex Action

Sometimes conscious action is too slow to prevent harm to the body, e.g. removing your hand from a hot plate! **Reflex action** speeds up the response time by missing out the brain completely. The spinal cord acts as the coordinator and passes impulses directly from a sensory neurone to a motor neurone via a relay neurone, which by-passes the brain. Reflex actions are automatic and quick.

Stimulus	Receptors	Coordinator	Effectors	Response
Drawing pin	Pain receptor	**Sensory Neurones** ▼ **Relay Neurone in Spinal Cord** ▼ **Motor Neurones** ▶	Muscles to hand	Withdraw hand

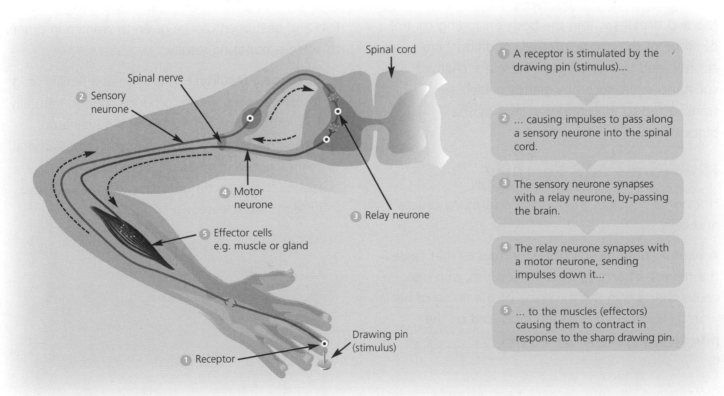

Spinal cord

Spinal nerve

2 Sensory neurone

4 Motor neurone

5 Effector cells e.g. muscle or gland

3 Relay neurone

1 Receptor

Drawing pin (stimulus)

1 A receptor is stimulated by the drawing pin (stimulus)...

2 ... causing impulses to pass along a sensory neurone into the spinal cord.

3 The sensory neurone synapses with a relay neurone, by-passing the brain.

4 The relay neurone synapses with a motor neurone, sending impulses down it...

5 ... to the muscles (effectors) causing them to contract in response to the sharp drawing pin.

Biology Unit 1a

Internal Conditions

Humans need to keep their internal environment relatively constant. Body temperature, and the levels of water, salts (ions) and blood sugar need to be carefully controlled.

- **Temperature** (ideally 37°C – the temperature at which most body enzymes work best.) Temperature is increased by shivering and narrowing skin capillaries. Temperature is decreased by sweating and expanding skin capillaries.
- **Water content**
  Water is gained by drinking, and lost by breathing via the lungs and sweating. Any excess is lost via the kidneys in urine.
- **Ion content** (sodium, potassium etc.)
  Ions are gained by eating and drinking. Ions are lost by sweating and excess is lost via the kidneys in urine.
- **Blood sugar (glucose) levels**
  Glucose provides the cells with a constant supply of energy. It is gained by eating and drinking.

How Conditions are Controlled

Many processes within the body (including control of some of the above internal conditions) are coordinated by **hormones**. These are chemical substances, produced by glands, which are transported to their target organs by the bloodstream.

Hormones and Fertility

Hormones regulate the functions of many organs and cells.

A woman naturally produces hormones that cause the release of an egg from her ovaries, and also cause changes in the thickness of the lining of her womb. These hormones are produced by the **pituitary gland** and the **ovaries**.

Natural Control of Fertility

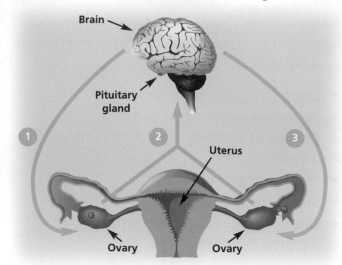

1. **Follicle stimulating hormone (FSH)** from the pituitary gland causes the ovaries to produce oestrogen and an egg to mature.
2. **Oestrogen**, produced in the ovaries, inhibits the production of FSH and causes the production of luteinising hormone (LH).
3. **LH**, also from the pituitary gland, stimulates the release of an egg in the middle of the menstrual cycle.

Artificial Control of Fertility

FSH and oestrogen can be given to women in order to achieve opposing results.

- **Increasing fertility:** FSH is given as a fertility drug to women who do not produce enough naturally to stimulate eggs to mature and be released.
- **Reducing fertility:** oestrogen is given as an oral contraceptive to inhibit FSH production. This means that eggs do not mature in the ovary, so no eggs are released.

You need to be able to evaluate the claims made by a manufacturer about a sports drink.

Example

SustainEnergy

This carbohydrate drink will help to increase your available energy, and improve hydration and performance when taken before and during exercise. You will develop endurance, and be able to exercise more intensely and for longer. It will also help you to recover more rapidly so that you can train more frequently.

SustainEnergy. For all your energy needs.

– High in glucose
– Rehydrates (contains water)
– Matches body ions
– No artificial additives

Benefits

- Contains glucose to provide cells with a constant supply of energy.
- Improves hydration by replacing water lost from the body via lungs when we breathe out and via skin when we sweat during exercise.
- Replaces ions lost through skin when we sweat.
- SustainEnergy should have a positive impact on the fitness of those who drink it.

Problems

- Encourages over-exercise before the body has chance to recover.
- No evidence that its claims are true.
- No reference to which of the body's ions are present.
- The claims could be influenced by the manufacturer's need to make a financial gain from this product.

It would be necessary to investigate this product further and to compare it with others on the market before arriving at a final conclusion.

How Science Works

You need to be able to evaluate the benefits of, and problems that may arise from, IVF treatment, including its impact on society.

Example

SCIE

Issue 19
January 2006

Natural Conception

Did you know that one in seven couples in the UK experiences delays in conceiving? Only a third of those trying for a baby become pregnant each month, although some of these will miscarry before they even know they are pregnant. The most common reasons for miscarriage / fertility problems include hormonal problems and blocked fallopian tubes in women, and a low sperm count in men.

What can Specialist Scientists do?

Once a couple has been referred to a fertility specialist (called a reproductive medicine specialist), the treatment they receive will depend on the cause of the problem and can range from hormone treatments such as FSH, which boosts egg production, to assisted conception techniques such as in vitro fertilisation (IVF).

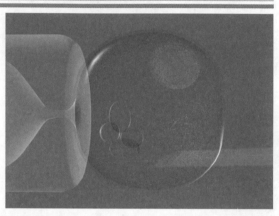

In Vitro Fertilisation

IVF involves removing eggs from the woman's ovaries and mixing them with her partner's sperm or donated sperm in a laboratory. A number of eggs are then placed back in the womb. This is a demanding treatment for the woman and the success rate is just 15 per cent. Many cycles of treatment may be required.

Although access to IVF is limited on the NHS, couples are now entitled to one cycle of treatment. To qualify, women must be between 23 and 39 and have a specific fertility problem (e.g. blocked fallopian tubes) or have failed to conceive for three years despite regular intercourse. A cycle of IVF at a private clinic costs around £2,000.

Benefits	Problems
• Can help a woman become pregnant. • Uses woman's own eggs and partner's own sperm. • Provides an alternative to adoption.	• Emotionally / physically demanding treatment. • Only 15% success rate. • Age restriction. • Costly. • Could lead to over population. • Uses NHS resources. • Increases expectation for babies on demand.

11.2

What can we do to keep our bodies healthy?

A nutritious, balanced diet and regular exercise are required to keep our bodies healthy. To understand this, you need to know...

- what a healthy diet consists of
- what can happen as a result of a poor diet
- how the metabolic rate varies
- how to balance cholesterols to maintain a healthy heart
- what the problems are with fats, salt and processed food.

A combination of a balanced diet and regular exercise is needed to keep our bodies healthy.

Metabolic Rate

This is the rate at which all the chemical reactions in the cells of the body are carried out. It varies with...

- the amount of activity you do – your metabolic rate increases with the amount of exercise you do and it stays high for some time after you have finished exercising
- the proportion of fat to muscle in your body
- your family history – it can be affected by inherited factors.

People who exercise regularly are usually fitter than those who don't.

The less exercise you take and the warmer it is, the less food you need.

Healthy Diets

A healthy diet contains the correct balance of the different foods your body needs:

- carbohydrates
- fats
- protein
- fibre
- vitamins
- minerals
- water.

The proportions required depend on an individual's body and lifestyle.

A person is **malnourished** if their diet is not balanced. A poor diet can lead to...

- a person being too fat or too thin
- deficiency diseases, for example, scurvy, which is caused by lack of vitamin C.

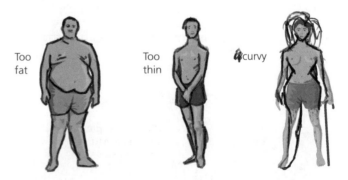

Too fat   Too thin   Scurvy

Health Problems Linked to Diet and Exercise

In the **developed** world (e.g. UK, USA) people are consuming too much food and taking too little exercise. The result is high levels of obesity and diseases linked to excess weight, such as...

- arthritis (worn joints)
- diabetes (high blood sugar)
- high blood pressure
- heart disease.

In the **developing** world (e.g. some parts of Africa and Asia) people suffer from problems linked to lack of food, such as...

- reduced resistance to infection
- irregular periods in women.

Biology Unit 1a

How to Improve the Diet

Two things we can control to improve our diets are...
- cholesterol
- salt.

Cholesterol

Cholesterol is naturally made in the liver and is found in the blood. Diet and inheritance factors affect how much cholesterol the liver makes.

Cholesterol is carried around the body by chemicals called **lipoproteins** (made from fat/lipid and protein). High levels of low-density cholesterol (bad cholesterol) in the blood increase the risk of disease of the heart and blood vessels.

- **Low-density lipoproteins** (LDLs) can cause heart disease.
- **High-density lipoproteins** (HDLs) are good cholesterols.

The balance of these is important for a healthy heart.

Salt

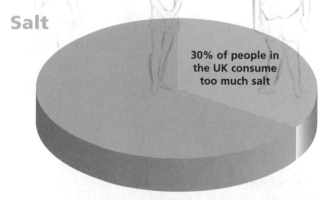

30% of people in the UK consume too much salt

Too much salt in the diet can lead to increased blood pressure. So you should...

- eat less **salt**
- eat less **processed food**, which often contains a high proportion of fat and/or salt
- eat less **saturated fats** e.g. butter, animal fat (these increase blood cholesterol)
- eat more **unsaturated fats** (monounsaturated and polyunsaturated fat) e.g. vegetable oil, some fish. These help to reduce blood cholesterol levels and improve the balance between good and bad lipoproteins.

Ideal amounts of cholesterol in the blood

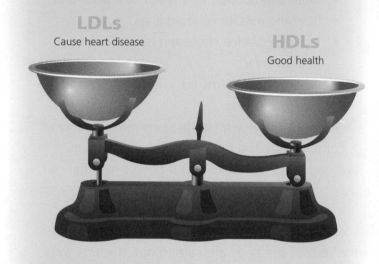

LDLs
Cause heart disease

HDLs
Good health

More...

Less...

You need to be able to evaluate information about the effect of food on health.

Example

To be healthy, the main thing is to ensure you have a balanced intake of protein, carbohydrates, essential fats, fruit, fibre, vitamins and minerals. The Western Approach to a healthy diet involves limiting your intake of salt, alcohol, caffeine and saturated fats, and eating at least five portions of fruit and vegetables per day. People should eat plenty of fresh and wholegrain foods and have only a moderate amount of sugar.

Benefits	Problems
• Balances protein, carbohydrates and vitamins daily throughout the year. • Foods are available all year round. • Encourages eating fruit and vegetables every day.	• Some people think that the body reacts best to foods that are seasonal and eaten at the time of the year when they are naturally available. • In order for certain foods to be available all year round, chemical/genetic assistance may be used to grow foods out of season.

The Oriental Approach involves eating foods in the season they are naturally grown, so foods such as salads, soft fruits, peas and beans are eaten in summer, whereas in winter, vegetables grown below ground, like carrots and turnips, are eaten.

All foods are categorised as being either 'warming' or 'cooling'. Warming foods include meats, pulses and ginger, and are boiled, grilled or fried. Cooling foods include lettuce, watercress and soft fruits that are eaten raw, cool or refrigerated.

Benefits	Problems
• Some people think this is the healthiest option because it involves eating seasonal food. • Encourages consumption of healthy, natural foods such as salad and fruit. • Foods are not genetically modified.	• The diet keeps changing which can upset some people's stomachs. • During certain times of the year, e.g. winter, the diet may be restrictive.

How Science Works

You need to be able to evaluate claims made by a slimming programme.

Example

April 2006

Slimm...

Slimmer April 2006

The all-new <u>low-carb</u> diet

Advertorial

It's easy to lose weight quickly on this new slimming programme. All you have to do is limit your carbohydrate intake.

You can consume a very small amount of carbohydrates from vegetables such as broccoli, but you are not allowed any carbohydrates from bread, pasta, potatoes or fruit.

- Eat unlimited quantities of protein and fats (e.g. meat, cheese, eggs)!
- No need to make yourself eat fruit!
- No need for exercise!

How does it work?

Managing the intake of carbohydrates is certain to lead to weight loss because without carbohydrates to provide energy, the body starts using up stored fat as the main source of energy.

Page 3

Benefits	Problems
• Low-carbohydrate diets can help you to lose weight very quickly in the short term. • Low-carbohydrate diets can seem like an easy way to lose weight. • You can still eat many of the foods that would be cut out on a conventional slimmer's diet, e.g. chips, cheese.	• Such a drastic change in diet can have a negative effect on the body. • Exercise is not encouraged by this slimming programme, but it is required for a person to be healthy – especially when they are consuming so much fat. • The body needs a healthy balance of foods to maintain good health: low-carbohydrate diets are not balanced and not good in the long term. • The body misses out on essential nutrients found in fruit, vegetables and grains. • Low-carbohydrate diets do not allow sufficient consumption of fruit and vegetables to meet the recommended daily allowance. • Long-term high intake of protein puts a strain on the kidneys. • Lack of energy (energy should come from carbohydrates). • In the absence of carbohydrates, protein (muscle) stores get used for energy, as well as fat.

11.3

How do we use/abuse medical and recreational drugs?

Drugs are used in medicine to cure illnesses and diseases. Drugs, alcohol and tobacco may also be used recreationally by people who like the effect they have. To understand this, you need to know about...

- the benefits and the harmful effects of drugs
- the stages in the development and testing of drugs
- thalidomide and its effects
- the effects of legal and illegal drugs
- the effects of tobacco and alcohol on the human body.

Drugs

Drugs are chemical substances which alter the way the body works. They can be beneficial but may also harm the body. Some drugs can be obtained from natural substances (many have been known to indigenous people for years). Others are synthetic (man-made) and need to be thoroughly tested and trialled in the laboratory to find out if they are toxic (poisonous). Then they are checked for side-effects on human volunteers.

Developing New Drugs

The flow chart below shows the stages in developing new drugs.

> **New drug made in a laboratory**
>
> ↓
>
> **Tested in laboratory for toxicity**
>
> ↓
>
> **Trialled on volunteers to check for side-effects**

Example: Thalidomide

- This drug was developed as a sleeping pill. It was tested and **approved** for this use.
- It was also found to be effective in relieving morning sickness in pregnant women. It had **not been tested** for this use.
- Many babies born to mothers who took the drug had severe limb abnormalities, so it was **banned**.
- Thalidomide was re-tested and is now used successfully to treat leprosy.

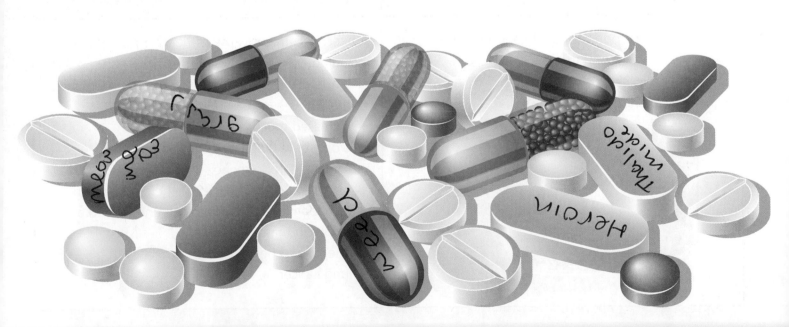

Biology Unit 1a

Legal and Illegal Drugs

Some drugs are used illegally for pleasure (recreation) but they can be very harmful.

Drugs alter chemical processes in people so they may become dependent or addicted to them. They may therefore suffer withdrawal symptoms if they do not have them. Symptoms may be psychological or physical (e.g. paranoia, sweating, vomiting).

Heroin and cocaine are examples of two very addictive drugs, which are used illegally.

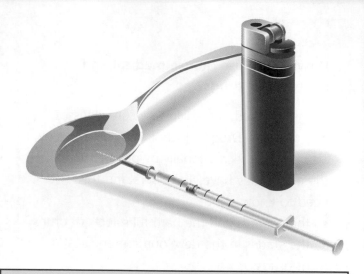

Alcohol	Effects
Contains the chemical ethanol.	• Alcohol is a depressant – it causes reactions to slow down. • Alcohol can lead to a lack of self-control. • Excess alcohol can lead to unconsciousness and even coma or death. • The long-term effects of alcohol can be liver damage (due to the liver having to remove all the toxic alcohol from the body) or brain damage.
Tobacco	**Effects**
Contains tar, carbon monoxide and nicotine (which is addictive) and the chemicals that cause cancer – carcinogens.	Tobacco is a major cause of health problems, including... • emphysema – alveoli damage due to coughing • bronchitis – increased infection due to increased mucus production • problems in pregnancy – tobacco smoke contains carbon monoxide, which reduces the oxygen-carrying capacity of the blood which can deprive a fetus of oxygen and lead to a low birth mass • arterial and heart disease • lung cancer.

You need to be able to evaluate the effect of statins on cardio-vascular disease.

Example

– *Why does cholesterol need to be reduced?*

High levels of cholesterol, especially the 'bad' type (LDLs) can cause the arteries to clog up with a thick fatty substance. The result is the narrowing of the arteries that take blood to heart muscle (coronary arteries). This narrowing and hardening of the arteries is called atherosclerosis, and can cause heart attacks. A sufferer will feel a heavy, tight chest pain and perhaps experience breathing difficulties. In very serious cases, a coronary artery may become blocked by a blood clot (thrombosis). This can cause severe pain and is life-threatening.

– *What are statins?*

Statins are drugs that work in the liver to reduce the manufacture of cholesterol. They have been found to be the most effective drugs for lowering LDL levels.

– *How long do you take them for?*

Statins are taken for life. They can reduce the chance of having a heart attack or a stroke by up to a third, and can increase the life expectancy of a person with a history of high cholesterol when taken long term.

– *Are there any side effects?*

They may cause headaches, sickness, diarrhoea, insomnia, liver problems, stomach upset, hepatitis and muscle aches. They cannot be taken by children, pregnant women or heavy drinkers.

– *Is there an alternative?*

If your doctor prescribes statins, you should take them. However, you can reduce the need for them if you stop smoking, eat a healthy diet with plenty of fruit and vegetables and low fat and salt content, and exercise regularly: moderate exercise three times a week reduces the risk of a heart attack by a third.

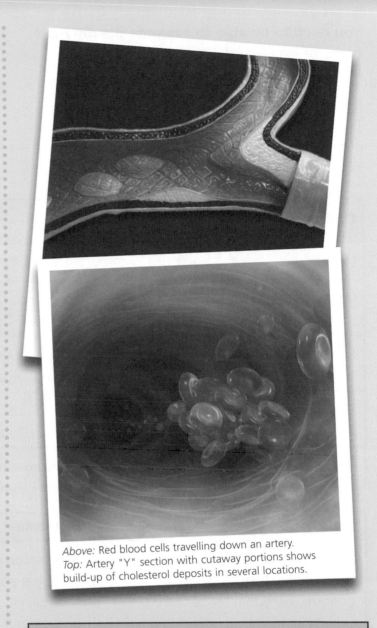

Above: Red blood cells travelling down an artery.
Top: Artery "Y" section with cutaway portions shows build-up of cholesterol deposits in several locations.

Benefits

- They reduce the manufacture of cholesterol.
- They reduce the risk of heart attack or stroke caused by cardio-vascular disease by up to a third.
- They are the most effective drugs for reducing LDLs.

Problems

- Statins can have many side effects.
- They cannot be taken by children, pregnant women or heavy drinkers.
- Availability of statins reduces the need for people to change their unhealthy lifestyles.
- They must be taken for life.

How Science Works

You need to be able to evaluate the different types of drugs and why some people use illegal drugs for recreation.

Example

The table below shows the different types of illegal drugs commonly used in the UK. Drugs are classified into class A, B and C; class A is the most dangerous.

Drug	Class	Details of Drug	Number of people using it regularly
Heroin	A	Sedative. Smoked or injected. Causes severe cravings, very addictive.	43 000
Cocaine	A	Stimulant, increases confidence, raises heart rate and blood pressure. Injected, inhaled or smoked. Causes cravings, very addictive.	755 000
Ecstacy	A	Stimulant, gives adrenaline rush, feeling of well-being, high body temperature, anxiety. Ingested in tablet form.	614 000
Amphetamines	A / B	Stimulant, increases heart rate. Ingested in tablet form. Can be very addictive and can cause paranoia.	483 000
Cannabis	C	Relaxant. Smoked. Can cause hallucinations.	3 364 000

Types of Drug Use	Problems
Experimental: when people try a drug for the first few times out of curiosity, boredom, or because their friends are doing it. Some do it to rebel against authority.	• A person is just as likely to have a bad reaction from trying a drug the first time as a person who uses drugs for recreation regularly. • It could lead to recreational use. • It could lead to trying harder drugs to get a new 'high'.
Recreational: when people use drugs in a regular but fairly controlled way. It is seen by some people as a way of relaxing.	• It could lead to dependent drug use. • It could lead to using harder drugs to get a new 'high'. • A person risks a bad reaction to drugs every time they use them. • It could lead to mental problems.
Dependent: when people are addicted to drugs and are dependent on the feeling it gives them. It is also physically addictive – the body needs the drug.	• People can not function without the drug. • People suffer withdrawal symptoms if they do not have the drug. • A person risks a bad reaction to drugs every time they use them. • It could lead to mental problems.

Drugs are illegal so there are no guarantees that you are getting what you think you are getting and they can be very expensive.

In all cases, a harmful substance is being put into the body, so there is always a risk of death.

You need to be able to evaluate claims made about the effect of cannabis on health and the link between cannabis and addiction to hard drugs.

Example

New concerns over cannabis use

A leading report published yesterday has sparked a fresh wave of concern about the dangers of using cannabis.

Concern about cannabis use is not isolated to the 21st century.

In Egypt in the 8th Century, laws were introduced which prohibited the use of 'hemp drugs' (cannabis). In the 19th Century, a large scale investigation into the health effects (physical and mental) of cannabis use was set up by the Indian Hemp Drugs Commission who concluded that the link between cannabis and mental injury was complex. In recent years, research in Scandinavia has linked cannabis to severe mental illness.

The new report backs up these claims that it is bad for your health, and suggests that in many cases users go on to use harder drugs, which can be extremely addictive.

— 1 —

The report claims that cannabis contains more tar and more cancer-causing chemicals than cigarettes; around 400 chemicals which are known to affect the brain.

It claims that its use affects blood pressure, causing fainting, or more severe problems for people with heart and circulation conditions. Although cannabis is not as addictive as alcohol, tobacco or amphetamines, many users do become psychologically addicted, which may then lead to them trying harder drugs.

Other reports, however, have said that the use of cannabis, unlike harder drugs, does not lead to major health problems, and few deny that it can have beneficial effects for patients suffering from conditions such as HIV, multiple sclerosis and cancer.

The recreational use of cannabis is still illegal in Britain although up to half of all young people have tried it.

— 2 —

Is smoking cannabis bad for your health?

Yes

- Cannabis has a higher concentration of cancer-causing substances (carcinogens) than tobacco.
- It has a higher tar content than tobacco so can lead to bronchitis, emphysema and lung cancer.
- It can increase the risk of fainting since it disrupts the control of blood pressure.
- It can lead to mental illness.
- It contains more than 400 chemicals. The main one that affects the brain is known as THC.
- People with heart and circulation disorders or mental illness can be adversely affected by it.
- It may be psychologically addictive.

No

- Its effects are beneficial to patients suffering from various medical conditions including HIV, multiple sclerosis and cancer.
- Unlike harder drugs, a government report has suggested that high use of cannabis isn't associated with major health or sociological problems.
- Cannabis is less addictive than amphetamines, tobacco or alcohol, and does less harm to the body.

Can smoking cannabis lead users to harder drugs?

Yes

- Cannabis may be a 'gateway' drug to more addictive and harmful substances such as heroin and cocaine.

No

- Many cannabis smokers never use any harder drugs.

How Science Works

You need to be able to explain how the link between smoking tobacco and lung cancer gradually became accepted.

During the 1940s and 1950s, there was a marked increase in deaths from lung cancer which prompted scientists to investigate the cause.

1940–1950 – Many scientists thought pollution was to blame for the increase in lung cancer deaths, whilst others believed the cause was the tar used in new roads.

Sir Richard Doll was commissioned by the Medical Research Council to investigate a possible link between smoking tobacco and lung cancer. He visited 2000 people suspected of having lung cancer across England and found that those who had the disease were heavy smokers. Those who did not have it did not smoke. However, the findings, published in 1950, were widely ignored.

1954 – The government accepted that there was a strong link between smoking tobacco and lung cancer.

1970s – In the 1970s the link began to be taken more seriously, and the media began to discuss it openly.

1990s – Some people in the tobacco industry continued to dispute claims of the link until as late as 1997, when they were sued by 40 US states to pay for the treatment costs of tobacco-related illnesses, and were forced to accept the evidence.

2000s – It is now accepted that people who smoke have an increased risk of lung cancer; the more people smoke, the more the risk is increased. The number of smokers in England has fallen (30% of men smoked in 2000 compared to 80% in 1950).

2006 – The UK Government passed a bill to ban smoking in all enclosed public places. It is already law in Scotland and will extend to England and Northern Ireland in 2007.

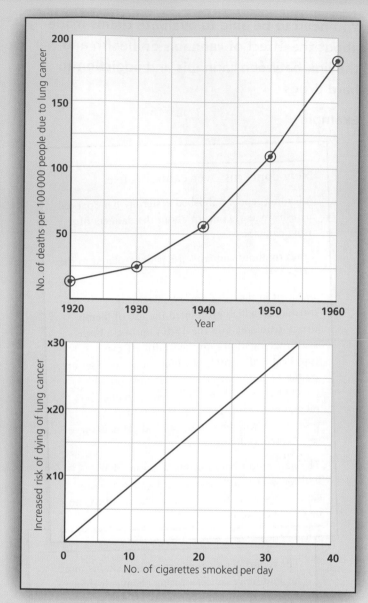

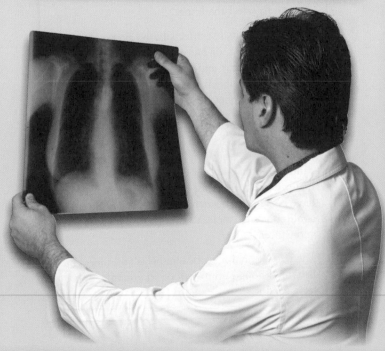

How Science Works

You need to be able to evaluate different ways of trying to stop smoking.

Example

A test was carried out to find the most effective way to stop smoking. The four methods tested were: nicotine patches, acupuncture, hypnosis and 'going cold turkey' (the **independent variables**).

400 participants who wanted to quit were divided into four equal groups. Each group tried one of the four methods for 2 months. The effectiveness of each method was measured by the number of people in each group who were still not smoking one year later (the **dependent variable**).

Because the study involved a large number of participants, it was important that similar people were selected to ensure the findings were **reliable**.

Therefore, people who smoked between 20 and 25 cigarettes a day were selected, and divided into groups so there was an equal number of men and women in each, **limiting the variables**.

Here are the results of the investigation.

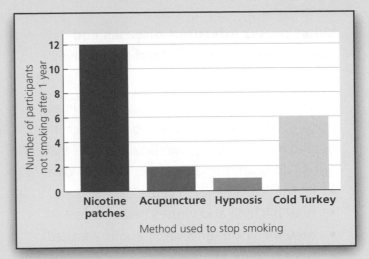

The bar graph shows us that nicotine patches are the most effective way to stop smoking. They are twice as effective as willpower alone (cold turkey).

Acupuncture and hypnosis are significantly less effective.

The conclusion is limited by the data and further tests would be needed to see if this were true for the whole population.

Method	Benefits	Problems
Nicotine patches (oversize sticking plasters containing nicotine).	• Fairly cheap. • Does not require expert help. • Easier than using willpower alone.	• Continues to put chemicals into the body. • Can become reliant on patches. • Unsuitable to use during pregnancy or if you have heart problems. • Can cause skin irritation or allergies.
Acupuncture (fine needles inserted in specific areas of the skin).	• Helps to restore the body's natural balance of health.	• Not proven to be very effective. • Must be administered by an expert. • Expensive.
Hypnosis (trained hypnotherapist suggests stopping while person is in a relaxed state).	• No side effects.	• No scientific evidence to support this. • Expensive. • Must be administered by an expert. • Not proven to be very effective.
Cold turkey (willpower only).	• No drugs or chemicals are used. • Quick. • No cost involved.	• Difficult to rely on willpower alone. • May experience withdrawal symptoms, e.g. mood swings, nausea.

Biology Unit 1a

11.4

What causes infectious diseases and how can our bodies defend themselves against them?

Microorganisms can thrive inside the human body, so the body has to try to stop them from getting in, and defend itself against those that do get in. To understand this, you need to know…
- how microorganisms cause disease
- how bacteria and viruses make us feel ill
- how medicines and vaccinations are used
- how immunisation works.

Bacteria and Viruses

Microorganisms that cause infectious diseases are called **pathogens**. Bacteria and viruses are the two main types of pathogen which may affect health.

Bacteria	Viruses
Very small.	Even smaller.
Reproduce very quickly.	Reproduce very quickly once inside living cells, which are then damaged.
Can produce toxins (poisons) which make us feel ill.	Can produce toxins (poisons) which make us feel ill.
Responsible for illnesses like tetanus, cholera, tuberculosis.	Responsible for illnesses such as colds, flu, measles, polio.

Defence against Pathogens

White blood cells form part of the body's **immune system** and help to fight infection by ingesting pathogens, producing antitoxins to neutralise toxins produced by the pathogens, and producing **antibodies** to destroy particular pathogens.

Treatment of Disease

The symptoms of disease are often alleviated using painkillers. You will be familiar with the mild versions of these, e.g. aspirin. Although painkillers are useful, they do not kill pathogens.

Antibiotics like penicillin are often used against bacteria. They kill infective bacteria inside the body, but cannot be used to kill viruses which live and reproduce inside cells. It is difficult to develop drugs which kill viruses without damaging the body's tissues.

Over-use of Antibiotics

Many strains of bacteria, including MRSA, have developed resistance to antibiotics as a result of natural selection.

Some individual bacteria in a particular strain have natural resistance. If the majority of the strain is wiped out by antibiotics, this leaves the field clear for the resistant bacteria to multiply quickly, passing on their resistance. It is therefore necessary to have a range of antibiotics and to select the one that is most effective for treatment of a particular infection.

Development of further resistance is avoided by preventing over-use of antibiotics.

Vaccination

A person can acquire **immunity** to a particular disease by being vaccinated (immunised).

1. An inactive / dead pathogen is injected into the body.
2. White blood cells produce antibodies to destroy the pathogen.
3. The body then has an acquired immunity to this particular pathogen since the white blood cells are sensitised to it and will respond to any future infection by producing antibodies quickly. An example is the MMR vaccine used to protect children against measles, mumps and rubella.

You need to be able to relate the contribution of Semmelweiss in controlling infection to solving modern problems with the spread of infection in hospitals.

Example

The work of Semmelweiss, and subsequent scientists, has led to the creation of many regulations which help to maintain hygiene standards in modern hospitals and reduce the chance of infections being spread.

1865

Semmelweiss dies of blood poisoning

The Hungarian doctor, Ignaz Semmelweiss, died today after contracting blood poisoning.

He will be remembered for his work in local hospitals where he reduced patient deaths on his wards from 12% to 1% by insisting that doctors washed their hands after surgery and before visiting another patient.

He had recognised that germs on surgeons' and doctors' hands were infectious and contagious and were responsible for many patients' deaths.

Frampton
General
Hospital

Health and Safety Regulations

- All staff must wash their hands thoroughly before and after having contact with each patient.

- All patients must wash their hands thoroughly.

- All surgical instruments must be sterilised before use.

- All hospital wards must be cleaned regularly with antibacterial cleaner.

- Doctors and surgeons must wear disposable face masks, gowns and gloves.

- All spillages of blood, bodily fluids, vomit, etc. must be cleared up immediately.

- All patients with infectious diseases must be isolated to prevent the disease spreading.

How Science Works

You need to be able to explain how the treatment of disease has changed as a result of increased understanding of the action of antibiotics and immunity...

... and evaluate the consequences of mutations of bacteria and viruses in relation to epidemics and pandemics, e.g. bird influenza.

Example

Genetically Modified Vaccine may be Answer to Bird Flu

Currently, scientists are trying to prevent an epidemic (large scale infection) of bird influenza becoming pandemic (a world wide infection) by developing new vaccinations. There are fears that the bird flu virus could mutate into a strain that can be transmitted between humans. US scientists are currently working on a genetically engineered vaccine that has been found to protect mice from the strains of bird flu that recently killed people in Asia and Europe. The vaccine, which was created from a genetically modified common cold virus, has been shown to stimulate the white blood cells to produce specific antibodies that may fight a number of strains of the bird flu virus.

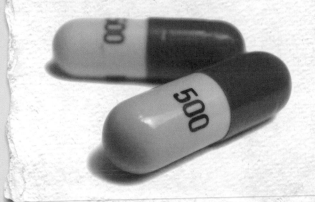

Treatment of disease changed drastically with the understanding of antibiotics and immunity.

Antibiotics are medicines which kill bacteria, so many bacterial infections and diseases, e.g. bronchitis and malaria, can be treated quite simply with a course of antibiotics. Patients suffering from illnesses which could once have led to death, now have a good chance of recovery through use of antibiotics.

People can acquire immunity to many diseases through vaccination, which means many, once common diseases, can now be prevented. Today, most young children are given vaccinations to immunise them from diphtheria, whooping cough, polio, meningitis and tuberculosis. Most are also given the MMR vaccine to immunise them against measles, mumps and rubella.

Vaccines are also available for tourists visiting places such as some parts of Africa and Asia, to protect them from diseases such as rabies and yellow fever. These diseases and illnesses could be fatal without modern medicine.

So what are the new problems facing today's scientists researching the prevention and cure of disease?

- Some strains of bacteria have developed resistance to antibiotics as a result of natural selection, e.g. MRSA (Methicillin-resistant Staphylococcus aureus). This results in the need for stronger antibiotics to be developed.
- Some bacteria and viruses have mutated (changed their form) so that existing drugs are no longer effective. The influenza (flu) virus can change rapidly, so a vaccine which combated its effect on the body one year will no longer be effective the following year. This means scientists are always having to develop new vaccines and find new ways to protect against these new strains.

You need to be able to evaluate the advantages and disadvantages of being vaccinated against a particular disease.

Example

issues

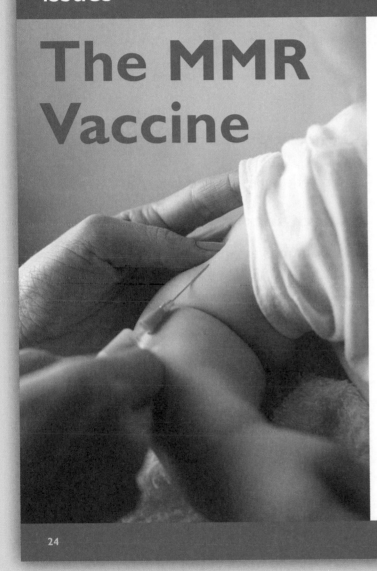

The MMR Vaccine

In Japan, scientists undertook a study of over 30 000 children born between 1988 and 1996 in the city of Yokohama. The triple vaccine (MMR) was made compulsory in 1989 and withdrawn in 1993, so they were able to compare how it affected those children who had been given the MMR vaccine and those that hadn't.

They counted the number of children who were diagnosed as being autistic by the age of 7. Their findings showed that for the children born in 1990, the number of cases was 86 per 10 000 children. For the children born in 1991, the figure was 56 per 10 000 children.

When the MMR was withdrawn in 1993, the children were given separate vaccinations. For children born in 1994, the number of cases of autism was 161 per 10 000.

As the number of cases of autism rose after the MMR vaccine was withdrawn, the scientists concluded that the MMR vaccine was not responsible.

24

Benefits of Vaccination against MMR	Problems with Vaccination against MMR
• The MMR vaccine immunises children against three potentially fatal diseases – mumps, measles and rubella. • The widespread use of the MMR vaccine prevents an epidemic of mumps, measles or rubella. • The MMR vaccination means children only need one jab, rather than three separate ones.	• Smaller studies have suggested a link between the MMR vaccine and autism in children. • Some larger studies do not rule out that MMR may trigger autism in a small number of children.

Biology Unit 1b

What determines where particular species live and how many of them there are?

Species adapt to live in their surrounding environments. How many live in a certain area depends on certain factors. To understand this, you need to know...
- what organisms need in order to survive
- how plants and animals compete
- how plants and animals adapt.

To survive, organisms need a supply of materials from their surroundings and from the other organisms there.

Competition

Organisms compete with each other for space / light, food and water.

Factor	Plants	Animals
Space / light	Need room to spread leaves and obtain light for photosynthesis.	Need space to breed and compete for a mate. Also territory to hunt in.
Food	Absorb nutrients from the soil.	Herbivores compete for vegetation and carnivores compete for their prey.
Water	Absorb water by their roots.	Need water in order to survive.

Animal populations are also affected by predators, disease and migration.

Plant populations are also affected by grazing by herbivores, and disease.

A **population** is the total number of individuals of the same species which live in a certain area, e.g. the number of field mice in a meadow. A **community** is all the organisms in a particular area, i.e. many populations of plants and animals.

When organisms compete in an area or habitat, those which are better adapted to the environment are more successful and usually exist in larger numbers, often resulting in the complete exclusion of other competing organisms.

Adaptations

Adaptations are special features or behaviour which make an organism particularly well-suited to its environment. They are part of the evolutionary process which 'shapes life' so that a habitat is populated by organisms which excel there.

Adaptations increase an organism's chance of survival; they are biological solutions to an environmental challenge. For example, some plants (e.g. roses and cacti) have thorns to prevent animals from eating them. Other organisms (e.g. blue dart frogs) have developed poisons and warning colours to deter predators.

Below is an example of another organism that is well suited to its environment.

Life in a Very Cold Climate – the Polar Bear
- Rounded shape means a small surface area to volume ratio to reduce heat loss.
- Large amount of insulating fat beneath the skin, which also acts as a food store.
- Thick greasy fur to add to insulation against the cold, and to repel water.
- White coat so it is camouflaged.
- Large feet to spread its weight on the ice.
- Powerful swimmer so that it can catch its food.

You need to be able to suggest how organisms are adapted to the conditions in which they live.

Example

A group of students from a school in North Yorkshire set off to the coast to investigate the effect of waves on organisms on the seashore.

They decided to base their study on the width and height of limpets in two rocky bays – Runswick Bay and Robin Hood's Bay – to see how they were adapted to their environment.

The rocks at Runswick Bay were large boulders. They were exposed to the force of the waves on one side but sheltered on the other side.

At Robin Hood's Bay, the sandstone outcrops were shelved as they stretched gradually out to sea.

RUNSWICK BAY

	Width of base of limpet shell (cm)	Height of limpet shell (cm)
Limpet 1	1.4	1.4
Limpet 2	2.4	1.5
Limpet 3	2.5	1.6
Limpet 4	2.4	2.5
Limpet 5	2.6	2.6
Limpet 6	3.5	2.1
Limpet 7	1.3	2.1
Limpet 8	2.3	1.9
Mean	2.3	2.0

ROBIN HOOD'S BAY

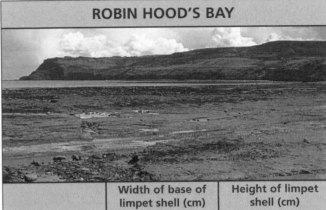

	Width of base of limpet shell (cm)	Height of limpet shell (cm)
Limpet A	2.5	2.6
Limpet B	2.9	3.6
Limpet C	3.0	2.8
Limpet D	2.5	3.7
Limpet E	2.6	3.6
Limpet F	2.5	3.9
Limpet G	2.1	3.3
Limpet H	2.0	2.9
Mean	2.4	3.3

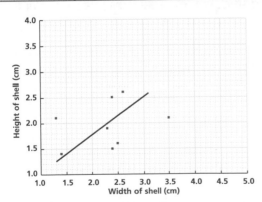

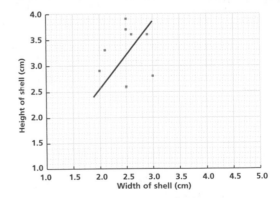

The data showed that at Runswick Bay, where the boulders are exposed to the waves, the limpet shells had a broad base compared to their height. This allowed them to resist the action of the waves.

The data from Robin Hood's Bay showed that the limpet shell bases were quite narrow compared to the height. The wave action here is not as forceful as at Runswick Bay so the limpet does not require such a broad base to hold it on the rocks.

How Science Works

You need to be able to suggest the factors for which organisms are competing in a given habitat.

Different species (e.g. plants, animals) can compete for certain factors. Different organisms of the same species have to compete against each other too.

Example 1: Red and Grey Squirrels need...	Example 2: Seaweed needs...
• **space:** red squirrels' natural habitat is woodland, but much has been destroyed, reducing the space available to them. Grey squirrels also live in woodland but they have been able to adapt to other habitats such as parks and gardens. • **food:** grey squirrels and red squirrels eat the same foods. However, grey squirrels can, if necessary, live on acorns, of which there are plenty. Red squirrels cannot and so this extra food gives grey squirrels a better chance of survival. • **shelter from prey:** both red and grey squirrels spend a lot of their time high up in the trees to escape attack from foxes and birds of prey.	• **light for photosynthesis:** many species of seaweed are found in shallow waters because they need light for photosynthesis and sunlight can only penetrate water up to a certain depth. • **water and nutrients:** unlike most other plants, seaweed absorbs water and nutrients through its surface, not through roots. This is why it needs to spend most of its time submerged. • **a 'holdfast' (somewhere to anchor):** because it doesn't have roots, seaweed needs to anchor on to a rock, or something similar, to stop itself from being swept out to sea.

Red Squirrel

Grey Squirrel

Spiral Wrack

Knotted Wrack

Bladder Wrack

Oar Weed

You need to be able to suggest reasons for the distribution of animals or plants in a particular habitat.

Some species adapt so that they can survive in conditions where their competitors cannot. This affects the distribution of organisms in a particular habitat.

Example

Species of Seaweed	Habitat	Reasons for distribution
Spiral wrack	Shallow water with long periods of exposure on the upper shore.	Contains more water when hydrated and loses it slowly. It does not have air bladders.
Knotted wrack	Mid-shore, spends less time exposed to the air.	Has single bladders and varying lengths of thallus (stalks). It contains less water.
Bladder wrack	The surface of the sea.	Is often covered so has less mucus and less water initially contained in it. It has double bladders to allow it to float.
Oar weed	The surface of the sea.	Cannot withstand drying out. It has very long thallus (stalks) and large flat fronds (leaves) like hands which are lifted by the tide.

11.6

Why are individuals of the same species different from each other? What new methods do we have for producing plants and animals with the characteristics we prefer?

Differences are due to inheritance and environment. Modern science can alter, add or remove genes to produce favourable characteristics. To understand this, you need to know about...

- genes in chromosomes
- sexual and non-sexual reproduction
- how plant cuttings produce identical plants
- modern cloning techniques
- genetic engineering and why it is used.

The Genetic Information

The nucleus of a cell contains **chromosomes**, which are made up of a substance called **DNA**. A section of a chromosome is called a **gene**. Genes carry information that controls the characteristics of an organism. Different genes control the development of different characteristics. During reproduction, genes are passed from parent to offspring (inherited).

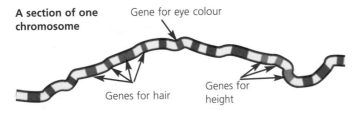

A section of one chromosome

Gene for eye colour

Genes for hair

Genes for height

Chromosomes come in pairs, but different species have different numbers of pairs, e.g. humans have 23 pairs. This example has just two pairs:

Cell

One of four chromosomes inside

Nucleus

Causes of Variation

Differences between individuals of the same species are called **variation**. Variation may be due to genetic causes (i.e. the different genes that have been inherited), or environmental causes (i.e. the conditions in which the organism has developed). Usually variation is due to a combination of genetic and environmental causes.

For example, identical twins will look exactly alike at birth, but their lifestyle will alter how they look. So if one twin has a diet high in fat and does no exercise, he will become fatter than his brother. This is an example of environmental factors. Genetics are responsible for things such as the colour of dogs' coats.

Effect of Reproduction on Variation

During **sexual reproduction** a sperm from a male fuses with an egg from a female. When this happens, the genes carried by the egg and the sperm are mixed together to produce a new individual.

This process is completely random, which produces lots of variation, even amongst offspring from the same parents.

Asexual reproduction means no variation at all, unless it is due to environmental causes.

Only one parent is needed and individuals who are genetically identical to the parent (clones) are produced. Bacteria reproduces asexually.

Biology Unit 1b

Reproducing Plants Artificially

Plants can reproduce **asexually** (i.e. without a partner) and many do so naturally. All the offspring produced asexually are **clones** (i.e. they are genetically identical).

Taking Cuttings

When a gardener has a plant with all the desired characteristics he may choose to produce lots of them by taking stem, leaf or root cuttings. These should be grown in a damp atmosphere until roots develop.

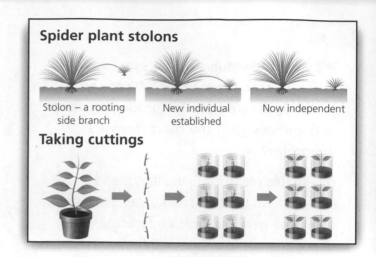

Spider plant stolons

| Stolon – a rooting side branch | New individual established | Now independent |

Taking cuttings

Cloning

Clones are genetically identical individuals. E.g. If you have a plant which has the ideal characteristics you can clone it to produce more plants with the same desired characteristics. This is exactly what is happening in modern agriculture.

Tissue Culture

1. Parent plant with the characteristics that you want.
2. A few cells are scraped off into several beakers containing nutrients and hormones.
3. A week or two later there are lots and lots of genetically identical plantlets growing. The same can be done to these.
4. This whole process must be aseptic (carried out in the absence of harmful bacteria) otherwise the new plants will rot.

Note, the offspring are genetically identical to each other and to the parent plant.

Embryo Transplants

Instead of waiting for normal breeding cycles farmers can obtain many more offspring by using their best animals to produce embryos which can be inserted into 'mother' animals.

1. Parents with desired characteristics are mated.
2. Embryo is removed before the cells become specialised...
3. ...then split apart into several clumps.
4. These embryos are then implanted into the uteruses of sheep who will eventually give birth to clones.

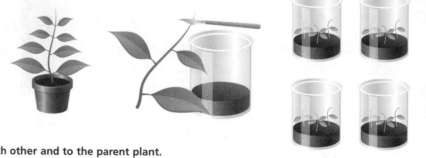

Prize ewe

Prize ram

Note, the offspring are genetically identical to each other, but not to the parents.

Adult Cell Cloning / Fusion Cell Cloning

1. DNA from a donor animal is inserted into an empty egg cell (nucleus removed)...
2. ...which then develops into an embryo.
3. The embryo is then implanted into the uterus of another sheep. Dolly the sheep was produced this way.

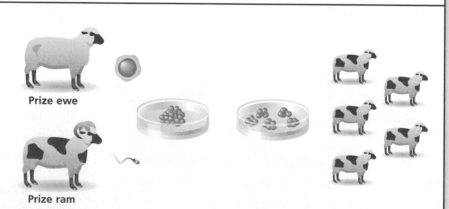

Reasons for Genetic Modification

Reasons for altering an organism's genetic make-up are...

- to improve the crop yield, e.g. to produce larger tomatoes, potatoes, wheat seed-heads, more oil from oilseed rape etc.
- to improve resistance to pests or herbicides, e.g. soya plants have been modified so that they are resistant to herbicides, allowing farmers to eliminate weeds without killing the crop
- to extend the shelf-life of fast-ripening crops such as tomatoes
- to harness the cell chemistry of an organism so that it produces a substance that you require, e.g. production of human insulin.

All these processes involve transferring genetic material from one organism to another. In animals and plants, genes are often transferred at an early stage of their development so that the organism develops with desired characteristics. These characteristics can then be passed onto the offspring if the organism reproduces asexually or is cloned.

Genetic Engineering

Insulin is the hormone that is produced by the pancreas and helps to control the level of glucose in the blood. Diabetics can't produce enough insulin and often need to inject it. **Human insulin** can be produced by genetic engineering, where genes from the chromosomes of humans and other organisms are cut out using enzymes.

1. Scientists use enzymes to cut a chromosome at specific places so they can remove the precise piece of DNA they want. In this case, the gene for insulin production is cut out.

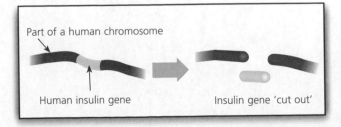

Part of a human chromosome

Human insulin gene   Insulin gene 'cut out'

2. Another enzyme is then used to cut open a ring of bacterial DNA (a plasmid). Other enzymes are then used to insert the piece of human DNA into the plasmid.

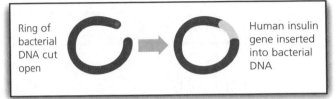

Ring of bacterial DNA cut open

Human insulin gene inserted into bacterial DNA

3. The plasmid is reinserted into a bacterium which starts to divide rapidly. As it divides the plasmid replicates and soon there are millions of them, each with instructions to make insulin.

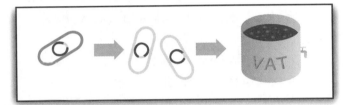

VAT

When the above process has been completed, the bacteria is cultured on a large scale and commercial quantities of insulin are then produced.

The Great Genetics Debate

Scientists have made great advances in their understanding of genes.

- They have identified genes that control certain characteristics.
- They can determine whether a person's genes may increase the risk of them contracting a particular illness, e.g. breast cancer.
- They may soon be able to 'remove' faulty genes and therefore reduce genetic diseases.

However, some people are concerned that...

- unborn children will be genetically screened and then aborted if their genetic make-up is faulty
- parents may want to choose the genetic make-up of their child
- some insurance companies may genetically screen applicants and refuse to insure people who have an increased genetic risk of an illness or disease. This may prevent these people being able to drive cars or buy homes due to lack of insurance.

How Science Works

You need to be able to make informed judgements about the economic, social and ethical issues concerning cloning and genetic engineering, including GM crops.

Argument for GM Crops	Argument against GM Crops
• They are more cost-effective (manufacturers claim higher yields). • They reduce pesticide use (according to a US study). • They can benefit human health (they can be enriched with nutrients). • They are safe for human consumption (according to the British Medical Association). • They could help the developing world by increasing yields. • They preserve natural habitats as less land is needed for agriculture.	• They increase pesticide use as farmers spray freely (according to a US study on maize). • Cross-contamination of non-GM crops could destroy the GM-free trade. • They mainly benefit big GM companies. • Unknown long-term health risks of antibiotic resistance (there is no actual evidence for this). • Increasing yields won't help the developing world (the problem is distribution of food, not lack of it). • Could affect wildlife since there are no weeds as a food source for animals.

Argument for Cloning Plants, Animals & Humans	Argument against Cloning Plants, Animals & Humans
• Traditional breeding methods are slow. • Can quickly predict characteristics of offspring. • Allows quick response to livestock / crop shortages. • Produces genetically superior stock. • Elimination of diseases such as diabetes. • Organ donation: a clone has matching tissue to the parent, so it would be able to donate an organ without the risk of the receiver rejecting the organ.	• Loss of livelihood by traditional farmers. • Risk of expression of 'unwanted' genes which adversely affect stock. • May cause backlash against cloned stock leading to market crashes. • Cloning companies may have monopoly on patent for clones. • Cloning is unnatural. • The fear of creating the 'perfect race'. • Human clone will not have 'parents'. • Cloning goes against the principles of some religions. • Abnormalities may occur in a clone. • Does not allow natural evolution.

11.7

Why have some species of plants and animals died out? How do new species of plants and animals develop?

Some species die out due to environmental changes. Other species survive better due to alterations in their genes which can sometimes result in a new species. To understand this, you need to know about...

- the theory of evolution
- similarities and differences between species
- why certain species have become extinct
- evolution and natural selection
- gene mutation.

The Theory of Evolution

The theory of **evolution** states that all living things which exist today, and many more that are now extinct, evolved from simple life forms which first developed 3 000 000 000 (3 billion) years ago.

Studying the similarities and differences between species can help us to understand evolution.

The Reasons for Extinction of Species

- Increased **competition** – Australian limpets were out-competed by British limpets and are now extinct.
- Changes in the **environment** – the mammoth was once well-adapted to live in the cold environment, but became poorly adapted for the current global climate.
- New **predators** – the dodo was hunted by humans, and animals introduced by humans.
- New **diseases**.

The Fossil Record

Fossils are the remains of plants or animals from many years ago which are found in rock. They provide evidence of how organisms have changed over time.

If we look at exposed rock strata, it is possible to follow the gradual changes which have taken place in an organism over time. Even though the fossil record is incomplete, these gradual changes confirm that species have changed over long periods of time providing strong evidence for evolution.

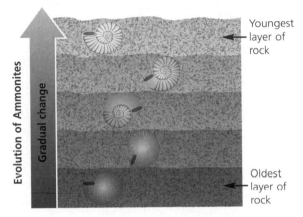

Youngest layer of rock

Oldest layer of rock

Evolution by Natural Selection

Evolution is the change in a population over a large number of generations that may result in the formation of a new species, the members of which are better adapted to their environment. There are five key points to remember.

1. Individuals within a population show variation (i.e. differences due to their genes).
2. There is competition between individuals for food and mates etc., also predation and disease keep population sizes constant in spite of the production of many offspring, i.e. there is a struggle for survival, and many individuals die.
3. Individuals better adapted to their environment are more likely to survive, breed successfully and produce offspring. This is 'survival of the fittest'.
4. These survivors will pass on their genes to their offspring resulting in an improved organism being evolved through **natural selection**.
5. Where new forms of a gene result from **mutation** there may be a more rapid change in a species.

How Science Works

You need to be able to...

- **identify the differences between Darwin's theory of evolution and conflicting theories**
- **suggest reasons why Darwin's theory of natural selection was only gradually accepted**

- **suggest reasons for the different theories and why scientists cannot be certain about how life began on Earth.**

Darwin's Theory

Charles Darwin sailed around the world in the 1830s collecting evidence for his 'theory of natural selection'. This states that...

- there is much variation in a species
- more offspring are produced than the environment can support (for example, food and breeding areas)
- only the ones best suited or adapted will survive and breed. This is known as natural selection or 'survival of the fittest'
- those that survive pass their genes onto their offspring. Eventually the species which is less suited will become extinct.

Darwin's theory was only gradually accepted because...

- religion had an important place in society
- it is difficult to prove
- many scientists did not (and some still don't) accept the theory
- attempts to demonstrate evolution through tests have failed.

The Conflicting Theories

1. **Creationist**
   This view states that each living thing was created separately and did not evolve. They view the gaps in the fossil records as evidence against evolution.

2. **Lamarck's Theory**
   Jean Baptiste Lamarck thought that living things changed throughout their lives and these changes were passed on to their offspring. So he had the idea that giraffes grew long necks to reach the highest leaves on a tree. He would have also believed that if a person learnt to play the piano, that person's children would be born able to play the piano. His was 'the theory of inheritance of acquired characteristics'.

3. **Intelligent Design (ID)**
   This view states that certain structures within cells, such as DNA and mitochondria, are far too complicated to have evolved over time so must have been put there by some other higher being or creator.

Reasons for the different theories may include...

- **religion:** people who are religious may not accept scientific theories because they believe in a creator
- **culture:** people's backgrounds can influence the way they think
- **evidence:** certain theories may have more evidence to support them than others
- **knowledge:** people believe what they know
- **status of theorists / scientists:** people may be more likely to believe the ideas of renowned scientists or prominent people.

Remember that there are many different theories and scientists cannot be absolutely certain about how life began on Earth because it is difficult to find evidence to prove any theory, and theories are based on the best evidence available at that time.

No-one experienced the beginning of life on Earth so it is impossible to ever be certain how it began. Even today, we are still finding out about things and developing our scientific knowledge.

How Science Works

You need to be able to interpret evidence relating to evolutionary theory.

Example

Sea Monster Fossils Discovered

Fossil evidence has been discovered of what appears to be a 'sea monster', thought to be 135 million years old.

The animal's large skull was found in an area in Argentina that was once part of the Pacific Ocean.

Measuring four metres (13 feet) in length, the *Dakosaurus* had four paddle-like limbs, thought to be used for balance. It had a tail like a fish which propelled it through the sea, and a head that bore a resemblance to a carnivorous dinosaur.

The fossil displays a short, high snout and big, serrated teeth similar to a crocodile's.

Dakosaurus' serrated tooth

Every other known marine reptile had a long snout and sharp, identical teeth, which were used to deal with their main prey – small fish.

Dakosaurus's unusual snout, sharp, jagged teeth and huge jaws suggest that it hunted for sea reptiles and other large marine creatures, using its teeth to bite into and chop up its prey.

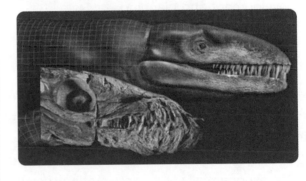

Identify and Interpret the Evidence Collected by the Scientists

1 Question

Was Dakosaurus related to today's crocodiles?

2 Evidence

For crocodile
- Large skull like a crocodile.
- Short, high snout similar to a crocodile.
- Serrated (jagged) teeth like a crocodile.

Against crocodile
- Tail like a fish.
- Paddle-like limbs, no legs.
- Large jaws and teeth suggest it preyed on large sea reptiles and other sea creatures.

3 Interpretation

- *State your view*
  Dakosaurus was a sea monster related to today's crocodiles.

- *Explain your view*
  This seems to be true because the fossils were similar to crocodiles – they had a short, high snout and serrated teeth.

- *Conclude*
  The characteristics are not found in marine reptiles. This means that Dakosaurus was a reptile with many similarities to today's crocodiles. However, unlike crocodiles, Dakosaurus was adapted to live in the sea as a sea creature.

Biology Unit 1b

11.8

How do humans affect the environment?

Humans affect the environment in many ways, resulting in changes to natural ecosystems and populations of species. Both the local and global environment may be harmed permanently as the human population increases. To understand this, you need to know…

- how the increasing human population results in pollution, waste and loss of raw materials
- how pollution can be indicated by living organisms
- what the effects of deforestation are
- how the atmosphere is affected by increasing levels of carbon dioxide and methane
- why there is a need for sustainable development and planning.

The Population Explosion

The standard of living for most people has improved enormously over the past 50 years and developments in science and medicine mean that people are now living for longer. The human population is therefore increasing exponentially (with accelerating speed).

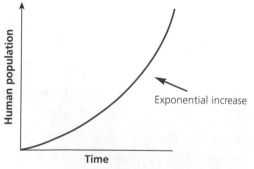

The rapid increase in the human population causes the following major problems…

- raw materials, including non-renewable energy resources, are being mined and quarried more intensively than ever before and they are being used up
- more and more domestic and industrial waste is being produced which means more landfill sites are needed

- improper handling of waste is leading to an increase in environmental pollution
- more land is taken up by farms to grow crops and keep animals
- towns and cities are expanding which means there is less land available for plants and animals.

Pollution

Human activities may pollute water, air and land:

- **water** – with sewage, fertiliser or toxic chemicals.
- **air** – with smoke and gases such as carbon dioxide, sulfur dioxide and oxides of nitrogen, which may contribute to acid rain.
- **land** – with toxic chemicals such as pesticides and herbicides, which may be washed from land into water.

Unless waste is properly handled and stored, more pollution will be caused.

Indicators of Pollution

Living organisms can be used as measures or indicators of pollution, for example…

- the absence of lichens (a blend of algae and fungus) can indicate air pollution
- the presence or absence of invertebrate animals can indicate water pollution, e.g. freshwater shrimp survive only in unpolluted water.

Deforestation

Deforestation involves the large-scale cutting down of trees for timber, and to provide land for agricultural use. This has occurred in many tropical areas with devastating consequences for the environment.

- Deforestation has increased the amount of CO_2 (carbon dioxide) released into the atmosphere due to the burning of the wood and also as a result of the decay of the wood by microorganisms.
- Deforestation has also reduced the rate at which carbon dioxide is removed from the atmosphere by photosynthesis.
- Deforestation reduces biodiversity and results in the loss of organisms that could be of future use.

Sustainable Development

It is important to improve the quality of life on Earth without compromising future generations. This is **sustainable development** and it is needed at local (towns), regional (countries) and global (worldwide) levels.

The Greenhouse Effect

The **Greenhouse Effect** describes how gases, such as methane and carbon dioxide, act like an insulating blanket by preventing a substantial amount of heat energy from 'escaping' from the Earth's surface into space. Without this effect the Earth would be a far colder and quite inhospitable place. However, the levels of these gases are slowly rising and so too is the overall temperature of the planet.

A rise in temperature by only a few degrees Celsius may lead to substantial climate changes and a rise in sea level.

- Methane and carbon dioxide gases reduce the amount of heat radiated into space.
- Deforestation reduces photosynthesis which removes CO_2.
- Burning the chopped-down wood, and industrial burning, produces CO_2.
- Increased microorganism activity on decaying material produces CO_2.
- Herds of cattle and rice fields produce methane, CH_4.

All of the above cause an increase in atmospheric carbon dioxide and methane which causes global warming.

Biology Unit 1b

Sustainable Development (cont.)

Sustainable development is concerned with three related issues:

- economic development
- social development
- environmental protection.

The United Nations Earth Summit in Rio de Janeiro in 1992 was arguably the first major event that resulted in a coordinated worldwide effort to produce sustained economic and social development that would benefit all the world's people, particularly the poor, whilst balancing the need to protect the environment by reducing pollution and ensuring resources are sustainable.

Sustainable resources are resources that can be maintained in the long term at a level that allows appropriate consumption or use by people. This often requires limiting exploitation by using quotas or ensuring the resources are replenished / restocked.

The Johannesburg Summit in 2002 led to the United Nations increasing efforts to support new developments whilst sustaining the planet.

Example 1: Cod in the North Sea

The UK has one of the largest sea fishing industries in Europe. To ensure the industry can continue and fish stocks can be conserved, quotas are set to prevent over-fishing.

In 2006 the European Union Fisheries Council made changes which included…

- increasing mesh size to prevent young fish being caught before they reach breeding age
- increasing quotas of certain other types of fish other than cod.

Example 2: Pine Forests in Scandinavia

Scandinavia uses a lot of pine wood to make furniture and paper, and to provide energy. To ensure the long-term economic viability of pine-related industries, companies replenish and restock the pine forests by planting a new sapling for each mature tree they cut down.

Endangered Species

When countries or companies neglect the ideas of sustainable development, various species can become **endangered**. Below are some examples.

- The red kite (bird of prey) was exploited for its feathers.
- The numbers of osprey were reduced as its habitats were destroyed.
- The red squirrel was endangered when the larger grey squirrel was introduced.

Many endangered species are now protected. For example, the Countryside Council for Wales provides legal protection for red squirrels; they cannot be trapped, killed or kept except under special licence. The red kite and osprey both have protected sites in Wales where they can live and breed undisturbed.

Education has become a powerful 'weapon' in protecting endangered species and promoting the ideas behind sustainable development.

You need to be able to analyse and interpret scientific data concerning environmental issues.

Example

Green Week
FACTSHEET

How pollution affects the environment

Sulfur dioxide (SO₂) and nitrogen dioxide (NO₂) are pumped into the atmosphere by power stations and industrial plants.

Once in the atmosphere, they dissolve in water vapour to form sulfuric acid and nitric acid.

These fall to the Earth as acid rain, which alters the pH of rivers and lakes.

Human activity often upsets the natural balance of ecosystems, or changes the environment so that some species find it difficult to survive. The presence or absence of certain species acts as a pollution indicator.

Acid rain has been a problem ever since the industrial revolution began. The main gases involved are sulfur dioxide (SO_2) and nitrogen dioxide (NO_2) which are emitted from power stations and industrial plants into the air. Here they dissolve in water vapour to form acids which fall to the Earth as acid rain.

Acid rain will affect the pH of rivers and lakes. Some aquatic creatures cannot survive in acidic conditions (i.e. pH levels less than 7).

Others, however, are more tolerant and can survive at quite low pH levels (i.e. highly acidic levels).

The chart opposite shows the levels of acidity that can be tolerated by four different aquatic species: freshwater mussels, mayfly nymphs, water boatmen, and frogs.

The presence and absence of certain 'indicator species' can provide evidence of pollution both in the recent past, and at present. For example…

- the presence of water boatmen alone indicates a quite high acidity (pH 3.5–5)
- the presence of frogs and the absence of freshwater mussels indicate some acidity (pH 5–6)
- the presence of frogs and mayfly nymphs, and the absence of freshwater mussels indicate some acidity (pH 5.5–6).

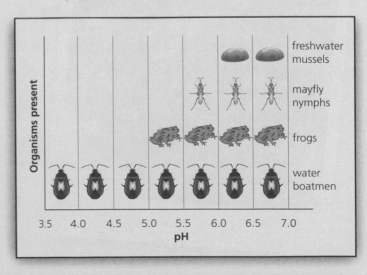

How Science Works

You need to be able to evaluate methods used to collect environmental data and consider their validity and reliability as evidence for environmental change.

Example

A power station was built upstream from a farmer's land. He was concerned about the effect that the power station was having on the local environment, so he contacted a team of scientists to carry out an investigation on the stream.

The scientists carried out a survey at the point where the shallow stream left the farmer's land. They decided to find out what the predominant species was in the stream to use as an indicator of the pH levels in the stream. They used the sweep net method to collect data.

The scientists found that the bloodworm was the predominant species. This indicates that the quality of the water was quite low. Bloodworms can tolerate poor water quality, whereas other species may be more sensitive to water quality and may, therefore, not be able to survive.

They concluded that the power station had reduced the quality of the water.

In this investigation the evidence gathered will be limited by the method used because...

* there was no control group to compare the results to – they only carried out the investigation at one point in the stream, and they did not know what the pH levels were before the power station was operating
* they carried out their investigation at the point where the stream left the farmer's land, so it did not taken into account the effect of the chemicals the farmer might use on his crops
* the sweep net method is not the most appropriate sampling method for a shallow stream
* there is no mention of how they determined what the predominant species was
* although bloodworms can survive in low quality water, they can also survive in better quality water, so it is not a very reliable measure
* it does not state how many times they repeated the experiment (if at all)
* other variables that might influence the results (e.g. season, weather) were not considered.

How Science Works

You need to be able to weigh up the evidence and form balanced judgements about some of the major environmental issues facing society, including the importance of sustainable development.

Example

Plight Of The Whale

The plight of the oceans' whales was highlighted in January 2006 when a Northern Bottlenose whale lost its way and swam up the River Thames in London. It struggled to find its way to the sea and marine experts were asked for their opinions about what to do. Sadly it died, but not before the 'whale debate' started again.

Whales have been hunted for hundreds of years. The Minke whale has now been hunted to such an extent that it could soon be extinct. In 1986, the International Whaling Commission agreed to ban whale hunting.

Some whaling communities in countries such as Norway lost income at first but they started to offer 'whale-spotting' trips to supplement their earnings. However, some scientists argued that there was a need to kill some whales for research purposes. Others said that the whales need to be alive in order to study their communication and migration.

The ban has now been lifted and some countries claim to be hunting whales for scientific research, but make a profit from the whale carcasses.

Home

Newsroom

News Archive

About Whales

Shop

Whale Watching

Kids' Corner

Links

Contact Us

Gallery

Sustainable development is concerned with the careful management of natural resources. It allows us to continue using these resources, whilst ensuring that stocks do not run out and that adequate levels are maintained for the future. For example, where animals are being taken out of the environment for food, or other reasons, it is important to ensure that enough individuals are left to breed and maintain future populations. This means that numbers must be monitored carefully, so that appropriate action can be taken when necessary.

Your judgement may not be based on evidence alone as other social factors may be relevant. To help you make your judgement about whaling, consider the following:

- certain viewpoints may be biased, e.g. whalers rely on hunting whales for their income so they will have a biased view
- evidence can be given too much weight or dismissed too lightly according to its political significance; the evidence might be downplayed if it upsets the public, e.g. the possible extinction of some whales could be dismissed by a government whose people rely upon whaling
- the status of a scientist may influence the weight placed on the evidence, e.g. a scientist with experience or professional status who presents evidence that whales can be studied without killing them is more likely to have his case heard than a lesser-known colleague.

Example Questions

If you are studying Specification A, you will have to complete a 30 minute objective test under exam conditions for each section (i.e. Biology 1a and Biology 1b). These consist of matching and multiple choice questions - see Questions 1 and 2 below.

If you are studying Specification B, you will have to complete a 45 minute written exam covering the whole of the unit (i.e. Biology 1). This will feature structured questions – see Question 3 below.

1   What is the purpose of a vaccination?

    A   To cure a patient who has the disease. .... ☐

    B   To treat the symptoms of the disease. .... ☐

    C   To provide relief from pain. .... ☐

    D   To provide long-term protection against a disease. .... ☑   *(1 mark)* $\frac{}{1}$

2   Which of the following statements is true for clones?

    A   All clones of the same organism are the same as Dolly the sheep. ... ☐

    B   All clones of the same organism are genetically different. .... ☐

    C   All clones of the same organism are genetically identical. .... ☑

    D   All clones of the same organism are twins. .... ☐   *(1 mark)* $\frac{}{1}$

3   Research has been carried out into the link between the number of cigarettes smoked per day and the risk of dying from lung cancer.

(a) In this graph, which factor is the independent variable?

    The number of cigarettes.

                                                  (1 mark)

(b) Which factor is the dependent variable?

    The risk of dying of cancer.

                                                  (1 mark)

(c) Suggest two factors that should have been kept the same in both groups.

    Age range AND an equal proportion of men and women.

                                                  (2 marks)

(d) What conclusion could the scientists have drawn from the graph?

    As the number of cigarettes smoked per day increases, the risk of dying from lung cancer also increases.

                                                  (1 mark) $\frac{}{5}$

---

1. Questions like this often appear as part of a set of questions relating to the same subject (e.g. vaccinations).
2. If you are unsure about the answer to a multiple-choice question, eliminate the options that are obviously wrong first.
3. Look at graphs carefully and make sure you understand what they show before answering any questions.
4. The independent variable is the one that is being controlled.
5. The dependent variable is the one that is measured each time the independent variable is changed, to see if there is a relationship between them.
6. Read the question carefully, this one asks for **two** factors so you would lose a mark if you only gave one.
7. You could name any factors that could potentially affect the dependent variable (risk of dying of lung cancer).
8. Describe what the data tells you – nothing else!

Key Words

Adaptation – the gradual change of a particular organism over generations to become better suited to its environment

Biodiversity – the variety among living organisms and the ecosystems in which they live

Carcinogen – a substance that causes cancer

Chromosome – a coil of DNA made up of genes, found in the nucleus of plant / animal cells

Clone – a genetically identical descendent of an organism

Deficiency disease – a disease caused by the lack of some essential element in the diet

Deforestation – the destruction of forests by cutting down trees

DNA (deoxyribonucleic acid) – nucleic acid molecules which contain genetic information and make up chromosomes

Effector – the part of the body, e.g. a muscle or a gland, which produces a response to a sensor

Embryo – a ball of cells which will develop into a human / animal baby

Enzyme – a protein which speeds up a reaction (a biological catalyst)

Evolve – to change naturally over a period of time

Extinct – a species that has died out

Fetus – an unborn animal / human baby

Fossil – remains of animals / plants preserved in rocks

FSH (Follicle Stimulating Hormone) – stimulates ovaries to produce oestrogen

Gene – part of a chromosome, composed of DNA

Gland – an organ in an animal body used for secreting substances

Herbicide – a toxic substance used to destroy unwanted vegetation

Hormone – a regulatory substance which stimulates cells or tissues into action

Infectious – a disease that is easily spread, through water, air, etc.

Ion – minerals such as sodium and potassium, that are needed by the body

Leprosy – a contagious bacterial disease affecting the skin and nerves

LH – Luteinising Hormone, stimulates changes in the menstrual cycle

Malnourished – suffering from lack of essential food nutrients

Menstrual cycle – the monthly cycle of hormonal changes in a woman

Metabolic rate – the rate at which an animal uses energy over a given time period

Methane – a colourless, odourless, inflammable gas

MRSA – Methicillin-resistant Staphylococcus aureus (or 'superbug'), an antibiotic-resistant bacterium

Mutation – a change in the genetic material of a cell

Neurone – specialised cell which transmits electrical messages or nerve impulses

Non-renewable – resources that cannot be replaced

Obesity – the condition of being very overweight

Pathogen – a disease causing microorganism

Pesticide – a substance used for destroying insects or other pests

Pituitary – a small gland at the base of the brain that produces hormones

Predator – an animal that hunts, kills and eats other animals

Receptor – a sense organ e.g. eyes, ears, nose, etc.

Recreation – for pleasure

Reflex action – an involuntary action, e.g. removing hand from hot plate

Saturated fats – animal fat, considered to be unhealthy

Sustainable – resources that can be maintained or replaced

Synapse – the gap between two nerve-cells

Toxin – a poison produced by a living organism

Vaccine – a liquid preparation used to make the body produce anti-bodies in order to provide protection against disease

Variation – differences between individuals of the same species

Chemistry Unit 1a

12.1

How do rocks provide building materials?

Industry makes use of naturally occurring rock to provide essential building materials. Limestone is used in the manufacture of cement, concrete and glass. To understand this, you need to know...

- what atoms and elements are
- how elements are arranged in the periodic table
- what a compound is and how it is formed
- why limestone is a useful resource
- how limestone is used to produce building materials.

Atoms

All substances are made of **atoms** (very small particles). Each atom has a small central **nucleus** made up of **protons** and **neutrons** that is surrounded by **electrons**.

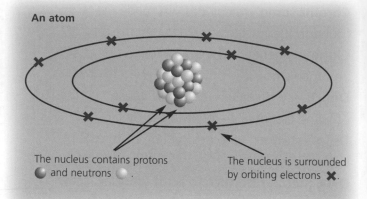

An atom

The nucleus contains protons and neutrons .

The nucleus is surrounded by orbiting electrons ✖.

Elements

A substance which contains only one sort of atom is called an **element**. There are about 100 different elements.

The atoms of each element are represented by a different chemical symbol, for example, O for oxygen, Na for sodium, C for carbon, and Fe for iron. Elements are arranged in the periodic table (see below). The groups in the periodic table contain elements that have similar properties.

Compounds

Compounds are substances in which the atoms of two or more elements are chemically combined, i.e. the atoms are held together by **chemical bonds** (not just mixed together).

When elements react, the atoms can form chemical bonds by...

- sharing electrons
- giving or taking electrons.

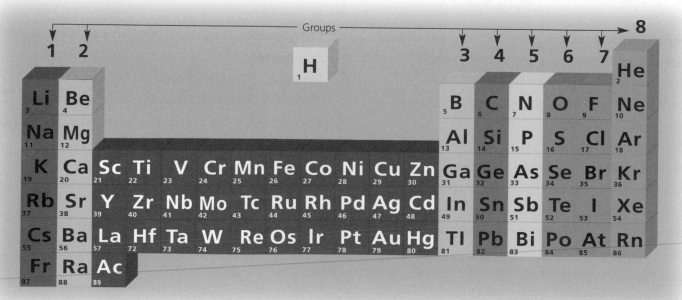

Chemical Formulae

Compounds are represented by a combination of numbers and chemical symbols called a **formula**, e.g. ZnO or $2H_2SO_4$.

Chemists use formulae to show...
- the different elements in a compound
- the ratio of atoms of each element in the compound.

In chemical formulae, the position of the numbers tells you what is multiplied. Smaller numbers that sit below the line (subscripts) only multiply the symbol that comes immediately before it, and large numbers that are the same size as the letters multiply all the symbols that come after, e.g. H_2O means (2 x H) + (1 x O)

2NaOH means 2 x (NaOH) or 2 x (Na + O + H).

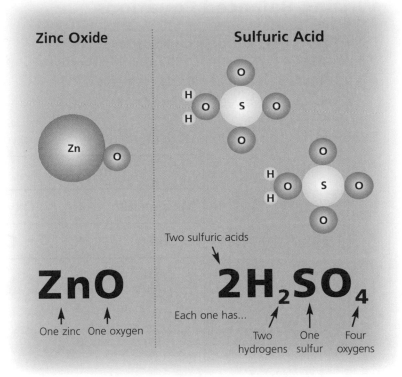

Zinc Oxide

Sulfuric Acid

Two sulfuric acids

ZnO

One zinc   One oxygen

$2H_2SO_4$

Each one has...   Two hydrogens   One sulfur   Four oxygens

Chemical Reactions

You can show what has happened during a reaction by writing a **word equation** with the substances that react (the **reactants**) on one side of the equation and the new substances formed (the **products**) on the other.

The total mass of the products of a chemical reaction is always equal to the total mass of the reactants.

This is because the products of a chemical reaction are made up from exactly the same atoms as the reactants – no atoms are lost or made!

That means chemical symbol equations must always be balanced: there must be the same number of atoms of each element on the reactant side of the equation as there is on the product side.

Example

Word equation...

Symbol equation...

This means that...

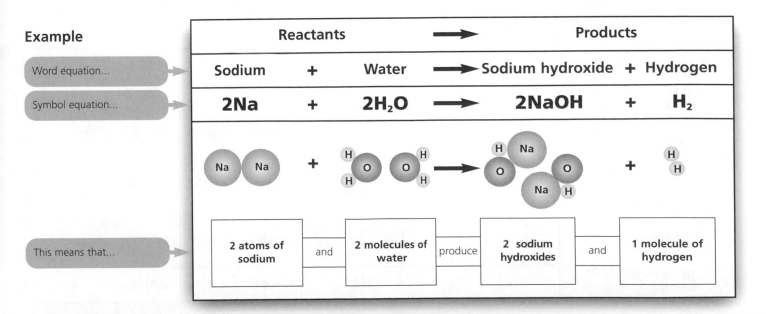

	Reactants		→	Products	
Word equation...	Sodium	+ Water	→	Sodium hydroxide	+ Hydrogen
Symbol equation...	2Na	+ $2H_2O$	→	2NaOH	+ H_2

| 2 atoms of sodium | and | 2 molecules of water | produce | 2 sodium hydroxides | and | 1 molecule of hydrogen |

Chemistry Unit 1a

Writing Balanced Equations

Follow these steps to write a balanced equation:

1 write a word equation for the chemical reaction

2 substitute in formulae for the elements or compounds involved

3 balance the equation by adding numbers in front of the reactants and/or products

4 write down a balanced symbol equation (see p.53).

Example 1 – The reaction between magnesium and oxygen.

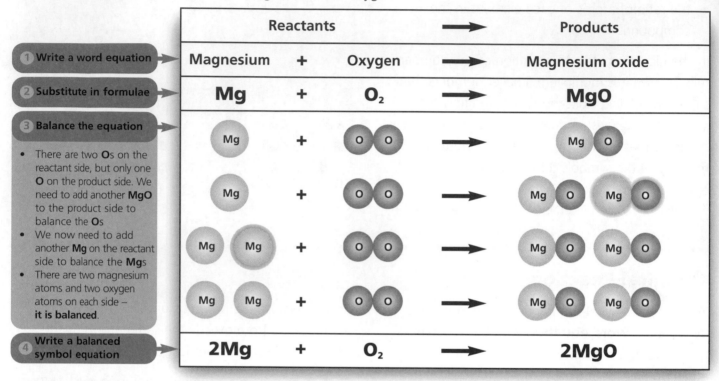

1 Write a word equation

2 Substitute in formulae

3 Balance the equation

- There are two **O**s on the reactant side, but only one **O** on the product side. We need to add another **MgO** to the product side to balance the **O**s
- We now need to add another **Mg** on the reactant side to balance the **Mg**s
- There are two magnesium atoms and two oxygen atoms on each side – **it is balanced**.

4 Write a balanced symbol equation

Reactants			→	Products
Magnesium	+	Oxygen	→	Magnesium oxide
Mg	+	O₂	→	MgO
2Mg	+	O₂	→	2MgO

Example 2 - The production of ammonia.

1 Write a word equation

2 Substitute in formulae

3 Balance the equation

- There are two **N**s on the reactant side, but only one **N** on the product side. We need to add another **NH₃** to the product side to balance the **N**s
- We now need to add two more **H₂**s on the reactant side to balance the **H₂**s
- There are two nitrogen atoms and six hydrogen atoms on each side – **it is balanced**.

4 Write a balanced symbol equation

Reactants			→	Products
Nitrogen	+	Hydrogen	→	Ammonia
N₂	+	H₂	→	NH₃
N₂	+	3H₂	→	2NH₃

Limestone

Limestone is a sedimentary rock which consists mainly of the compound **calcium carbonate**. It is cheap, easy to obtain and has many uses.

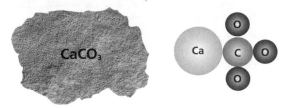

1 Building Material

Limestone can be **quarried** and cut into blocks, and used to build walls of houses in regions where it is plentiful.

Over time it can be eroded by acid rain, but this is a very slow process.

2 Neutralising Agent

Alkalis in soil can be 'washed out' by acid rain. Excess acidity in soils can cause crop failure. Powdered limestone can correct this but it works quite slowly.

When calcium carbonate is heated in a kiln it decomposes. This reaction is called **thermal decomposition** and it causes the calcium carbonate to break down into **calcium oxide (quicklime)** and **carbon dioxide**. Carbonates of other metals decompose in a similar way.

| Calcium carbonate (limestone) | heat → | Calcium oxide (quicklime) | + | Carbon dioxide |

The calcium oxide (quicklime) can then be reacted (slaked) with water to produce **calcium hydroxide (slaked lime)**.

| Calcium oxide (quicklime) | + | Water | → | Calcium hydroxide (slaked lime) |

Calcium hydroxide (like all hydroxides), is a strong **alkali**. It can be used to neutralise soils and lakes much faster than powdered limestone. *N.B. The carbonates of other metals behave very similarly when they are heated.*

3 Glass

Glass is made by mixing powdered limestone, sand and soda (sodium carbonate) and heating the mixture until it melts. When cool, it is transparent.

| Limestone | + | Sand | + | Soda | heat → | Glass |

4 Cement, Mortar and Concrete

Powdered limestone and powdered clay are roasted in a rotary kiln to produce dry **cement**.

When the cement is mixed with sand and water it produces **mortar**, which is used to hold together bricks and stone during building.

When the cement is mixed with water, sand and gravel (crushed rock) a slow reaction takes place where a hard, stone-like building material, called **concrete**, is produced.

How Science Works

You need to be able to consider and evaluate the environmental, social and economic effects of exploiting limestone and producing building materials from it.

Advantages	Disadvantages
• Limestone is found naturally, so can be quarried relatively easily. • Using local stone to build new houses makes them 'fit in' with older houses. • Better roads will be built to cope with quarry traffic. • Creates more jobs locally. • Other industries (e.g. cement makers) will be attracted to the area, providing more job opportunities. • The quarry might invest in the local community in a bid to 'win over' the locals.	• Could be more expensive to quarry limestone than to use another building material. • Quarries destroy the landscape and the habitats of animals and birds. • Increased traffic to and from the quarries. • Noise pollution. • Health problems arising from the dust particles, e.g. asthma. • Reduced tourism in the area.

You need to be able to evaluate the advantages and disadvantages of using limestone, concrete and glass as building materials.

Material	Advantages	Disadvantages
Limestone	• Widely available. • Easy to cut. • Cheaper than many other building materials, e.g. marble. • Can be used to produce cement, concrete and glass.	• Susceptible to acid rain – the dilute acid dissolves the limestone very slowly, wearing it away.
Concrete	• Can be moulded into different shapes, e.g. panels and blocks which can be put together easily in buildings. • Quick and cheap way to construct buildings. • Does not corrode, so is a good alternative to metal. • Can be reinforced using steel bars so that it is safer and has a wider range of uses.	• Low tensile strength* and can crack and become dangerous, especially in high-rise buildings. • Looks unattractive.
Glass	• Transparent, therefore useful for windows and parts of buildings where natural light is wanted. • Can be toughened or made into safety glass.	• Breaks easily. • Not always the cheapest and safest option.

All of these materials are resistant to fire and rot, and are strong enough to resist attack from animals and insects, which make them a better choice than wood. However, there may be cheaper, safer and more aesthetically pleasing materials that are also suitable for the job.

*Tensile strength refers to a material's ability to resist breaking when under tension.

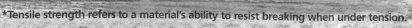

12.2

How do rocks provide metals and how are metals used?

Metals have lots of uses in our homes, workplaces and environment. Metals begin life as an ore: a naturally occurring mineral (or rock). To understand how these rocks provide metals and how we then use them, you need to know...

- what an ore is
- how we obtain different metals (reactive and unreactive)
- what properties and uses different metals have.

Ores

The Earth's crust contains many naturally occurring elements and compounds called **minerals**. A metal **ore** is a mineral or mixture of minerals from which economically viable amounts of pure metal can be **extracted**. This can change over time.

Extracting Metals from their Ores

The method of extraction depends on how reactive the metal is. Unreactive metals like gold exist naturally. They are obtained through physical processes such as panning.

Most metals are found as **metal oxides** or compounds that can be easily changed into a metal oxide. To extract a metal from its oxide the oxygen must be removed by heating the oxide with another element in a chemical reaction. This process is called **reduction**.

Metals that are less reactive than carbon can be extracted from their oxides by heating them with carbon. (The carbon is a more reactive element, so it will displace the metal and form a compound with the oxygen.)

Iron

Iron oxide can be reduced in a blast furnace to produce iron.

Molten **iron** obtained from a blast furnace contains roughly 96% iron and 4% carbon and other metals. Because it is impure, the iron is very brittle with limited uses. To produce **pure iron**, all the impurities would have to be removed.

The atoms in pure iron are arranged in layers, which can slide over each other easily. This makes pure iron soft and malleable – it can be easily shaped. However, it is too soft for many practical uses.

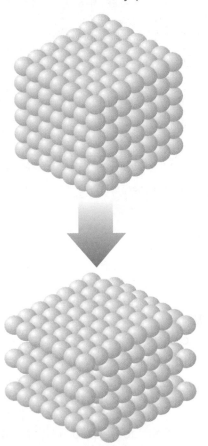

The properties of iron can be changed by mixing it with small quantities of carbon or other metals to make **steel**, which is an **alloy**.

Chemistry Unit 1a

Alloys

An alloy is a mixture which contains a metal and at least one other element. The added element disturbs the regular arrangement of the metal atoms so that the layers do not slide over each other so easily. Alloys are, therefore, usually stronger and harder than pure metal. Many of the metals we use everyday are alloys.

Pure copper, gold and aluminium are too soft for many uses. They are mixed with small amounts of similar metals to make them harder for everyday use.

Steel

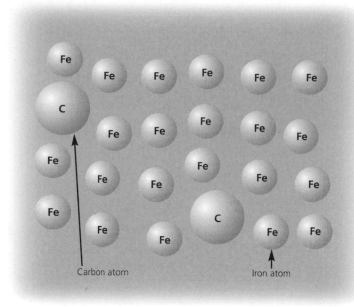

Carbon atom   Iron atom

Carbon is added to iron to make the alloy steel. A majority of iron is converted into steel.

To make steel, the molten iron from a blast furnace is transferred into another furnace. Here it is mixed with recycled scrap metal and pure oxygen is passed into the mixture. The oxygen reacts with the non-metal impurities such as carbon, silicon and sulfur to produce acidic oxides.

Alloys like steel are developed to have the necessary properties for a specific purpose. In steel, the amount of carbon and / or other elements determines its properties:

- steel with a high carbon content is hard and strong, e.g. screwdrivers
- steel with a low carbon content is soft and easily shaped. Mild steel (0.25% carbon) is easily pressed into shape, e.g. cars
- steel which contains chromium and nickel is called stainless steel. It is hard and resistant to corrosion, e.g. knives and forks.

Smart Alloys

Smart alloys belong to a group of materials that are being developed to meet the demands of modern engineering and manufacturing. These materials respond to changes in their environment, e.g. temperature, moisture, pH and electrical and magnetic fields.

Smart alloys (also called shape memory alloys) remember their shape. They can be deformed, but will return to their original shape (usually when they are heated).

Alloys of nickel-titanium, silver-cadmium, copper-aluminium-nickel and copper-zinc-aluminium can possess the shape memory effect. They are useful in thermostats; car, plane and helicopter parts; and flexible spectacle frames.

The Transition Metals

In the centre of the **Periodic Table**, between Groups 2 and 3, is a block of metallic elements called the **transition metals**. These include: iron, copper, platinum, mercury, chromium, titanium and zinc.

These metals are **hard** and mechanically **strong**. They have **high melting points** (except mercury – which is liquid at room temperature).

Transition metals, like all other metals, are **good conductors** of heat and electricity, and can also be easily bent or hammered into shape.

These properties make transition metals very useful as structural materials, and as electrical and thermal conductors.

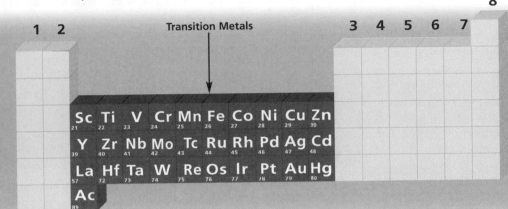

Extracting Transition Metals

Copper, aluminium and titanium, unlike iron, cannot be extracted from their ores by reduction with carbon. They are extracted through a process called **electrolysis**.

Electrolysis is very complex – there are lots of different stages – and requires a large amount of energy. This makes it very expensive. So, we should recycle metals wherever possible to…
- save money and energy
- make sure we don't use up all the natural resources
- reduce the amount of mining because it is damaging the environment.

Copper

Copper is useful for **electrical wiring** and **plumbing** but natural supplies of ores containing large quantities of copper are limited. If we continue to use them they will run out completely.

Scientists are trying to find ways to extract copper from other ores which contain less copper but are more abundant.

Aluminium

Aluminium is **resistant to corrosion**. A reaction between the aluminium and oxygen from the air produces a thin 'skin' which prevents further corrosion. It is for this reason that greenhouses don't have to be painted. However, for some uses of aluminium, a thicker layer of this protective oxide is needed.

Aluminium has a **low density** so it is very light. It is used for…
- drink cans
- window frames
- lightweight vehicles
- aeroplanes.

Titanium

Titanium is **strong** and **resistant to corrosion**. It is used in…
- aeroplanes
- nuclear reactors
- replacement hip joints.

How Science Works

You need to be able to consider and evaluate the social, economic and environmental impacts of exploiting metal ores, of using metals and of recycling metals.

Example

Local Village Launches National Campaign

The villagers of Littlehampton are speaking out to show us all how we can help to reduce the damage being done to our environment.

A large metal extraction plant was built near Littlehampton 15 years ago and the village has suffered from the effects of the industry ever since. The plant has had a detrimental impact not only on the look of the area but also on its environment. The pollution has made its way into rivers and streams, and the local wildlife group reports that certain species are dwindling in number.

These bad effects are not only limited to wildlife. The noise that comes from the factory is annoying, but more worrying is the dramatic increase in the number of local people who suffer from asthma as a result of the dust particles discharged into the air.

Now, after proposals to extend the plant have been revealed, villagers have joined together to recycle metals and want to encourage others to do the same. Campaign spokesman, Bob Jeffries, 42, says, 'We know that metals are useful materials and that extraction needs to be done, but we hope to encourage people to recycle what they can. This should reduce the demand for newly extracted metals and remove the need for new plants. Not only will we be improving our standard of living but we will also be helping to reduce the pressure and impact on our environment'.

Recycling is a much better option because it uses less energy, which makes it a much cheaper process. The more times a material is recycled, the more cost-effective it becomes.

Councillors listened to the views of local residents and agreed to implement a recycling scheme. Five large recycling bins have been brought in to the car park at the local supermarket. Said councillor Cilla Jackson, 56, 'The scheme has had a much better response than we had hoped for; I just hope the enthusiasm for it is maintained'. *For information on how you can do your bit go to www.recyclenow.com*

Method	Advantages	Disadvantages
Extracting metals	• Provides jobs and income locally. • Provides raw materials for industry. • Local facilities (e.g. roads) will be improved to cope with additional traffic.	• Destroys the landscape. • Losses to tourism. • Noise and dust pollution. • Traffic problems.
Recycling metals	• Saves energy (e.g. less energy used to recycle aluminium than to electrolyse the ore it comes from). • Less pollution produced because fewer materials are sent to landfill sites, which are ugly and take up space. • Less pressure placed on environment (the more material that is recycled, the less pressure to find new materials to mine, extract, etc.).	• Individual apathy. • Availability and collection of recycling facilities.

How Science Works

You need to be able to evaluate the advantages and disadvantages of using metals as structural materials and as smart materials.

Use of Metal	Advantages	Disadvantages
Structural material	• Hard, tough and strong. • Do not corrode easily. • Can be bent or hammered into shape. • Alloys of metals are harder than pure metals.	• Iron is naturally very soft so needs to be mixed with other metals to form steel. • Conduct electricity and heat – this might not be what is wanted. • Some metals, particularly iron, can be corroded by water and other chemicals – this weakens and eventually wears away the metal. • The supply of metal ores from the Earth's crust is decreasing as more is extracted – eventually the supplies will run out.
Smart material	• Can be produced by mixing metals which have many advantageous properties over the original metals. • Good mechanical properties, e.g. strong and resist corrosion. • Can return to their original shape when heated (known as the shape-memory effect) – used in thermostats, coffee pots, hydraulic fittings. • More bendy than normal metals, therefore harder to damage. • Have new properties, such as pseudo-elasticity, which can be exploited in diverse ways, such as in glasses frames, bra underwires and orthodontic arches. • Can be changed by passing an electrical current or a magnetic field through them or by heating. • Not much temperature change required (sometimes as little as 10°C) to change the molecular structure.	• Expensive to manufacture. • Fatigue easily – a steel component can survive for around 100 times longer than a smart material under the same pressure.

Chemistry Unit 1a

12.3

How do we get fuels from crude oil?

Crude oil is found in rocks and can be used to produce fuels. To understand this, you need to know...

- the difference between a compound and a mixture
- how crude oil can be fractionally distilled to produce fuels
- that most fuels contain carbon and hydrogen and sometimes sulfur
- what happens when fuels are burned; the effect that sulfur has on the environment.

Crude Oil

Crude oil is a mixture of compounds, most of which are molecules made up of carbon and hydrogen atoms only, called **hydrocarbons**. These hydrocarbon molecules vary in size. This affects their properties and how they are used as fuels. The larger the hydrocarbon (the greater the number of carbon and hydrogen atoms in a molecule)...

- the less easily it flows, i.e. the more viscous it is
- the less easily it ignites, i.e. the less flammable it is
- the less volatile it is, i.e. it doesn't vaporise as easily
- the higher its boiling point.

Short-chain hydrocarbon

Long-chain hydrocarbon

A **mixture** consists of two or more elements or compounds which are not chemically combined together, so the properties of the substances in the mixture remain unchanged and specific to that substance. This makes it possible to separate the substances in a mixture by physical methods such as **distillation**.

Fractional Distillation

Crude oil on its own isn't very useful. However, different hydrocarbons have different boiling points which means that crude oil can be separated into different parts, or **fractions**, by **fractional distillation**. Most of the hydrocarbons obtained are alkanes (see p.63).

In fractional distillation, the oil is evaporated (by heating) and then allowed to condense at a range of different temperatures. This is when it forms fractions, each of which contains hydrocarbon molecules with a similar number of carbon atoms. This is done in a fractionating column (see below).

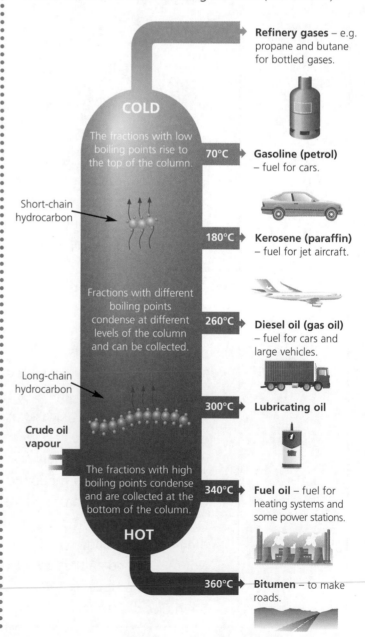

Refinery gases – e.g. propane and butane for bottled gases.

COLD

The fractions with low boiling points rise to the top of the column.

Short-chain hydrocarbon

70°C **Gasoline (petrol)** – fuel for cars.

180°C **Kerosene (paraffin)** – fuel for jet aircraft.

Fractions with different boiling points condense at different levels of the column and can be collected.

260°C **Diesel oil (gas oil)** – fuel for cars and large vehicles.

Long-chain hydrocarbon

300°C **Lubricating oil**

Crude oil vapour

The fractions with high boiling points condense and are collected at the bottom of the column.

340°C **Fuel oil** – fuel for heating systems and some power stations.

HOT

360°C **Bitumen** – to make roads.

Alkanes (Saturated Hydrocarbons)

The 'spine' of a hydrocarbon is made up of a chain of carbon atoms. When these are joined together by single carbon carbon bonds we say the hydrocarbon is saturated and it is known as an **alkane**. To put it simply…

- hydrogen atoms can make 1 bond each

- carbon atoms can make 4 bonds each

- the simplest alkane, methane, is made up of 4 hydrogen atoms and 1 carbon atom.

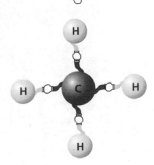

The general formula for alkanes is C_nH_{2n+2}. A more convenient way of representing alkanes is as follows…

Methane, CH₄

$$H - \underset{\underset{H}{|}}{\overset{\overset{H}{|}}{C}} - H$$

Ethane, C₂H₆

$$H - \underset{\underset{H}{|}}{\overset{\overset{H}{|}}{C}} - \underset{\underset{H}{|}}{\overset{\overset{H}{|}}{C}} - H$$

Propane, C₃H₈

$$H - \underset{\underset{H}{|}}{\overset{\overset{H}{|}}{C}} - \underset{\underset{H}{|}}{\overset{\overset{H}{|}}{C}} - \underset{\underset{H}{|}}{\overset{\overset{H}{|}}{C}} - H$$

In alkanes, all the carbon atoms are linked to 4 other atoms by single bonds. This means that all their bonds are 'occupied' (the alkane is saturated) so they are fairly unreactive, although they do burn well. The shorter-chain hydrocarbons release energy more quickly by burning, so there is a greater demand for them as fuels.

Burning Fuels

As fuels burn they produce waste products, which are then released into the atmosphere. The waste products produced depend on which elements are present in the fuel. Most fuels contain carbon and hydrogen, but many also contain some sulfur.

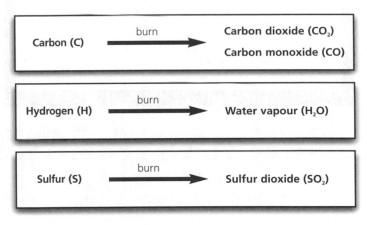

| Carbon (C) | $\xrightarrow{\text{burn}}$ | Carbon dioxide (CO₂) |
| | | Carbon monoxide (CO) |

| Hydrogen (H) | $\xrightarrow{\text{burn}}$ | Water vapour (H₂O) |

| Sulfur (S) | $\xrightarrow{\text{burn}}$ | Sulfur dioxide (SO₂) |

- CO₂ causes 'global warming' due to the Greenhouse Effect.
- SO₂ causes acid rain. Removing the sulfur before burning, or removing the SO₂ from the waste gases, can reduce this. However, both of these add to the cost.

Power stations remove sulfur dioxide from the waste gases produced when combustion takes place to reduce the pollution they give out.

Particles may also be released, which causes global dimming (a reduction in the amount of sunlight reaching the Earth's surface).

How Science Works

You need to be able to consider and evaluate the social, economic and environmental impacts of the uses of fuels.

Example

Forget Fossil Fuels...

When hydrocarbons are burned they release harmful waste gases into the air. Burning fossil fuels has a considerable impact on the environment and its inhabitants. The solution is to use fewer fossil fuels by using alternative energy resources, using existing resources more efficiently and by making changes to lifestyles, such as car-sharing to reduce fuel consumption, etc.

...Switch to Sugar!

Brazilian motorists have been converting their petrol-guzzling cars so they can be powered by ethanol. Ethanol, better known as grain alcohol, is easily distilled from sugar cane, and is a cheap alternative to petrol. This new use for sugar cane has greatly affected the farmers – never has there been such a high demand for sugar! This in turn has helped to push up the price of sugar to an all-time high. Scientists hope that the use of sugar cane as a viable alternative to petrol will grow, because it burns more cleanly than usual fuels and produces less of the harmful gas, carbon monoxide. However, it is not all good news. Alcohol releases less energy than petrol when it burns and it can be a health risk to filling station attendants.

You need to be able to evaluate developments in the production and uses of better fuels, for example, ethanol and hydrogen.

Example

Is Rocket Fuel the Way Forward?

Experts are carrying out research to find out if hydrogen gas, which is currently used as rocket fuel, could be an answer to our pollution problem. Hydrogen can be produced by passing an electric current through water, and when it burns it releases a lot of energy. Unlike other fuels which produce harmful gases when burnt, hydrogen produces only water vapour, which does not pollute the atmosphere. A major consideration is the costs involved because the production of hydrogen requires a lot of electricity. It could also be quite risky because hydrogen is flammable so it needs to be stored under special conditions.

Fuel	Advantages	Disadvantages
Fossil fuel	• Power stations provide jobs. • Provides energy for homes and industry. • Does not take up much space.	• Produces pollutants. • Causes global warming due to the Greenhouse Effect. • Non-renewable source so is in danger of running out.
Ethanol	• Does not affect the performance of the car. • Can save money. • Made from renewable resources. • Less carbon emissions. • Less carbon monoxide produced.	• Need to pay out to convert engine. • Much more sugar will need to be grown to meet demand. • Price of sugar is likely to rise due to increased demand. • When used as a fuel, alcohol can be a health risk. • Produces less energy than petrol when it burns.
Hydrogen	• Burning releases lots of energy. • No harmful gases produced, only water vapour which does not harm the environment.	• Expensive to produce from electricity. • Difficult to store safely.

12.4

How are polymers and ethanol made from oil?

Fractions produced from the distillation of crude oil can be cracked and used to make polymers, and ethene can be used to make ethanol. To understand this, you need to know…
- how hydrocarbons are cracked
- how fuels can be produced from cracking
- how ethanol is produced
- about the properties and uses of polymers.

Cracking Hydrocarbons

Longer-chain hydrocarbons can be **cracked** or broken down into shorter chains, which release energy more quickly by burning.

Hydrocarbons are cracked by heating them until they vaporise, then passing the vapour over a heated catalyst, where a thermal decomposition reaction takes place.

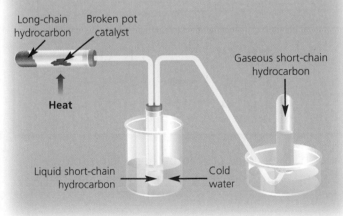

Apparatus used for cracking in the laboratory

Long-chain hydrocarbon | Broken pot catalyst

Heat

Gaseous short-chain hydrocarbon

Liquid short-chain hydrocarbon → ← Cold water

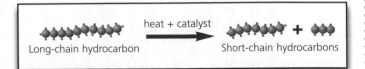

Long-chain hydrocarbon   heat + catalyst   Short-chain hydrocarbons

The products of cracking include alkanes and unsaturated hydrocarbons called **alkenes**. Some of the products are useful as fuels.

Making Alcohol from Ethene

Ethanol is an **alcohol**. It can be produced by reacting steam with ethene at a moderately high temperature and pressure in the presence of a catalyst, phosphoric acid.

Ethene + Steam — phosphoric acid → Ethanol

Ethanol can be used as a…
- solvent
- fuel
- component in alcoholic drinks.

Alkenes (Unsaturated Hydrocarbons)

We have already seen that carbon atoms can form single bonds with other atoms; they can also form double bonds. Some of the products of cracking are hydrocarbon molecules with at least one double bond; this is an unsaturated hydrocarbon and it is known as an alkene.

The general formula for alkenes is C_nH_{2n}. The simplest alkene is ethene, C_2H_4, which is made up of 4 hydrogen atoms and 2 carbon atoms. As you can see in the diagram below, ethene contains one double carbon carbon bond.

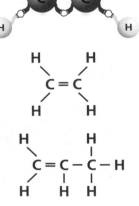

Here is another way of representing alkenes…

Ethene, C_2H_4

Propene, C_3H_6

Not all the carbon atoms are linked to 4 other atoms; a double carbon carbon bond is present instead. Because they are not 'fully occupied', i.e. they are unsaturated, they are useful for making other molecules, especially **polymers**.

Chemistry Unit 1b

Polymerisation

Because alkenes are unsaturated (have a double bond), they are very reactive. When small alkene molecules (monomers) join together to form long-chain molecules (polymers) without producing another substance, it is called **polymerisation**.

The properties of polymers depend on what they are made from and the conditions under which they are made. The materials commonly called plastics are all synthetic polymers. They are produced commercially on a very large scale and have a wide range of properties and uses. Polymers and plastics were first discovered in about 1933.

Making Poly(ethene) from Ethene

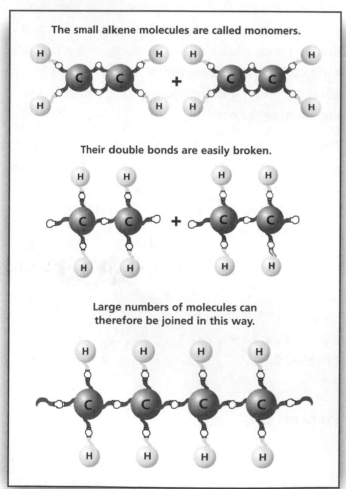

The small alkene molecules are called monomers.

Their double bonds are easily broken.

Large numbers of molecules can therefore be joined in this way.

The resulting long-chain molecule is a polymer – in this case poly(ethene), often called polythene. Poly(propene) can be made in a similar way.

Representing Polymerisation

A more convenient form of representing polymerisation is…

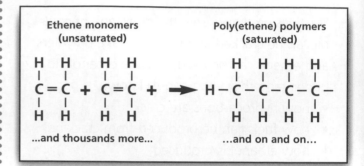

General Formula for Polymerisation

This formula can be used to represent the formation of any simple polymer:

$$n \left[\begin{matrix} | & | \\ C = C \\ | & | \end{matrix} \right] \longrightarrow \left[\begin{matrix} | & | \\ C - C \\ | & | \end{matrix} \right]_n$$

where n is a very large number

For example, if we take 'n' molecules of propene we can produce poly(propene), which is used to make crates and ropes:

$$n \left(\begin{matrix} H & CH_3 \\ | & | \\ C = C \\ | & | \\ H & H \end{matrix} \right) \xrightarrow[\text{catalyst}]{\text{pressure}} \left[\begin{matrix} H & CH_3 \\ | & | \\ C - C \\ | & | \\ H & H \end{matrix} \right]_n$$

And 'n' molecules of chloroethene can produce polychloroethene (also known as polyvinyl chloride or PVC):

$$n \left(\begin{matrix} H & Cl \\ | & | \\ C = C \\ | & | \\ H & H \end{matrix} \right) \xrightarrow[\text{catalyst}]{\text{pressure}} \left[\begin{matrix} H & Cl \\ | & | \\ C - C \\ | & | \\ H & H \end{matrix} \right]_n$$

Polymers are classified by the reactions by which they are formed.

Polymers

Polymers have many useful applications and new uses are being developed.

Polymers and composites are widely used in medicine and dentistry:

- Implantable materials are used for hard and soft tissue surgery, replacing and fusing damaged bone and cartilage.
- Hard-wearing anti-bacterial dental cements, coatings and fillers have been produced.
- Hydrogels can be used as wound dressings.
- Silicone hydrogel contact lenses have been developed over the last few years. Research has shown that people who wear this type of contact lens have a 5% lower risk of developing severe eye infections.

They can be used to coat fabrics with a waterproof layer. Smart materials, including shape memory polymers, are also increasingly more common.

Specific polymers can have different uses, e.g.

Polyvinyl Chloride (PVC) can be used to make waterproof items and drain pipes and can also be used as an electrical insulator.

Polystyrene is used to make the casing for electrical appliances, and it can be expanded to make protective packaging.

Poly(ethene) is commonly used to make plastic bags and bottles.

Poly(propene) can be used to make crates and ropes.

Disposing of Plastics

Because plastic is such a versatile material and it is cheap and easy to produce we tend to generate a large amount of plastic waste.

There are various ways of disposing of plastics, unfortunately some of them have an impact on the environment.

1 Landfill Sites

The problem with most plastics is that they are non-biodegradable. Microorganisms have no effect on them, so they will not decompose and rot away. The use of landfill sites means that plastic waste builds up. However, research is being carried out on the development of biodegradable plastics.

2 Burning

Burning plastics produces air pollution. The production of carbon dioxide contributes to the Greenhouse Effect which results in global warming. Some plastics cannot be burned at all because they produce toxic fumes.

How Science Works

You need to be able to evaluate the social and economic advantages and disadvantages of using products from crude oil as fuels or as raw materials for plastic and other chemicals.

Crude oil is one of our most important natural resources. It is hard to imagine what our lives would be like without the products we can get from crude oil. Transport would come to a standstill, there would be no more plastics and detergents, and the pharmaceutical industry would not be able to get essential raw materials, so medicines would run out.

Crude oil can be used to make tough, lightweight, waterproof and breathable fabrics for clothes; paint for cars; dyes; packaging and communication equipment. However, it is important to weigh up the advantages of the products we can get from crude oil against the disadvantages of using it as a raw material.

Advantages of Crude Oil

- Refining crude oil provides jobs.
- The fractions of crude oil have many uses.
- Provides raw materials for industry.
- Provides fuel for transport.

Disadvantages of Crude Oil

- Oil spills damage the environment.
- Air pollution.
- Increases global warming.
- Produces non-biodegradable material.

You need to be able to consider and evaluate the social, economic and environmental impacts of the uses, disposal and recycling of polymers.

Plastics (polymers) are everywhere. There is a wide range of polymers with different, highly useful physical properties: some polymers are flexible, others are rigid; some have a low density, whereas others are very dense. They can be transparent or opaque. They are waterproof and resistant to corrosion and they can be used as a protective layer.

However, although polymers are relatively cheap to produce, the cost to society and the environment needs to be considered. Pollution, and its effects on residents who live near polymer-producing factories, is a major issue. And the disposal of polymers once they have been used needs to be addressed, as burning them produces harmful and sometimes toxic gases.

Advantages of Polymers

- Cheap to make.
- Many uses because of their different properties.
- Provides jobs in firms which make the polymer and the product.
- Some polymers can be recycled, melted down and made into something else which saves valuable natural resources.
- If polymers are used instead of wood, fewer trees will have to be cut down.

Disadvantages of Polymers

- People do not like to live near polymer-producing industrial works.
- Some people think plastic products look cheap compared with natural materials.
- Made from oil, a non-renewable resource.
- Most plastics are not biodegradable so there is a problem of how to get rid of them.
- Landfill sites are ugly.
- Give off toxic fumes when they burn.
- Sorting types of polymers for recycling can be expensive.

How Science Works

You need to be able to evaluate the advantages and disadvantages of making ethanol from renewable and non-renewable sources.

Using Non-renewable Sources

Ethanol can be produced by reacting steam with ethene at a moderately high temperature and pressure in the presence of the catalyst, phosphoric acid.

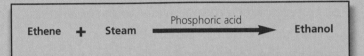

Ethene **+** Steam —Phosphoric acid→ **Ethanol**

Using Renewable Sources

Ethanol can also be produced by the fermentation of sugars. Water and yeast are mixed with the raw materials at just above room temperature. Enzymes, which are biological catalysts found in the yeast, react with the sugars to form ethanol and carbon dioxide. The carbon dioxide is allowed to escape from the reaction vessel, but air is prevented from entering it. The ethanol is separated from the reaction mixture by fractional distillation when the reaction is over.

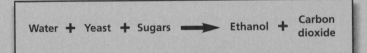

Water **+** Yeast **+** Sugars **→** Ethanol **+** Carbon dioxide

One problem with the production of ethanol is that it can be oxidised by air (in certain conditions) to produce ethanoic acid. The presence of ethanoic acid results in alcoholic drinks turning sour.

Method	Advantages	Disadvantages
Reacting ethene with steam	• Fast rate of production. • High-quality ethanol produced. • Can be produced continuously. • Best method for making large quantities.	• Uses non-renewable sources.
Fermentation	• Renewable. • Can be produced in batches. • Fairly high-quality ethanol produced after fractional distillation. • Best method for making small quantities.	• Slow rate of production. • Ethanol not as good quality as that produced by reacting ethene with steam.

Chemistry Unit 1b

12.5

How can plant oils be used?

Oils can be extracted from plants and used for many purposes. To understand this, you need to know...

- how oils are extracted from plants
- the properties and uses of oils.

Getting Oil from Plants

Many plants produce fruit, seeds and nuts that are rich in **oils**, which can be extracted and changed into consumer products. Some common examples you might find in the food you eat are...

- sunflower oil
- olive oil
- oilseed rape
- palm kernel oil.

Oil can be extracted from plant materials by pressing (crushing) them or by distillation. This removes the water and other impurities from the plant material.

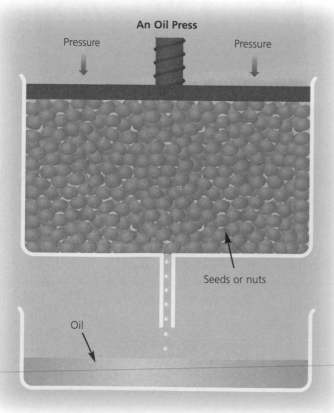

An Oil Press

Pressure

Pressure

Seeds or nuts

Oil

Vegetable Oils

Vegetable oils are important **foods** and **fuels** as they provide nutrients and a lot of energy. Some vehicles can now be converted to use vegetable oils as their fuel instead of petrol or diesel.

Vegetable oils contain double carbon carbon bonds, so they are described as **unsaturated**. They can be detected using bromine water. They react with the orange-coloured bromine water to decolourise it. The bromine becomes part of the compound by breaking the double bond. For example...

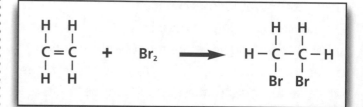

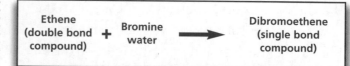

Oils do not dissolve in water as the liquids have different densities. A mixture of oil and water is called an **emulsion**. If oil and water are mixed thoroughly, droplets of oil can be seen dispersed in the water.

Emulsions are thicker than oil or water and have a better texture, appearance and coating ability. They have many uses, e.g. salad dressing and ice cream.

If you mix some olive oil and vinegar together you can make a salad dressing. However, it does not stay mixed for very long as the water particles in the vinegar clump together and the oil particles clump together. The mixture can be seen to separate into two layers. You can make the salad dressing last longer by adding some mustard to it before shaking the mixture up. This stops the separate layers forming. The mustard is an emulsifying agent. Many different emulsifying agents are used in the manufacture of food to stop vegetable oils and water forming separate layers.

The Manufacture of Margarine

As a general guide, the more double carbon carbon bonds present in a substance, the lower its melting point. This means that unsaturated fats, e.g. vegetable oils, tend to have melting points below room temperature and are called oils.

For some purposes you might need a solid fat, for example, to spread on your bread or to use to make cakes and pastries. You can raise the melting point of an oil to above room temperature by removing some or all of the double carbon carbon bonds.

When ethene and hydrogen are heated together in the presence of a nickel catalyst, a reaction takes place which removes the double carbon carbon bonds to produce ethane. This process is called **hydrogenation**.

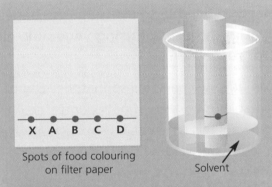

Margarine is manufactured from unsaturated vegetable oils like sunflower oil. The oil is reacted with hydrogen, at a temperature of around 60°C in the presence of a nickel catalyst and some of the double bonds are hydrogenated. Removing more double bonds makes the margarine harder.

Additives

Many processed foods have different substances added to them to improve their look, texture or flavour or to help preserve them. Some of these additives are natural, but the majority are produced by the chemical industry.

Additives have to be shown in the list of ingredients on the label. Some of the additives that are allowed to be added to foods are called E-numbers.

Chemical Analysis

Chemical analysis can be used to identify additives in food. **Chromatography** is a method used to identify artificial colours.

Chromatography identifies unknown substances, by comparing them to known substances. A sample of four known substances (A, B, C and D) and the unknown substance (X) are put on a 'start line' on a piece of paper, which is then dipped into a solvent. As the solvent is absorbed by the paper, it dissolves the samples and carries them up the paper. The substances will move up the paper by differing amounts due to different substances having different solubilities. Substance X can be identified by comparing the horizontal spots.

Apparatus for chromatography

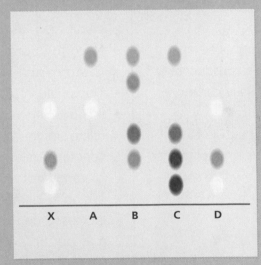

Spots of food colouring on filter paper

Solvent

By comparing food colourings A, B, C and D to substance X, we can see that substance X is food colouring D.

A chromatogram showing how the food colourings have split into their dyes

How Science Works

You need to be able to evaluate the effects of using vegetable oils in food and the impacts on diet and health.

Oils have many uses. However, the amount of saturated fats we consume needs to be carefully controlled to reduce the risk of heart disease.

Vegetable oil is a healthy alternative to using fats derived from animals because it contains monounsaturated fats which can lower blood cholesterol levels, and it contains no cholesterol.

However, it is important to remember that you should not consume too much of any oil because this would not lead to a healthy balanced diet. Where possible, unsaturated fats such as olive oil should be used to reduce the health risks. However, using other oils occasionally would not be too bad for your health.

You need to be able to evaluate the benefits, drawbacks and risks of using vegetable oil to produce fuels.

Cars can now be converted so that they can be run on vegetable oil, instead of petrol or diesel. Although in many ways this is a more environmentally friendly option, it has not yet become widespread, and only a few cars have been converted.

Advantages	Disadvantages
• Cheaper than diesel or petrol. • Fewer pollutant gases produced – virtually carbon neutral. • No change to performance of car. • Renewable source	• High cost of conversion kit. • Need to inform Customs and Excise. • The smell. • Inconvenience of filling up your car – vegetable oil currently not an option at garages. • Increased demand may put up prices for food made using vegetable oil.

You need to be able to evaluate the uses, benefits, drawbacks and risks of ingredients and additives in foods.

Food additives are substances that are put into foods for various reasons. Some types of additives that are used in foods are...

- colourings (e.g. curcumin, E100) replace natural colouring of the food that can be lost during cooking
- flavourings (e.g. monosodium glutamate, E621) enhance and replace flavours that can be lost during processing
- emulsifiers and stabilisers (e.g. lecithin, E322) mix ingredients that would normally separate to give a consistent texture
- antioxidants (e.g. ascorbic acid or vitamin C, E300) help to stop substances from combining with oxygen in the air, which would make the food 'go off'
- preservatives (e.g. sulfur dioxide, E220) prevent food from rotting due to bacteria and moulds
- sweeteners (e.g. sorbitol, E420) make food sweeter.

Although additives can be very useful, we need to carefully weigh up the benefits of using them against the risks involved.

Advantages	Disadvantages
• Can increase the appeal of food. • Can extend the shelf-life of food. • Can reduce the energy in food (good for slimming products). • Can be better for teeth (e.g. sweetener).	• Introduces substances that are not needed by the body. • Can cause headaches, allergies and asthma attacks. • Can adversely affect behaviour, particularly in children, e.g. hyperactivity. • Some are so harmful they have been banned in some countries.

12.6

What are the changes in the Earth and its atmosphere?

The Earth is protected by the atmosphere, which has remained fairly constant for the last 200 million years but is now changing. To understand this, you need to know…

- about the structure of the Earth
- about tectonic activity
- what the atmosphere consists of.

Structure of the Earth

The Earth is nearly spherical and has a layered structure that consists of…

- a thin crust – thickness varies between 10km and 100km
- a mantle – extends almost halfway to the centre and has all the properties of a solid even though it does flow very slowly
- a core (made of nickel and iron) – over half of the Earth's radius with a liquid outer part and a solid inner part.

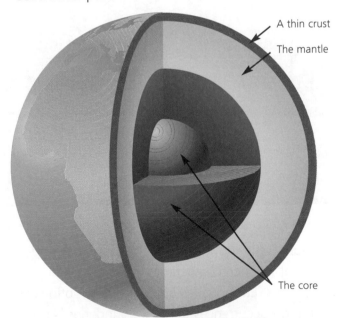

A thin crust

The mantle

The core

The average density of the Earth is much greater than the average density of the rocks which form the crust, because the interior is made of a different, denser material than that of the crust.

Although there doesn't seem to be much going on, the Earth and its crust are very dynamic. Rocks at the Earth's surface are continually being broken up, reformed and changed in an ongoing cycle of events, known as the rock cycle. It is just that the changes take a very long time.

Tectonic Theory

At one time people used to believe that features on the Earth's surface were caused by shrinkage when the Earth cooled, following its formation. However, as scientists have found out more about the Earth, this theory has now been rejected.

A long time ago, scientists noticed that the east coast of South America and the west coast of Africa have…

- similar patterns of rocks, which contain fossils of the same plants and animals, e.g. the Mesosaurus

Mesosaurus

- closely matching coastlines.

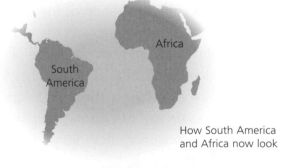

Africa

South America

How South America and Africa now look

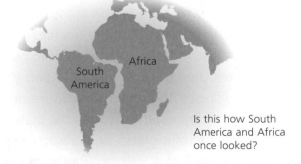

Africa

South America

Is this how South America and Africa once looked?

Tectonic Theory (continued)

This evidence led Alfred Wegener to propose that, even though they are now separated by thousands of kilometres of ocean, South America and Africa had at one time been part of a single land mass.

How it once was

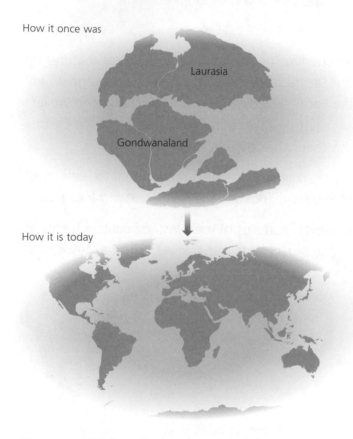

How it is today

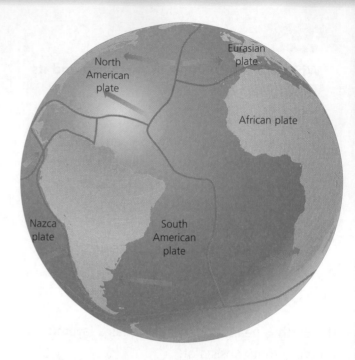

He proposed that the movement of the crust was responsible for the separation of the land (or continental drift), which explains the movement of the continents from how they were (as Gondwanaland and Laurasia) to how they look today. This is known as **tectonic theory**. Unfortunately, Wegener was unable to explain *how* the crust moved and it took more than 50 years for scientists to discover this.

We now know that the Earth's lithosphere (the crust and the upper part of the mantle) is 'cracked' into several large pieces called **tectonic plates**. Intense heat, released by radioactive decay deep in the Earth, causes hot molten rock to rise to the surface at the boundary between the plates, causing the tectonic plates to move apart very slowly, at speeds of a few centimetres per year.

In convection in a gas or a liquid, the matter rises as it is heated, then as it gets further away from the heat source it cools and sinks down again. The same happens in the Earth. The hot molten rock rises to the surface, creating new crust. The older crust, which is cooler, then sinks down where the convection current starts to fall. This causes the land masses on these plates to move slowly across the globe.

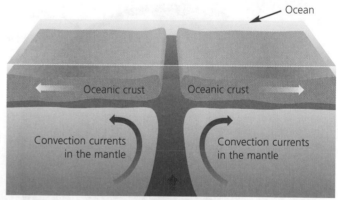

Hot molten rock

Although the movements are usually small and gradual, they can sometimes be sudden and disastrous. Earthquakes and volcanic eruptions are common occurrences at plate boundaries. As yet, scientists cannot predict when these events will occur, due to the difficulty in taking appropriate measurements, but at least they do know where these events are likely to occur.

Tectonic Plate Movement

The movement of the tectonic plates can happen suddenly due to a build up in pressure, and can sometimes have disastrous consequences, e.g. earthquakes and tsunamis. Tectonic plates can move in three ways:

1 Slide Past Each Other

When plates slide, huge stresses and strains build up in the crust which eventually have to be released in order for movement to occur. This 'release' of energy results in an earthquake. A classic example of this is the West Coast of North America (especially California).

2 Move Away from Each Other – Constructive Plate Boundaries

When plates move away from each other at an oceanic ridge, fractures occur. Molten rock rises to the surface, where it solidifies to form new ocean floor. This is known as sea floor spreading. Because new rock is being formed, these are called **constructive** plate boundaries.

3 Move Towards Each Other – Destructive Plate Boundaries

As plates are moving away from each other in some places it follows that they must be moving towards each other in other places. When plates collide, one is forced under the other, so these are called **destructive** plate boundaries. Earthquakes and volcanoes are common on destructive plate boundaries.

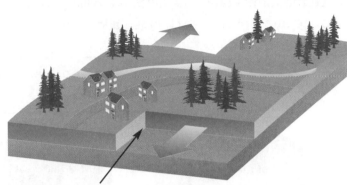

An earthquake will occur along the line where the two plates meet

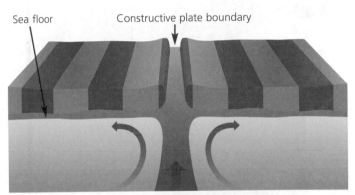

Sea floor · Constructive plate boundary

Magma rising

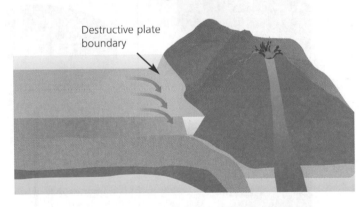

Destructive plate boundary

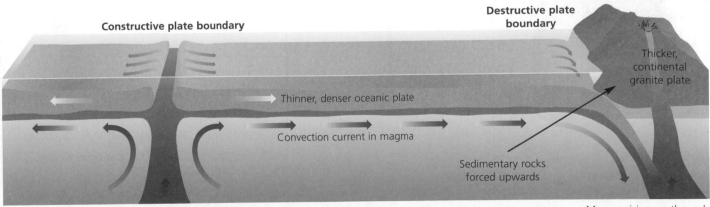

Constructive plate boundary

Destructive plate boundary

Thicker, continental granite plate

Thinner, denser oceanic plate

Convection current in magma

Sedimentary rocks forced upwards

Magma rising and solidifying to form new ocean floor (few centimetres per year)

Magma rising up through continental crust

Chemistry Unit 1b

The Earth's Atmosphere

Since the formation of the earth 4.6 billion years ago the atmosphere has changed a lot. The timescale, however, is enormous because one billion years is one thousand million (1 000 000 000) years!

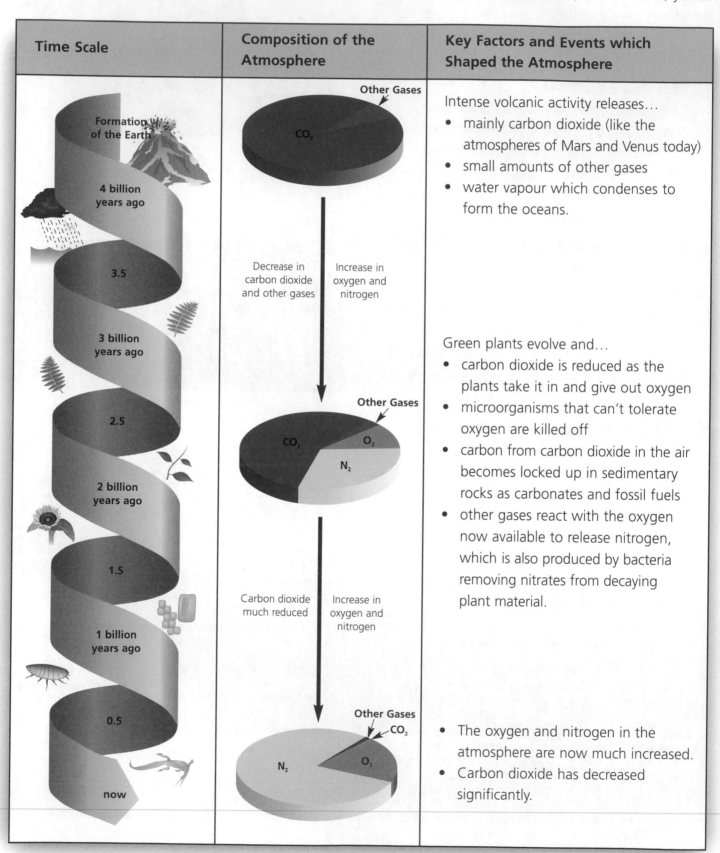

Time Scale	Composition of the Atmosphere	Key Factors and Events which Shaped the Atmosphere
Formation of the Earth 4 billion years ago 3.5 3 billion years ago 2.5 2 billion years ago 1.5 1 billion years ago 0.5 now	**Other Gases** CO₂ Decrease in carbon dioxide and other gases / Increase in oxygen and nitrogen **Other Gases** CO₂ / O₂ / N₂ Carbon dioxide much reduced / Increase in oxygen and nitrogen **Other Gases** CO₂ / N₂ / O₂	Intense volcanic activity releases... • mainly carbon dioxide (like the atmospheres of Mars and Venus today) • small amounts of other gases • water vapour which condenses to form the oceans. Green plants evolve and... • carbon dioxide is reduced as the plants take it in and give out oxygen • microorganisms that can't tolerate oxygen are killed off • carbon from carbon dioxide in the air becomes locked up in sedimentary rocks as carbonates and fossil fuels • other gases react with the oxygen now available to release nitrogen, which is also produced by bacteria removing nitrates from decaying plant material. • The oxygen and nitrogen in the atmosphere are now much increased. • Carbon dioxide has decreased significantly.

Composition of the Atmosphere

Our atmosphere has been more or less the same for about 200 million years. The pie chart (below) shows how it is made up. Water vapour may also be present in varying quantities (0–3%). The noble gases (in Group 0 of the periodic table) are all chemically unreactive gases and are used in filament layers and electric discharge tubes. Helium is much less dense than air and is used in balloons.

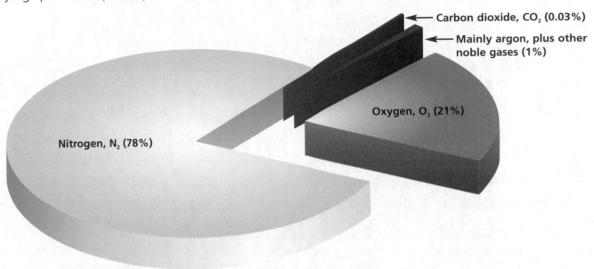

Carbon dioxide, CO_2 (0.03%)

Mainly argon, plus other noble gases (1%)

Oxygen, O_2 (21%)

Nitrogen, N_2 (78%)

Changes to the Atmosphere

The level of carbon dioxide in the atmosphere today is increasing due to…

- volcanic activity – geological activity moves carbonate rocks deep into the Earth. During volcanic activity they may release carbon dioxide back into the atmosphere.
- burning of fossil fuels – burning carbon, which has been locked up in fossil fuels for millions of years, releases carbon dioxide into the atmosphere.

The level of carbon dioxide in the atmosphere is reduced by the reaction between carbon dioxide and sea water. Increased carbon dioxide in the atmosphere increases the reaction between carbon dioxide and sea water. This reaction produces insoluble carbonates (mainly calcium) which are deposited as sediment, and soluble hydrogen carbonates (mainly calcium and magnesium). These form the sedimentary rocks in the Earth's crust.

How Science Works

You need to be able to explain why the theory of crustal movement (continental drift) was not generally accepted for many years after it was proposed.

About 200 years ago, most geologists thought that the Earth had gone through a period of being extremely hot and so consequently had dried out and contracted, or shrunk, as it cooled. Features of the Earth, such as mountain ranges, were thought to have been wrinkles that formed in the Earth's crust as it shrank.

At this point, insufficient data had been collected to show that the continents were in fact moving, and nobody produced any evidence to contradict the theory of the Earth shrinking until the early 1900s.

Then Alfred Wegener studied certain features of the Earth (see p.73–74), which prompted him to propose his theory of continental drift in 1915. This theory proposed that the Earth is made up of plates which have moved slowly apart. Most geologists at the time said that this theory was impossible, although a few did support Wegener.

In the 1950s scientists were able to investigate the ocean floor and found new evidence to support Wegener's theory. They discovered that although he was wrong about some aspects, the basis for his theory was correct.

By the 1960s, geologists were convinced by the theory of continental drift and can now use it to explain many geological features and occurrences caused by moving tectonic plates. Evidence now shows that the sea floor is spreading outwards and convection currents in the mantle cause movement of the crust.

You need to be able to explain why scientists cannot accurately predict when earthquakes and volcanic eruptions will occur.

To understand how earthquakes and volcanic eruptions occur, we need to consider the movement of the tectonic plates. They can stay in the same position for some time, resisting a build up of strain, and then when the strain becomes too great they can suddenly move.

However, it is impossible to predict exactly when this will happen because the plates do not move in regular patterns. Scientists can measure the strain in underground rocks to see if they can calculate when an earthquake is likely to happen, but they are unlikely to be able to give an exact forecast.

A volcano erupts when molten rock rises up into the spaces between the rocks near the surface. Scientists have instruments which can identify these changes, and therefore warn of imminent eruptions. However, sometimes the molten rock cools, so the magma does not reach the surface and the volcano does not erupt. So, other factors which are hard to predict can affect whether a volcano erupts or not.

Therefore, despite having very sophisticated equipment which monitors volcano activity and areas prone to earthquakes, scientists cannot always predict exactly when they might happen.

How Science Works

You need to be able to explain and evaluate the effects of human activities on the atmosphere.

Most human activities, especially those used to create heat and energy, can produce pollutants which are harmful to the atmosphere. Some of these activities and their impact on the atmosphere are listed below:

The burning of fossil fuels creates the gases sulfur dioxide and carbon dioxide. Sulfur dioxide contributes to the formation of acid rain which can erode buildings and add acid to lakes and the soil.

The carbon dioxide content of the air used to be roughly constant (0.03%) but it has been increased by the growth in population, which raises energy requirements.

Deforestation means less photosynthesis takes place. An increase in the level of carbon dioxide is believed to be responsible for global warming and climate change.

The combustion of petrol and diesel involves the reaction of nitrogen and oxygen at very high temperatures in car engines to provide oxides of nitrogen which are pollutants. Carbon monoxide is produced by the incomplete combustion of fuels. It is a poisonous gas which eventually oxidises into carbon dioxide, which leads to global warming.

So, what can we do to reduce the pollutants? Humans need to create energy to heat homes, power their cars, etc. but we need to look at the effect various fuels have on the environment and consider alternative methods of producing energy in order to limit the impact we have on the planet.

- Cars fitted with catalytic converters reduce the levels of carbon monoxide and oxides of nitrogen.
- Alternative forms of energy can reduce pollutants, e.g. wind farms and hydroelectricity.
- Power stations can use fuels which reduce atmospheric pollution.

The European Union and the United Kingdom have made laws to control the pollution levels. These laws need to be regulated and monitored, and every country needs to control their pollution levels.

Example Questions

If you are studying Specification A, you will have to complete a 30 minute objective test under exam conditions for each section (i.e. Chemistry 1a and Chemistry 1b). These consist of matching and multiple choice questions – see Questions 1 and 2 below.

If you are studying Specification B, you will have to complete a 45 minute written exam covering the whole of the unit (i.e. Chemistry 1). This will feature structured questions – see Question 3 below.

1   The elements in the periodic table are arranged in groups.

Which of these statements best describes a periodic group?

A A group contains elements with similar properties. .... ☑

B A group contains elements in alphabetical order. .... ☐

C A group contains a random selection of elements. .... ☐

D A group contains elements that react with each other. .... ☐   *(1 mark)*   ① 1

2   Crude oil is made up of hydrocarbons. What is a hydrocarbon?

A A mixture of lots of different elements. .... ☐

B A molecule made up of only carbon and hydrogen atoms. .... ☑

C A compound of carbon and water. .... ☐

D One of the elements in the periodic table. .... ☐   *(1 mark)*   ② 1

3   The boiling points of eight hydrocarbons are displayed in the following table:

No. of carbon atoms in the hydrocarbon	1	2	3	4	5	6	7	8
Boiling point °C	-150	-98	-45	2	32	66	98	120

(a) Suggest a hypothesis that could have been investigated when the data in the table was collected.

The number of carbon atoms in a hydrocarbon will affect its boiling point.

(1 mark)

(b) What is the independent variable?

The number of carbon atoms in the hydrocarbon.

(1 mark)

(c) What is the dependent variable?

The boiling point.

(1 mark)

(d) If you drew a line graph of these results which variable would you put on the horizontal axis?

The independent variable (number of carbon atoms in hydrocarbon).

(1 mark)

(e) Describe the relationship between the two variables in the results table.

A positive correlation: as the number of carbon atoms increases, the boiling point of the hydrocarbon increases.

(1 mark)

(f) Name one key variable you should control in order to make this investigation a fair test.

Amount (volume) of hydrocarbon tested.

(1 mark)

(g) Suggest one change you could make to your method in order to improve the accuracy of these results.

Measure each of the boiling points more than once and find the mean.

(1 mark)   ⑦ 7

① If you are unsure about the answer to a multiple-choice question, eliminate the options that you know are wrong first.

② Read the question and all the options carefully. For this one, the clue is in the name!

③ A hypothesis suggests the relationship between two variables. It is always a statement (never a question)!

④ The independent variable is the one being controlled.

⑤ The dependent variable is measured each time the independent variable is changed, to see if there is a relationship between the two.

⑥ The independent variable always goes on the horizontal axis (or x-axis).

⑦ Only comment on what the data tells you – nothing else!

⑧ In a fair test, only the independent variable can affect the dependent variable. All outside variables are kept the same.

⑨ Repeating measurements helps identify errors, and finding the mean (average) gives a best estimate of the true value.

Key Words

Alkane – a saturated hydrocarbon

Alkene – an unsaturated hydrocarbon (with at least one double carbon carbon bond)

Alloy – a mixture of two or more metals or a mixture of one metal and a non-metal

Atom – the smallest part of an element which can enter into chemical reactions

Catalyst – a substance that increases the rate of a chemical reaction, whilst remaining chemically unchanged itself

Chemical formula – a way of showing the elements present in a substance

Chemical reaction – a process in which one or more substances are changed into others

Compound – a substance consisting of two or more elements chemically combined together

Decompose – to break down

Element – a substance that consists of only one type of atom

Emulsion – a mixture of oil and water

Fossil fuels – fuels formed in the ground, over millions of years, from the remains of dead plants and animals

Fuel – a substance that releases heat or energy when combined with oxygen

Hydrocarbon – a compound containing only hydrogen and carbon

Hydrogenation – the process in which hydrogen is used to harden vegetable oils

Molecule – the simplest structural unit of an element or compound

Non-biodegradable – a substance that does not decompose naturally

Ore – a naturally occurring mineral from which a metal can be extracted

Polymer – a giant long-chained hydrocarbon

Sedimentary rocks – rocks formed by the accumulation of sediment

Smart alloy – an alloy which can change shape and then return to its original shape

Tectonic plates – huge sections of the Earth's crust which move relative to one another

13.1

How is heat (thermal energy) transferred and what factors affect the rate at which it is transferred?

Heat can be transferred from hotter places to colder places by three different methods: conduction, convection and radiation. To transfer heat effectively, with minimal heat loss, we need to know which method is the most efficient in a particular case. To understand this, you need to know…

- the differences between the transfer methods
- which surfaces are good absorbers or emitters of radiation
- the factors that affect the rate of heat transfer.

Conduction

Conduction is the transfer of heat energy without the substance itself moving. The structure of metals makes them good conductors of heat. As a metal becomes hotter, its tightly packed particles gain more kinetic energy and vibrate. This energy is transferred to cooler parts of the metal by delocalised electrons, which move freely through the metal, colliding with particles and other electrons.

N.B. an electron is a subatomic particle (see p.99).

Poker

Heat energy is conducted up the poker as the hotter parts transfer energy to the colder parts

Convection

Convection is the transfer of heat energy through movement. This occurs in liquids and gases and creates convection currents.

In a liquid or gas, the particles nearest the heat source move faster causing the substance to expand and become less dense than in the colder parts. The warm liquid or gas will rise up and colder, denser liquid or gas moves into the space created (close to the heat source).

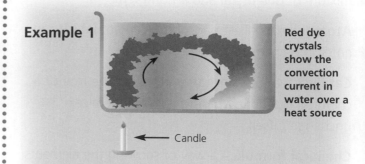

Example 1

Red dye crystals show the convection current in water over a heat source

← Candle

Example 2

Circulation of air caused by a radiator

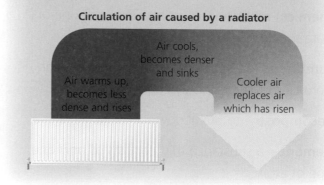

Air cools, becomes denser and sinks

Air warms up, becomes less dense and rises

Cooler air replaces air which has risen

Radiation

Thermal, or infra red, **radiation** is the transfer of heat energy by electromagnetic waves; no particles of matter are involved.

All objects emit and absorb radiation. The hotter the object, the more energy it radiates. How much radiation is given out or taken in by an object depends on its surface, shape and dimensions.

An object will emit or absorb energy faster if there is a big difference in temperature between it and its surroundings. The rate of heat transfer can be slowed down by the use of insulation, which provides a barrier.

Under similar conditions, different materials transfer heat at different rates. At the same temperature…

- dark matt surfaces emit more radiation than light shiny surfaces
- dark matt surfaces absorb more radiation than light shiny surfaces.

You need to be able to evaluate ways in which heat is transferred in and out of bodies and ways in which the rates of transfer can be reduced.

Every year, people in the UK spend a lot more money on energy (gas and electricity) to heat their homes than they need to. This is because energy gets lost and wasted.

An uninsulated house can lose up to 75% of heat through the roof, walls, windows, floors and doors. Heat energy is transferred from homes into the environment by...

- **conduction** – through the walls, floor, roof and windows
- **convection** – convection currents coupled with cold draughts from gaps in doors and windows cause heat energy to rise up to the roof space where it is easily lost
- **radiation** – through the walls, roof and windows.

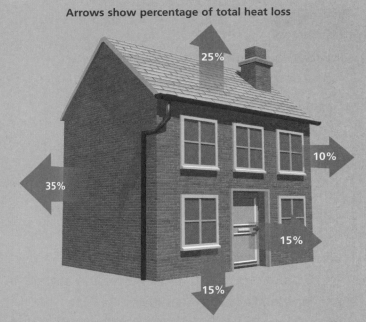

Arrows show percentage of total heat loss

Insulating a house will help it to retain the heat in winter, and also help to keep it cool in the summer. The table below outlines how heat can be lost and how this loss can be reduced.

Where Heat is Lost	Preventative Measure	Benefits	Problems
Roof	Roof insulation – traps a layer of air between fibres or insulating material.	• Can reduce heat loss by 20–25%. • Many different methods to suit all homes.	• Needs to be laid by an expert. • Expensive.
Under doors and windows	Draught excluders – keeps as much warm air inside as possible.	• Can reduce heat loss by up to 15%. • Cheap and easy to install.	• Must make sure that air vents are not blocked – need fresh air to circulate to prevent dry rot.
Walls	Cavity wall insulation and internal thermal boards.	• Can reduce heat loss by 35%.	• Expensive.
Windows	Double glazing – traps air between two sheets of glass. Curtains – stops heat loss through convection.	• Double glazing can reduce heat loss by up to 10%. • Curtains are cheap and easy to install.	• Double glazing is expensive.
Floor	Carpets, rugs and underfloor insulation can help to stop heat loss through the floor.	• Carpets and rugs are easy to install.	• Underfloor insulation is expensive.

Physics Unit 1a

13.2

What is meant by the efficient use of energy?

Devices can transform (change) energy from one form into another. When energy is transformed, not all of it is transformed into useful energy; some of it is wasted. To understand energy efficiency, you need to know...

- how energy is transferred
- how energy is wasted
- what happens to useful and wasted energy
- how efficiency is measured.

Transferring and Transforming Energy

When devices transfer energy, only part of the energy is usefully **transferred** to where it is wanted and in the form that it is wanted. The remaining energy is **transformed** in a non-useful way, mainly as heat energy that goes into the surroundings, and is known as **wasted** energy.

The **wasted** and the **useful** energy are eventually transferred to their surroundings which become warmer.

No energy is destroyed or created, it is just changed into a different form (transformed). However, the energy becomes increasingly spread out, so it is difficult for any further useful energy transfers to occur.

Efficiency of Devices

The greater the proportion of energy that is usefully transformed, the more **efficient** we say the device is. Opposite are examples of the efficiency of two devices.

- A car engine is 20% efficient. Much more energy is wasted (in heat and sound), than is transformed into useful kinetic energy.
- A microwave is 60% efficient. More energy is transformed into useful heat, light and kinetic energy than is wasted (as heat and sound).

Electrical energy
200 joules/sec

Wasted energy
Heat 150 joules/sec

Useful energy
Light 20 joules/sec

Useful energy
Sound 30 joules/sec

Only a quarter of the energy supplied to a television is usefully transformed into light and sound. Therefore it is only 25% efficient.

How Science Works

You need to be able to describe the intended energy transfers / transformations and the main energy wastages that occur with a range of devices, and calculate the efficiency of a device using:

$$\text{Efficiency} = \frac{\text{Useful energy transferred by device}}{\text{Total energy supplied to device}}$$

Some examples are shown in the table below.

Name of Device and Intended Energy Transfer	Energy In	Energy Out		Efficiency
		Useful	Wasted	
Standard light bulb – electrical energy to light energy	100 joules/sec	Light: 20 joules/sec	Heat: 80 joules/sec	$\frac{20}{100}$ x 100% = **20%**
Low energy light bulb – electrical energy to light energy	25 joules/sec	Light: 20 joules/sec	Heat: 5 joules/sec	$\frac{20}{25}$ x 100% = **80%**
Kettle – electrical energy to heat energy	2000 joules/sec	Heat (in water): 1800 joules/sec	Heat: 100 joules/sec Sound: 100 joules/sec	$\frac{1800}{2000}$ x 100% = **90%**
Electric motor – electrical energy to kinetic energy	500 joules/sec	Kinetic: 300 joules/sec	Heat: 100 joules/sec Sound: 100 joules/sec	$\frac{300}{500}$ x 100% = **60%**

You need to be able to evaluate the effectiveness and cost effectiveness of methods used to reduce energy consumption.

Method	Benefits	Problems
Switching lights off when leaving a room.	• Easy and simple way to reduce energy consumption.	• People forget or don't like being in a dark house.
Energy-efficient light bulbs.	• Use less power so cost less to run. • Less wasted energy. • Last longer than standard bulbs.	• More expensive to buy.
Using electrical equipment during the night, e.g. washing machine.	• Cheaper time of day for using electricity.	• Can be noisy and keep people awake.
More efficient tumble driers, or letting clothes dry naturally.	• Driers with a sensor stop automatically when the clothes are dry, which saves energy.	• New driers are expensive to buy. • Cannot hang clothes out to dry if it is raining.
Tankless water heater.	• Water is heated when needed so less energy used to heat unnecessary water, and keep it heated.	• Some units do not have enough power to supply to more than one tap at a time.

Physics Unit 1a

Why are electrical devices so useful?

Electrical energy can be transferred easily across large distances and therefore is very suitable to use in our homes and industries. To understand this, you need to know...

- what energy transformations electrical devices bring about
- how energy and power are measured
- how electricity is transferred
- how transformers are used
- what happens when voltage is increased.

Energy Transformation

Most of the energy transferred to homes and industry is electrical energy, because it is easily transformed to...

- heat (thermal) energy, e.g. an electric fire
- light energy, e.g. a lamp
- sound energy, e.g. stereo speakers
- movement (kinetic) energy, e.g. an electric whisk.

The **power** of an appliance is measured in **watts (W)** or **kilowatts (kW)**, and **energy** is normally measured in **joules (J)**.

The amount of energy transformed by an electrical appliance depends on...

- how long the appliance is switched on
- how fast the appliance can transform energy.

Energy Transfer

Electricity generated at power stations is transferred to homes, schools and factories all over the country by a network of cables called the National Grid.

Transformers are used to change the voltage of the alternating current supply before and after it is transmitted through the National Grid.

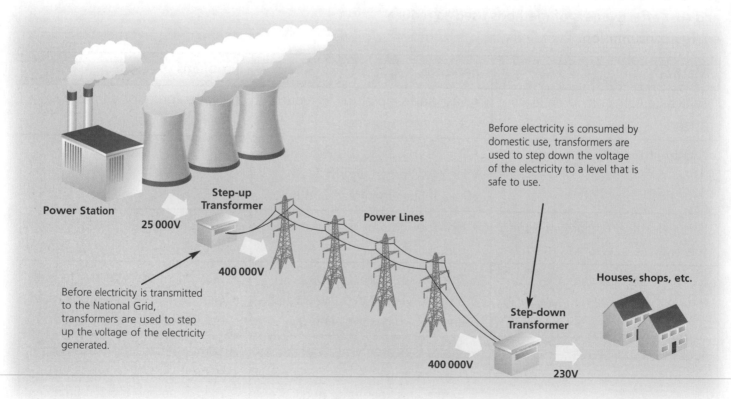

Power Station

25 000V

Step-up Transformer

400 000V

Before electricity is transmitted to the National Grid, transformers are used to step up the voltage of the electricity generated.

Power Lines

Before electricity is consumed by domestic use, transformers are used to step down the voltage of the electricity to a level that is safe to use.

Step-down Transformer

400 000V

230V

Houses, shops, etc.

Reducing Energy Loss During Transmission

The higher the current that passes through a wire the greater the amount of energy that is lost as heat from the wire. So we need to transmit as low a current as possible through the power lines.

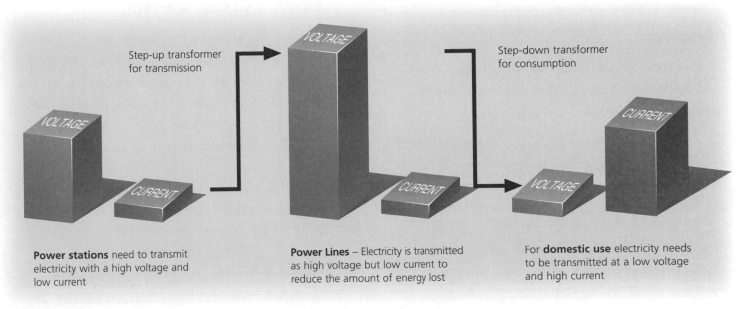

Step-up transformer for transmission

Step-down transformer for consumption

Power stations need to transmit electricity with a high voltage and low current

Power Lines – Electricity is transmitted as high voltage but low current to reduce the amount of energy lost

For **domestic use** electricity needs to be transmitted at a low voltage and high current

Calculating the Amount and Cost of Energy Transferred

The **amount of energy** transferred from the mains can be calculated using the following equation...

Energy transferred (kilowatt-hour, kWh)	=	Power (kilowatt, kW)	X	Time (hour, h)

The **cost of energy** transferred from the mains can then be calculated using the following equation...

Total cost	=	Number of kilowatt-hours	X	Cost per kilowatt-hour

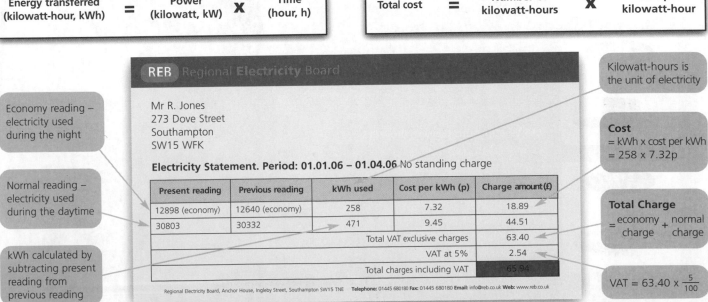

Economy reading – electricity used during the night

Normal reading – electricity used during the daytime

kWh calculated by subtracting present reading from previous reading

REB Regional **Electricity** Board

Mr R. Jones
273 Dove Street
Southampton
SW15 WFK

Electricity Statement. Period: 01.01.06 – 01.04.06 No standing charge

Present reading	Previous reading	kWh used	Cost per kWh (p)	Charge amount (£)
12898 (economy)	12640 (economy)	258	7.32	18.89
30803	30332	471	9.45	44.51
			Total VAT exclusive charges	63.40
			VAT at 5%	2.54
			Total charges including VAT	65.94

Regional Electricity Board, Anchor House, Ingleby Street, Southampton SW15 TNE   **Telephone:** 01445 680180 **Fax:** 01445 680180 **Email:** info@reb.co.uk **Web:** www.reb.co.uk

Kilowatt-hours is the unit of electricity

Cost
= kWh x cost per kWh
= 258 x 7.32p

Total Charge
= economy charge + normal charge

VAT = 63.40 x $\frac{5}{100}$

How Science Works

You need to be able to compare and contrast different electrical devices that can be used for a particular application, and calculate the amount of energy transferred from the mains using...

Energy transferred (kilowatt-hour, kWh)	=	Power (kilowatt, kW)	X	Time (hour, h)

Example

Mr and Mrs Jones are shopping for a new shower for their house. They see three different showers advertised (see below).

They work out the advantages and disadvantages of each model in order to decide which one will be the most suitable for their needs. They also need to work out how much energy will be needed to power each one. They have calculated that every morning they each have a shower lasting, on average, 12 minutes, whilst their young son, Nick, has a shorter shower lasting 6 minutes (total time = 12 + 12 + 6 = 30 mins or 0.5 hours).

Using the formula they calculate how much energy will need to be transferred from the mains to power each shower:

Power x Time = Energy
7kW: 7 x 0.5   = 3.5kWh
8.5kW: 8.5 x 0.5 = 4.25kWh
9.5kW: 9.5 x 0.5 = 4.75kWh

To compare the showers they work out...
- the 7kW shower will require the least amount of energy from the mains, but it does have a less powerful spray, fewer options and needs to be connected to a hot water tank
- the 8kW shower will require more energy than the 7kW shower, but is has a more powerful spray. It is also connected to the hot water tank
- the 9.5kW shower is more expensive to buy and requires more energy, but it has a much more powerful spray, more functions and can be connected to a cold water tank. This will be more useful for a family as they won't have to wait for the water to heat up.

7kW standard shower
- connects to hot water tank
- medium power jet
- suitable for any household
- choice of 3 colours

£50
7kW

8.5kW electric shower
- connects to hot water tank
- three function power selector
- 12% more power than a standard 7kW shower
- fully temperature stabilised for maximum comfort

£89
8.5kW

9.5kW supreme power shower
- connects to cold water supply
- 42% more power than average 7kW shower
- great for large families
- triple function – low, medium and high jet
- multi-spray shower head with massage function

£120
9.5kW

13.4

How should we generate the electricity we need?

Various energy sources can be used to generate the electricity that we need. We need to understand the benefits and costs associated with each method to select the best one to use in a particular situation. To understand this, you need to know...

- how energy is produced
- about renewable and non-renewable energy sources
- the advantages and disadvantages of using different energy sources.

Fuels are substances which release useful amounts of energy when they are burnt.

Non-Renewable Energy Sources

Coal, oil and gas are energy sources which are formed over millions of years from the remains of plants and animals. They are called **fossil fuels** and are responsible for most of the energy that we use. However, because they cannot be replaced within a lifetime, they will eventually run out. They are therefore called **non-renewable** energy sources.

Non-renewable Fossil Fuels

Coal   Oil   Gas

Nuclear fuels such as uranium and plutonium are also non-renewable. Nuclear fission is the release of nuclear particles that collide with other atoms causing a chain reaction that generates huge amounts of heat energy. However, nuclear fuel is not burnt like coal, oil or gas to release energy and is not classed as a fossil fuel.

Generating Electricity from Non-Renewable Energy Sources

In power stations, fossil fuels and wood are burnt to release heat energy, which boils water to produce steam. This steam drives turbines which are attached to an electrical generator.

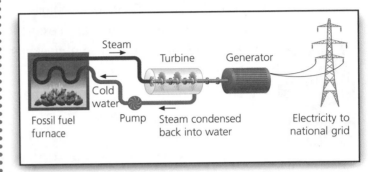

Nuclear fuel is used to generate electricity in a similar way. A reactor is used to generate heat by nuclear fission. A heat exchanger is used to transfer the heat energy from the reactor to the water which turns to steam and drives the turbines.

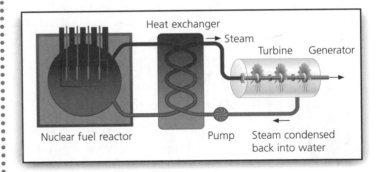

Wood

Although burnt for energy, wood is not a fossil fuel, nor is it non-renewable. It is classed as a **renewable** energy source since trees can be grown relatively quickly to replace those which are burnt to provide energy for heating.

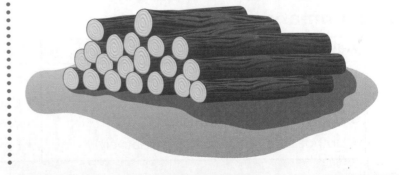

Physics Unit 1a

Comparing Non-Renewable Sources Of Energy

The energy sources below are used to provide most of the electricity we need in this country through power stations. Some of the advantages and disadvantages of each one are listed below.

Source	Advantages	Disadvantages
Coal	• Relatively cheap and easy to obtain. • Coal-fired power stations are flexible in meeting demand and have a quicker start-up time than their nuclear equivalents. • Estimates suggest that there may be over a century's worth of coal left.	• Burning produces carbon dioxide (CO_2) and sulfur dioxide (SO_2). • Produces more CO_2, per unit of energy than oil or gas does. (CO_2 causes global warming.) • SO_2 causes acid rain unless the sulfur is removed before burning or the SO_2 is removed from the waste gases. Both of these add to the cost.
Oil	• Enough oil left for the short to medium term. • Relatively easy to find, though the price is variable. • Oil-fired power stations are flexible in meeting demand and have a quicker start-up time than both nuclear-powered and coal-fired reactors.	• Burning produces CO_2 and SO_2. (CO_2 causes global warming, SO_2 causes acid rain.) • Produces more CO_2 than gas per unit of energy. • Often carried between continents on tankers leading to the risk of spillage and pollution.
Gas	• Enough natural gas left for the short to medium term. • Can be found as easily as oil. • No SO_2 is produced. • Gas-fired power stations are flexible in meeting demand and have a quicker start-up time than nuclear, coal and oil-fired reactors.	• Burning produces CO_2, although produces less than coal and oil, per unit of energy. (CO_2 causes global warming.) • Expensive pipelines and networks are often required to transport it to the point of use.
Nuclear	• Cost and rate of fuel is relatively low. • Can be situated in sparsely populated areas. • Nuclear power stations are flexible in meeting demand. • No CO_2 or SO_2 produced.	• Although there is very little escape of radioactive material in normal use, radioactive waste can stay dangerously radioactive for thousands of years and safe storage is expensive. • Building and de-commissioning is costly. • Longest comparative start-up time.

Summary

Advantages	Disadvantages
• Produce huge amounts of energy. • Reliable. • Flexible in meeting demand. • Do not take up much space (relatively).	• Pollute the environment. • Cause global warming and acid rain. • Will eventually run out. • Fuels often have to be transported over long distances.

Renewable Energy Sources

Renewable energy sources are those that will not run out because they are continually being replaced. Many of them are 'powered' by the Sun or Moon. The gravitational pull of the Moon creates tides and the Sun causes...

- evaporation which results in rain and flowing water
- convection currents, which result in winds, which in turn create waves.

Generating Electricity from Renewable Energy Sources

Renewable energy sources can be used to drive turbines or generators directly. In other words, nothing needs to be burnt to produce heat.

The table below shows the most common methods of generating energy from renewable energy sources.

Wind Turbines
Wind can be used to drive huge turbines, which, in turn, drive generators. Wind turbines are usually positioned on the top of hills so they are exposed to as much wind as possible.

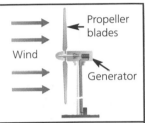

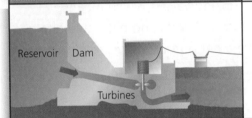

Solar Cells and Panels
Solar cells and panels are made of a semiconductor material (usually silicon) which captures the heat energy and transforms it into electrical energy.

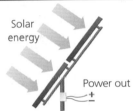

Hydroelectric Dam
Water that is stored in a reservoir above the power station is allowed to flow down through the pipes to drive the turbines, which produces a lot of power.

Tidal Barrage
As the tide comes in, water flows freely through a valve in the barrage. This water then becomes trapped. At low tide, the water is released from behind the barrage through a gap which has a turbine in it. This drives a generator.

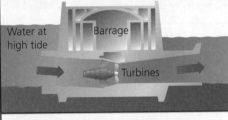

Nodding Duck
Nodding ducks are found in the sea. The motion of the waves makes the 'ducks' rock and this movement is translated into a rotary movement which, in turn, drives a generator.

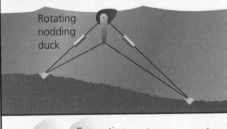

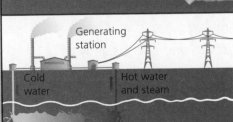

Geothermal
In some volcanic areas, hot water and steam rise naturally to the surface, having been heated up by the decay of radioactive substances (e.g. uranium) within the Earth. This steam can be used directly to drive turbines which, in turn, drive generators.

Physics Unit 1a

Comparing Renewable Sources of Energy

The energy sources listed below use modern technology to provide us with a clean, safe alternative source of energy. Some of their advantages and disadvantages are given.

Source	Advantages	Disadvantages
Wind	• No fuel and little maintenance required. • No pollutant gases produced. • Once built they provide energy when the wind is blowing. • Can be built offshore.	• Need a lot to produce a sizable amount of electricity, which means noise and visual pollution. • Electricity output depends entirely on the strength of the wind. • Not very flexible in meeting demand unless the energy is stored. • Capital outlay can be high to build them.
Tidal and Waves	• No fuel required. • No pollutant gases produced. • Once built they provide 'free' energy. • Barrage water can be released when demand for electricity is high.	• Tidal barrages, across estuaries, are unsightly, a hazard to shipping, and destroy the habitats of wading birds, etc. • Daily variations of tides and waves affect output. • High initial capital outlay to build them.
Hydro-electric	• No fuel required unless storing energy to meet future demand. • Fast start-up time to meet growing demand. • Produce large amounts of clean, reliable electricity. • No pollutant gases produced. • Water can be pumped back up to the reservoir when demand for electricity is low, e.g. in the night.	• Location is critical and often involves damming upland valleys which means flooding farms, forests and natural habitats. • To achieve a net output (aside from pumping) there must be adequate rainfall in the region where the reservoir is. • Very high initial capital outlay (though worth the investment in the end).
Solar	• Ideal for producing electricity in remote locations. • Excellent energy source for small amounts. • Produces free, clean electricity. • No pollutant gases produced.	• Dependent on the intensity of light; more useful in sunny places. • High cost per unit of electricity produced compared to all other sources, except non-rechargeable batteries.

Summary

Advantages	Disadvantages
• No fuel costs during operation. • No chemical pollution. • Often low maintenance. • Do not contribute to global warming or produce acid rain.	• With the exception of hydroelectric, they produce small amounts of electricity. • Take up lots of space and are unsightly. • Unreliable (apart from hydroelectric), depend on the weather and cannot guarantee supply on demand. • High initial capital outlay.

You need to be able to compare and contrast the particular advantages and disadvantages of using different energy sources to generate electricity.

Example

The Lonsdale News, Tuesday June 13 2006   12

Power to the People

The little village of Bukestead was in uproar yesterday after proposed plans were unveiled for a nuclear power station to be built just 10 miles away from the village on the top of the moor. The local area is well known for its beautiful countryside and is a carefully controlled breeding area for many birds. However, increasing demand for electricity means that new electricity generating plants need to be built and this site is considered to be most suitable. Its isolated location and the large number of jobs it will create, have made nuclear power a popular choice with some people.

However, opinion is strongly divided as to the best use of the land, with renewable energy options being cited by many as a better alternative.

Join the debate. Write to your local MP or councillor and have your say.

6 Moorland Road
Bukestead
Derbyshire

Mrs J Smith (MP)
Derby Council Offices
134 High Street
Derby

19th June

Dear Mrs Smith

I was appalled to read about the proposed nuclear power station. The blight on the countryside, the traffic and the horror of a nuclear leak would be unthinkable! What would happen to the local countryside, farms and the breeding grounds for migrating birds that has been so carefully built up? The local roads would be constantly clogged up with tankers travelling to and from the plant, some carrying highly dangerous waste for disposal. Not to mention the expense of building the site!

This land would be ideal for a farm of wind turbines. The constant strong winds on the hill, coupled with adequate space for 10 to 15 turbines, would be sufficient to produce a sizable amount of electricity. There would be no pollution, no fuel and little maintenance required, just clean, free energy. I hope you will consider the alternatives.

Yours sincerely,

Anne Pentwhistle

Anne Pentwhistle
(A very concerned local resident)

26 Hill View
Bukestead
Derbyshire

Mrs J Smith (MP)
Derby Council Offices
134 High Street
Derby

17th June

Dear Mrs Smith

I am writing in support of the proposed nuclear power station.

The isolated position on the hill would be ideal. Nuclear leaks are so uncommon that no real threat would be posed and the local economy would greatly benefit from the number of jobs created.

I know that reasons are being cited for the use of 'green' electricity – big solar panels, huge wind turbine farms and the like. These are unfeasible solutions; they could never fulfil the demand, and they themselves would visually pollute the countryside. Everyone says, 'not on my door step', but nuclear is flexible, non-pollutant and will provide the electricity needed for the area.

I whole-heartedly support your plans.

Yours sincerely,

A. Pollard

Local resident

13.5

What are the uses and hazards of the waves that form the electromagnetic spectrum?

The uses and hazards of electromagnetic radiations depend upon their wavelength and frequency. To understand this, you need to know…

- the different types of electromagnetic radiation
- the uses and dangers of each type of radiation
- the difference between analogue and digital signals.

Electromagnetic Radiation

Electromagnetic radiations are disturbances in an electric field. They travel as **waves** and move energy from one place to another. Each type of electromagnetic radiation…

- has a different **wavelength** and a different **frequency**
- travels at the same speed (300 000 000m/s) through a vacuum (e.g. space).

Electromagnetic radiations (such as light) form a continuous range called the electromagnetic spectrum.

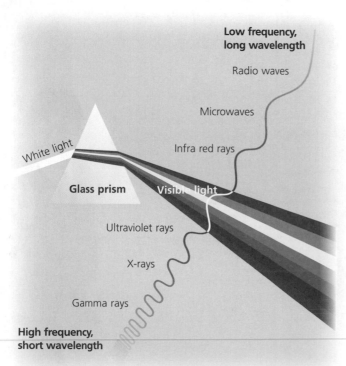

Radio waves, microwaves and infra red rays all have a longer wavelength and a lower frequency than visible light.

Ultraviolet waves, X-rays and gamma rays all have a shorter wavelength and a higher frequency than visible light.

Electromagnetic radiation can be **reflected** and **refracted**. Different wavelengths of electromagnetic radiation are reflected, absorbed or transmitted differently by different substances and types of surface, e.g. black surfaces are particularly good absorbers of infra red radiation.

When a wave is **absorbed** by a substance, the energy it carries is absorbed and makes the substance heat up. It may also create an **alternating current** of the same frequency as the radiation. This principle is used in television and radio aerials, which receive information via radio waves.

Electromagnetic waves obey the wave formula:

$$\text{Wave speed (metre/second, m/s)} = \text{Frequency (hertz, Hz)} \times \text{Wavelength (metre, m)}$$

Visible Light

Light is one type of electromagnetic radiation which, together with the other various types of radiation, is in the electromagnetic spectrum.

The seven 'colours of the rainbow' form the **visible spectrum** which, as the name suggests, is the only part of the electromagnetic spectrum that we can see.

The visible spectrum is produced because white light is made up of many different colours. These are refracted by different amounts as they pass through a prism – red light is refracted the least and violet the most. Visible light can be used for communication through optical fibres and for vision and photography.

Electromagnetic Waves	Uses	Effects
Radio Waves	• Transmitting radio and TV signals between places – waves with longer wavelengths are reflected by the ionosphere (an electrically charged layer in the atmosphere) so they can send signals between points regardless of the curve of the Earth's surface.	• Certain cancers can be treated with radio waves. • High levels of exposure for short periods can increase body temperature leading to tissue damage, especially to the eyes.
Microwaves	• Satellite communication networks and mobile phone networks. • Cooking – microwaves are absorbed by water molecules causing them to heat up.	• May damage or kill cells because they are absorbed by water in the cells, leading to the release of heat. Therefore, care must be taken in the use of microwaves.
Infra Red Rays	• Grills, toasters and radiant heaters. • Remote controls for televisions and video recorders. • Optical fibre communication.	• Absorbed by skin and felt as heat. • Excessive amount can cause burns.
Visible Light	**See p.94**	**See p.94**
Ultraviolet Rays	• Security coding – a surface coated with special paint absorbs UV and emits visible light. • Suntanning and sunbeds.	• Passes through skin to the tissues below. Darker skin allows less penetration and provides more protection. • High doses of this radiation can kill cells and a low dose can cause cancer.
X-rays	• Producing shadow pictures of bones and metals.	• Passes through soft tissues (although some is absorbed). • High doses can kill cells and a low dose can cause cancer.
Gamma Rays	• Killing cancerous cells. • Killing bacteria on food and surgical instruments.	• Passes through soft tissues – although some is absorbed. • High doses of this radiation can kill cells and a low dose can cause cancer.

Physics Unit 1b

Communication Using Electromagnetic Waves

Sound, e.g. speech or music, can be sent over long distances if it is converted into electrical signals which match the frequency and amplitude (the maximum disturbance caused) of the sound waves.

These electrical signals can then be sent using…

- **Cables** – copper cables weaken the signal during transmission. To boost the signal, regular amplification of the signal is required.
- **Electromagnetic waves** – a radio wave (called a 'carrier') is used to carry the electrical signal from a transmitter. This produces a **modulated** wave.

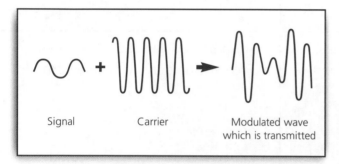

Signal   Carrier   Modulated wave which is transmitted

The modulated wave is picked up by the aerial in a radio and is demodulated (i.e. the carrier wave is removed) to leave the original signal. This is what comes out of a loudspeaker.

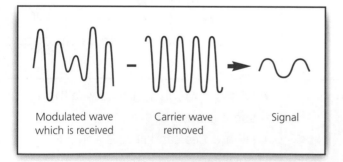

Modulated wave which is received   Carrier wave removed   Signal

Optical Fibres

Information can also be transmitted using optical fibres where the electrical signal is converted into light or infra red pulses. These waves travel in curved paths.

More information can be sent this way than by sending electrical signals through cables of the same diameter, and there is less weakening of the signal along the way.

Analogue and Digital Signals

Analogue signals vary continually in amplitude and / or frequency. They are very similar to the sound waves of speech or music.

Digital signals do not vary. They have discrete values, usually **on (I)** or **off (0)**; there are no in-between states. The information is a series of pulses.

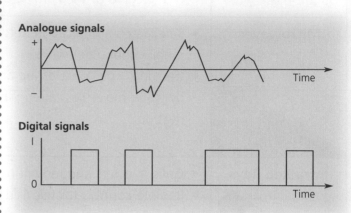

Analogue signals

Digital signals

Digital Versus Analogue

Digital signals are of a better quality than analogue signals and there is no change in the signal information during transmission. More information can be transmitted in this way in a given time via cable, optical fibre or carrier wave. Digital signals can also be easily processed by computers.

When analogue signals are transmitted, they become weaker and can also pick up additional signals or noise (interference). The transmitted signals have to be amplified at selected intervals to counteract the effects of the weakening.

Different frequencies within analogue signals weaken by different amounts. During amplification, these differences and any background noise are also amplified, causing a deterioration in the signal quality.

Digital signals also weaken during transmission, but the pulses are still recognisable as 'on' or 'off'. The signals are unaffected by noise which usually has a low amplitude and is recognised as an 'off' state. When amplified, the quality of the digital signal is retained.

How Science Works

You need to be able to evaluate the possible hazards associated with the use of different types of electromagnetic radiation.

Example

It's Good to Talk – Or Is It?

New findings raise concerns that mobile phones could cause cancer and other health problems.

Swedish scientists studying the effects of electromagnetic radiation on red blood cells have found that levels of radiation, equivalent to those emitted by mobile phones, have a significant effect on the attractive forces between cells.

Up until now, the conventional view has been that radio waves could only cause damage at a cellular level if they carried enough energy to break chemical bonds or 'fry' tissue. These new findings might suggest that mobile phones do in fact emit enough energy to affect the bonds.

Experts, however, have been quick to point out that the results were obtained through tests on small groups of cells and provide no real evidence of a danger to health.

There have been other suggestions in the past that mobile phones can cause brain tumours and Alzheimer's disease, but so far research has been inconclusive.

Mobile Phones are Safe

New study has found no link between mobile phones and cancer.

Scientists studying the possible links between mobile phones and brain tumours have reported today that they have found no correlation between using mobile phones and the risk of developing glioma – the most common type of brain tumour.

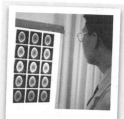

The study of 2 682 people across the UK looked at 966 individuals with diagnosed glioma and 1 716 individuals without the condition. It concluded that although a large percentage of the cancer sufferers reported their tumours to be on the side of the head where they held the phone, for regular mobile phone users, there was no increased risk of developing glioma.

Using mobile phones

Benefits	Problems
• Easy, convenient method of communication, especially in a vulnerable situation – when car breaks down, alone at night, feel threatened etc. • Can be used to access the Internet, take pictures, and watch television/video clips. • Easy way to keep in contact when away from home or abroad, e.g. text messages. • Many different networks available. • Can help in solving crime as mobile phones can be tracked.	• Some studies have linked mobile phone use with brain tumours and Alzheimer's disease. • Studies are still being carried out and the long-term effects of using mobile phones are not known. • Increasingly, advertising is targeted at younger age groups who would be more vulnerable to any health implications.

How Science Works

You need to be able to evaluate methods to reduce exposure to different types of electromagnetic radiation.

Prolonged exposure to many types of electromagnetic radiation is considered harmful. There are ways in which exposure can be reduced.

Example

Health Issues
Your questions answered

Is Sunbathing Unhealthy?

I love sunbathing and going out in the Sun, but I have recently become concerned about the effects and dangers of exposure to the Sun. Could you please give me some advice as to the safest methods of dealing with the Sun and UV radiation?
Claire, aged 16, Southampton

As you know, some exposure to sunlight can be enjoyable. However, too much can be dangerous, causing immediate effects such as sunburn, blistering of the skin and heat stroke, whilst longer-term effects can include skin cancer, cataracts, wrinkling and ageing of the skin. Some scientists believe that too much UV radiation can even impair the immune system.

However, don't worry, there are some simple ways to ensure that you can enjoy the Sun and the benefits of UV light, whilst minimising the risks.

Wear sunglasses. Fashion sunglasses won't be enough though, you must get sunglasses that block 99–100% of UV light.

Wear a hat with a wide brim. A hat is very important to stop your brain from overheating which leads to sunstroke.

Protect other areas of your body with clothing. Make sure you choose light materials: anything too heavy and you could overheat.

Always use a high factor sun cream. For it to be effective you must reapply frequently, especially if you have been swimming.

Avoid the hottest parts of the day, between 11am and 3pm. I know this may seem restrictive, but the Sun is most intense, and most damaging, during these times.

Avoid sunlamps and tanning parlours. I know that these can often make you feel good, or help medical conditions such as SAD (seasonal affective disorder) or eczema, but they are damaging to your skin.

Keep hydrated: drink lots of water – this will help your skin to cope with the effects of the Sun better.

Apply lots of aftersun lotion to help protect your skin.

13.6

What are the uses and dangers of emissions from radioactive substances?

Radioactive substances constantly emit radiation from the nuclei of their atoms. Some nuclear radiations can be very useful but others can be dangerous. To understand nuclear radiation, you need to know...

- the basic structure of an atom
- what an isotope is
- the properties and uses of radioactive substances
- the meaning of 'half-life'
- the effect of radiation on living organisms.

Each atom has a small central **nucleus** made up of **protons** and **neutrons**. This nucleus is surrounded by **electrons**. Here is a helium atom.

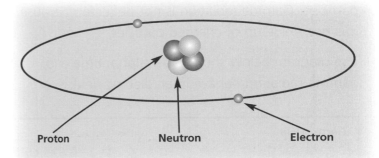

Proton　　Neutron　　Electron

Isotopes

Although all the atoms of a particular element have the same number of protons, they can have a different number of neutrons. These are called **isotopes**.

Radiation

Some substances give out radiation all the time, regardless of what is done to them. These substances are said to be **radioactive**. Radiation is released from the nucleus as the result of a change in the structure of the atom.

There are three types of radiation:

- **alpha (α)** – an alpha particle is a helium nucleus (a particle made up of two protons and two neutrons)

- **Beta (β)** – a beta particle is a high-energy electron which is ejected from the nucleus
- **Gamma (γ)** – high-frequency electromagnetic radiation.

When radiation collides with atoms or molecules, it can knock electrons out of their structure, creating a charged particle called an **ion**.

The relative ionising power of each type of radiation is different, as is their power to penetrate different materials and their range in air.

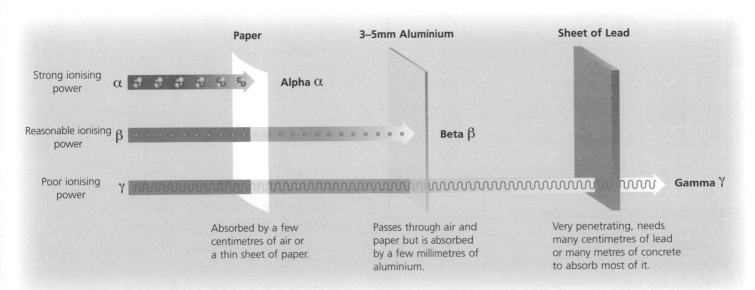

Paper　　3–5mm Aluminium　　Sheet of Lead

Strong ionising power　α　　Alpha α

Reasonable ionising power　β　　Beta β

Poor ionising power　γ　　Gamma γ

Absorbed by a few centimetres of air or a thin sheet of paper.

Passes through air and paper but is absorbed by a few millimetres of aluminium.

Very penetrating, needs many centimetres of lead or many metres of concrete to absorb most of it.

Electric and Magnetic Fields

Alpha and beta radiation are deflected by electric and magnetic fields. This is because they are charged particles. Gamma radiation is not deflected because it is not made up of charged particles.

The diagram below shows how alpha, beta and gamma radiation behave in an electric field:

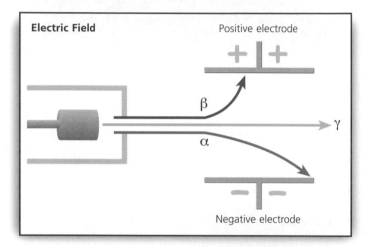

- **Alpha** (➤) particles are positively charged and are deflected towards the negative electrode.
- **Beta** (➤) particles are negatively charged and are deflected towards the positive electrode.
- **Gamma** (➤) radiation is not deflected by the electric field.

The diagram below shows how alpha, beta and gamma radiation behave in a magnetic field:

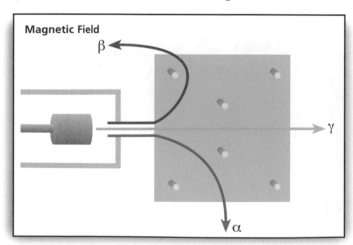

- **Alpha** (➤) and **beta** (➤) particles are deflected.
- **Gamma** (➤) radiation is not affected by the magnetic field.

Common Uses of Radiation

- Sterilisation – gamma rays can be used to sterilise medical instruments and food because they destroy germs and bacteria.
- Treating cancer – gamma radiation can be used to destroy cancerous cells. A high calculated dose is used from different angles so that only the cancerous cells are destroyed.

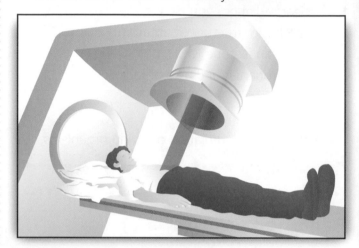

- Controlling the thickness of materials – when radiation passes through a material some of it is absorbed. The greater the thickness of the material, the greater the absorption of radiation. This can be used to control the thickness of different manufactured materials, e.g. paper production at a paper mill (see below).

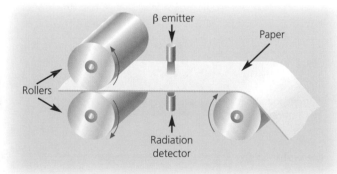

If the paper is too thick then less radiation passes through to the detector, and a signal is sent to the rollers which move closer together.

- Tracers – a tracer is a small amount of a radioisotope (radioactive isotope), which is put into a system. Its progress through the system can be traced using a radiation detector.

Acute Dangers

The ionising power of alpha, beta and gamma radiation can damage molecules inside healthy living cells, which results in the death of the cell.

Damage to cells in organs can cause cancer. The larger the dose of radiation the greater the risk of cancer.

The damaging effect of radiation depends on whether the source is located inside or outside the body. If the source is outside the body...

- α cannot penetrate the body and is stopped by the skin
- β and γ can penetrate the body to reach the cells of organs and be absorbed by them.

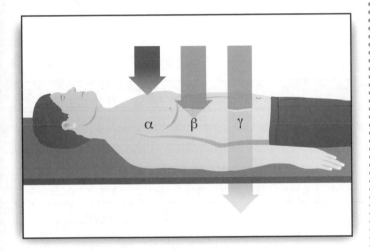

If the source is inside the body...
- α causes most damage as it is easily absorbed by cells causing the most ionisation
- β and γ cause less damage as they are less likely to be absorbed by cells.

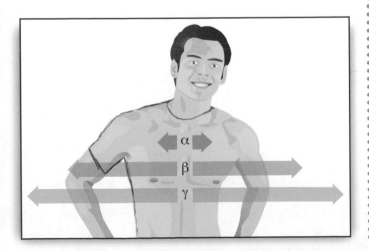

Half-life

The **half-life** of a radioactive isotope is a measurement of the rate of radioactive decay. It is the time it takes for...

1 the number of nuclei of the isotope (those which have not decayed) in a sample to halve **or**

2 the count rate (the number of atoms which decay in a certain time) of a sample containing the isotope to halve.

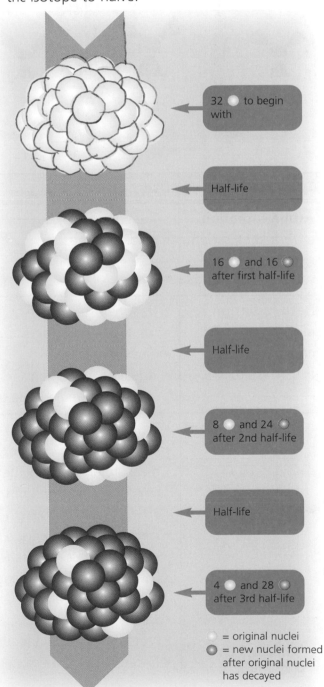

32 ⚪ to begin with

Half-life

16 ⚪ and 16 ◉ after first half-life

Half-life

8 ⚪ and 24 ◉ after 2nd half-life

Half-life

4 ⚪ and 28 ◉ after 3rd half-life

⚪ = original nuclei
◉ = new nuclei formed after original nuclei has decayed

How Science Works

You need to be able to evaluate the possible hazards associated with the use of different types of nuclear radiation.

The risks to humans from radiation differ depending on the type of radiation and the source. We need to understand these risks so that appropriate safety precautions can be taken.

Type of Radiation	Uses	Dangers
Alpha radiation e.g. radium, radon, uranium, thorium.	• Treating cancer, e.g. mouth cancer. • Smoke alarms.	• Cannot penetrate the skin, but harmful if materials emitting alpha radiation enter the body, e.g. are inhaled or swallowed. • Difficult to detect through other materials.
Beta radiation e.g. strontium-90, carbon-14, tritium, sulfur-35.	• Treatment of thyroid disorders. • Luminous signs, dials and gauges. • Carbon dating. • Industrial instruments for gauging thickness of materials (e.g. in paper mills).	• Can penetrate human skin cells and cause skin damage. • Materials emitting beta radiation may be harmful if they enter the body.
Gamma radiation e.g. iodine-131, caesium-137, cobalt-60, radium-226.	• Treating cancer. • Industrial control systems which measure and control the flow of liquids or ensure packages (of food, drugs etc.) are filled to the correct level. • Industrial instruments, e.g. in geological surveys, assessing sites for mining and construction and gauging thickness of materials in steel mills. • Sterilising medical equipment. • Pasteurising certain foods and spices. • Tracers (used in medicine and agriculture).	• Very penetrating, so even sealed sources can be a hazard. • Can easily penetrate the body and damage/kill cells in the internal organs. • Can cause cancer. • High doses can kill.

You need to be able to evaluate measures that can be taken to reduce exposure to nuclear radiation.

The transportation and application of radioactive substances is carefully controlled by government rules and regulations to minimise the risks to the general public. Authorised personnel who handle radioactive substances or operate machinery follow strict guidelines. These vary depending on the risk factor involved. The table below lists some measures that can be taken to reduce / prevent exposure to different types of radiation.

External Exposure – Beta and Gamma

- Minimise time of exposure.
- Maximise distance from the source of radiation.
- Wear protective clothing (and remove it before leaving a restricted area).
- Avoid direct handling of radioactive materials, i.e. use implements like forceps and tongs.
- Use protective shields, screens and containers.
- Use instruments that can detect levels of radiation, e.g. Geiger-Müller counter or liquid scintillation counter.
- Use materials which can provide a shield against radiation, e.g. lead, concrete and water.
- Wear a film badge which monitors the degree of exposure to radiation (see below right).

Internal Exposure – Alpha, Beta and Gamma

- Wear chemical fume hoods and protective masks to prevent inhalation.
- Never consume or store food and drink close to a radioactive source.
- Wear protective clothing.
- Ensure that any cuts or wounds are sealed up.
- Minimise amount of radioactive material to be handled.

People who work in the nuclear industry and are regularly exposed to radiation often wear a badge to monitor their degree of exposure. The badge contains photographic film, which (after developing) becomes darker the more radiation it has been exposed to. In this way, radiation exposure can be carefully monitored.

How Science Works

You need to be able to evaluate the appropriateness of radioactive sources for particular uses, including as tracers, in terms of the types of radiation emitted and their half-lives.

The properties of different radioactive substances make them suited to different uses.

Example 1 – Medical Tracers

Doctors use radioactive chemicals called tracers to help detect damage to the internal organs. Once the tracer enters the body, it builds up in the damaged or diseased part of the body. Radiation detectors can then be used to detect where the problem is. These can be linked to computers which produce an image showing the distribution of the radioactive chemical. Problem areas are highlighted by a high concentration.

Because it is being used inside the body, the radioactive tracer must be non-toxic. It also needs to have a short half-life, so that it breaks down quickly after use. Gamma and beta sources are used because they pass out of the body easily. An alpha source is never used because it would be quickly absorbed and cause damage.

Technium-99 is a gamma emitter often used for this purpose. It has a half-life of 6 hours. This gives the doctors enough time to detect the problem, but ensures that the chemical does not stay in the body for too long.

Example 2 – Industrial Tracers

Any leaks in a pipeline can be found by injecting a gamma-emitting isotope into the system. The tracer will leak out into the soil where the pipe is broken. Because of the penetrating nature of gamma rays, the leak will be easy to detect through several feet of soil.

A short half-life radioisotope is used so that it does not remain in the environment any longer than is necessary after the leak has been detected.

Example 3 – Controlling the Thickness of Materials

Radiation is absorbed by material through which it passes. This effect can be used to monitor the thickness of materials in production. Beta rays can be used to control the thickness of paper, and gamma rays can be used to control the thickness of metal.

Radiation	Use	Suitability
Gamma	Medical and industrial tracers.	Can pass out of the body or pipeline easily. Short half-life so does not stay in the body or environment for long.
	Controlling the thickness of metal.	Passes through thin metals, but is absorbed by heavier metals, e.g. lead.
Beta	Medical tracers.	Easily transferred out of the body.
	Controlling the thickness of paper.	Passes through paper but is absorbed by thin metals.
Alpha	Medical tracers.	Unable to transfer out of the body, would be quickly absorbed and cause damage – never used.
	Controlling the thickness of paper.	Absorbed by paper, so cannot be detected.

13.7

What do we know about the origins of the Universe and how it continues to change?

Current evidence suggests that the Universe started from a 'big bang' at a small point, from which mass and space expanded violently and rapidly, and is still expanding. To understand this, you need to know...

• how we study the Universe
• about red shift and how it supports the 'big bang' theory.

Observing the Universe

Observations of the Universe can be carried out from space or on Earth. One method of observation is to use a telescope.

Different types of telescope can detect visible light or other electromagnetic radiations, e.g. radio waves or X-rays.

Reflecting Telescopes

This type of telescope reflects light using mirrors.

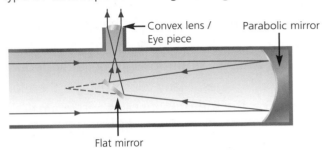

Refracting Telescopes

This telescope refracts light at each end using lenses.

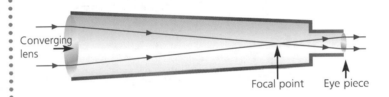

Radio Telescopes

As the name suggests, these telescopes pick up radio waves instead of light waves. Radio waves are much longer than light waves, so to be able to receive good signals, radio telescopes need large antennas or arrays of smaller antennas working together.

The radio waves are emitted by bodies in space. Most radio telescopes use a parabolic dish to reflect the radio waves to a receiver, which detects and amplifies the signal.

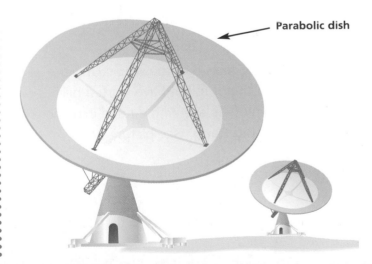

Physics Unit 1b

Using Telescopes

On Earth

Observing the Universe from the Earth is limited by the atmosphere. Interference from the atmosphere, clouds, weather storms or light pollution reduces the quality of images. Many telescopes are therefore placed on the top of mountains and in areas with low levels of pollution to reduce interference.

In Space

Putting telescopes into space so that they orbit the Earth outside the atmosphere means the images produced are not affected by atmospheric interference, e.g. the Hubble Telescope (see p.107).

Red Shift

If a wave source is moving away from, or towards, an observer there will be a change in the observed wavelength and frequency.

If a source of light moves away from us, the wavelengths of the light in its spectrum are longer than if it was not moving. This is known as **red shift** because the wavelengths 'shift' towards the red end of the spectrum (see p.94).

There is a red shift in light observed from most distant galaxies, which means that they are moving away from us very quickly (see picture 1).

This effect is exaggerated in galaxies which are further away, which means that the further away a galaxy is, the faster it is moving away from us (see picture 2).

This evidence suggests that the whole Universe is expanding and that it might have started billions of years ago, from one place with a huge explosion, known as the '**Big Bang**' (see picture 3).

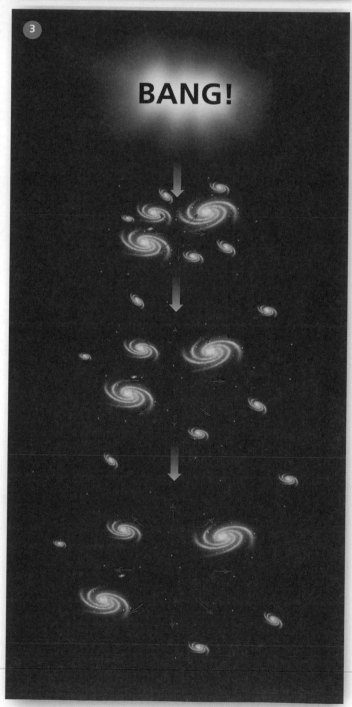

BANG!

How Science Works

You need to be able to compare and contrast the particular advantages and disadvantages of using different types of telescopes on Earth and in space to make observations of, and deductions about, the Universe.

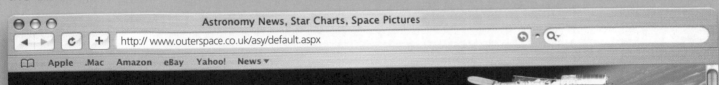

○ ○ ○   Astronomy News, Star Charts, Space Pictures

◀ ▶ C +   http:// www.outerspace.co.uk/asy/default.aspx   ⊙ ^ Q▾

📖   Apple   .Mac   Amazon   eBay   Yahoo!   News ▾

ABOUT ASTRONOMY

ASTRO FOR KIDS

THE STARRY SKY

THE SUN

MOONS AND PLANETS

METEORS

COMETS

THE AURORA

USING BINOCULARS

TELESCOPES

   ABOUT

   HOW TO USE

PHOTOGRAPHY

The main types of telescope used to observe the Universe from Earth are reflecting telescopes, refracting telescopes and radio telescopes.

Type	Advantages	Disadvantages
Reflecting Telescope	• Cheap. • Accurate colour representation.	• Limited to visible light. • Need cleaning and realigning frequently. • Poorer image quality than refracting telescope. • Produce inverted (upside down) images. • Bulky compared to refracting telescopes of same strength. • Can only be used at night.
Refracting Telescope	• Produce sharp, detailed images. • Portable. • Easy to maintain.	• Limited to visible light. • Images have a halo of false colours around them. • More expensive than reflecting telescopes. • Produce inverted images. • Can only be used at night.
Radio Telescope	• Unaffected by light so can be used 24 hours a day. • Can be used to accurately map the Universe. • Detect emissions of gas between stars that are not visible to the human eye.	• Require massive / multiple antenna. • Require a large, permanent site. • Very expensive to set up.

The Hubble Space Telescope belongs to a family of optical telescopes called catadioptrics. They use both mirrors and lenses to overcome a lot of the disadvantages associated with reflecting and refracting telescopes. They produce sharp, detailed images with accurate colours and they are smaller than reflectors and cheaper than refractors of the same strength.

In 1990, NASA went to great expense and risk to launch the Hubble Space Telescope. Within weeks of the launch, it became apparent that there were serious problems with the optical system. Although the first images appeared to be sharper than ground-based images, the telescope failed to achieve a final sharp focus. The problem was found to be a wrongly shaped mirror, which was replaced in 1993. Since then, the telescope has been visited regularly for servicing and updates. These visits are costly processes.

So, what are the advantages to science of having an optical telescope in space?

Optical Telescope in Space	Optical Telescope on Earth
Advantages • Can be used 24 hours a day. • Clear pictures as no light pollution, clouds or storms. **Disadvantages** • Very expensive to build, put up and maintain / repair. • Cannot focus on near objects.	**Advantages** • Cheaper to build, service and repair. **Disadvantages** • Can only be used at night and if skies are clear. • Has to be placed in a remote position due to light pollution.

Example Questions

If you are studying Specification A, you will have to complete a 30 minute objective test under exam conditions for each section (i.e. Physics 1a and Physics 1b). These consist of matching and multiple choice questions - see Questions 1 and 2 below.

If you are studying Specification B, you will have to complete a 45 minute written exam covering the whole of the unit (i.e. Physics 1), This will feature structured questions – see Question 3 below.

1 1   Every year large amounts of heat energy are lost from our homes.

Reducing this energy loss helps to cut energy bills and save money.

Which of these methods would not help to reduce heat loss from the home?

A Installing double glazing. .... ☐

B Installing a fire guard. .... ☑

C Fitting roof insulation. .... ☐

D Fitting draught excluders. .... ☐ *(1 mark)* ①

2 2   Gamma rays can be hazardous to humans.

Which statement describes why they are dangerous?

A Gamma rays can penetrate the body and be absorbed by organs. .... ☑

B Gamma rays kill cancer cells. .... ☐

C Gamma rays cannot pass through paper. .... ☐

D Gamma rays cannot get out of the body. .... ☐ *(1 mark)* ①

3 3 a) What causes a turbine in a fossil fuel power station to turn?

Fuel is burnt to heat water, producing steam which turns the turbine.

(1 mark)

4 b) Two resources that can be used to generate electricity are nuclear fuel and wind. In the table below, give one advantage and one disadvantage for each resource used to generate electricity.

Nuclear Fuel	Wind
Advantage	**Advantage**
Flexible in meeting demand.	No pollutant gases produced.
Disadvantage	**Disadvantage**
Produces radioactive waste.	Produces small amounts of electricity.

5

(4 marks) ③

① Read the question carefully. If you missed the word 'not' you would get this simple question wrong!

② If you are unsure about the answer to a multiple-choice question, eliminate the options that are obviously wrong or not relevant to the question first.

③ The amount of space and number of marks available is a clue to how much information you need to provide. This question requires a short, succinct answer.

④ Make sure you answer all the questions in full. This question requires four responses in total (an advantage and a disadvantage for two different methods).

⑤ Where there are several possible answers, choose one that you are certain is correct.

Key Words

Atom – the smallest part of an element that displays the chemical properties of the element

Conductor – a substance that readily transfers heat or energy

Current – the flow of electric charge through a conductor

Efficiency – the ratio of energy output to energy input, expressed as a percentage

Energy – the ability to do work, measured in joules

Half-life – the time taken for half the atoms in radioactive material to decay

Ions – a charged particle formed when an atom gains or loses electrons

Isotope – atoms of the same element but with a different number of neutrons

Kilowatt – a unit for measuring power, equal to 1000 watts

Kilowatt hour – the amount of electrical energy used by a 1 kilowatt device in 1 hour

Non-renewable – energy sources that cannot be replaced in a lifetime

Power – the rate of doing work, measured in watts

Reflection – a wave (e.g. light or sound) that is thrown back from a surface

Refraction – the change in direction of a wave as it passes from one medium to another

Renewable – energy sources that can be replaced

Telescope – a device that magnifies distant images

Thermal energy – heat energy

Transfer – to move energy from one place to another

Transform – to change energy from one form into another, e.g. electrical energy to heat energy

Transformer – an electrical device used to change the voltage of alternating currents

Transmission – the sending of information or electricity over a communications line or a circuit

Voltage – potential difference, expressed in volts

How Science Works Key Words

Here are the words that might be used in your test / exam, with a definition so you know exactly what you are being asked.

Accuracy – how correct or exact something is. The more times you repeat an experiment, the closer the average value (mean) of the results will be to the true value.

Analyse – look at in detail

Apply – relate to, put to practical use

Calculate – work out

Consider – think about

Construct – make, put together

Contrast – look at the differences between

Describe – put into words

Determine – decide, conclude

Discuss – talk about

Evaluate – determine the worth of

Evidence – results of an experiment or facts that you can use to prove or disprove a theory

Explain – put into words

Fair test – a test where conditions are controlled so no factors other than the one you are changing / controlling have an effect on what is being measured

Impact (social, economic, environmental) – an effect

Informed judgements – a balanced view based on information

Interpret – explain the meaning of

Precision – exactness, only a small spread / range of results

Predict – make a good guess at what you expect to happen

Recognise – notice, accept or be aware of

Relate – make a connection to something (like a real life situation or other experiments, etc.)

Reliability – dependability of the results, based on how accurate the measuring instruments are

Sketch – a drawing

Suggest reasons for – think of possible reasons for

Theory – an idea about what will happen

Variables – something that changes during the course of an investigation

Independent variable – the variable you change and have control over

Dependent variable – the variable (output) you measure

Index

A

Accuracy 10-11
Adaptations 34-36
Additives 71-72
Alcohol 24, 65, 68
Alkanes 63
Alkenes 65
Alloys 57-58
Alpha particles 99-104
Alternating current (ac) 94
Aluminium 59
Analogue signals 96
Antibiotics 30, 32
Antibodies 30
Asexual reproduction 37-38
Atmosphere 76-77, 79
Atoms 52

B

Bacteria 30-33
Beta particles 99-104
Big bang 106
Blood sugar 16
Brain 14-15

C

Cannabis 27
Cell cloning 38
Chemical
    analysis 71
    bonds 52
    equations 53-54
    formulae 53
    reactions 53
Cholesterol 20, 25
Chromatography 71
Chromosomes 37
Cloning 38, 40
Competition 34, 36, 41
Compounds 52
Conclusions 7, 12
Conduction 82-83
Conscious action 15
Continental drift 74, 78
Convection 82-83
Copper 59
Cracking (hydrocarbons) 65
Creationism 42
Crude oil 62, 68

D

Darwin, Charles 42
Data 8
Deforestation 45
Diet 19-22
Digital signals 96
Disease 30, 41
Distribution (of organisms) 36
DNA 37
Drugs 23-29

E

Earth (structure of) 73
Economic issues 12
Electromagnetic waves 94-98
Electrical devices 84-86, 88

Electricity 84-93
Electrons 52, 99
Elements 52
Embryo transplants 38
Endangered species 46
Energy 82-93
Environment 41, 44-49
Environmental issues 12
Ethical issues 12
Evaluation 12-13
Evidence 7
Evolution 41-43
Exercise 19
Extinction 41

F

Fair Test 10
Fats 20
Fertility 16, 18
Fossil fuels 89-90
Fossils 41, 43
Fractional distillation 62
FSH 16, 18
Fuels 62-64, 72

G

Gamma radiation 99-104
Gamma rays 94-95
Genes 37
Genetics 37-40
Greenhouse effect 45

H

Habitat 36
Half-life 101, 104
Heat 82-83
Hormones 16
How Science Works
    6-13, 17-18, 21-22, 25-29,
    31-33, 35-36,40 ,42-43,
    47-50, 56, 60-61, 64, 68-69,
    72, 78-79
Hydrocarbons 62-66
Hypotheses 8

I

Illegal drugs 24, 26
Immune system 30
Immunity 30, 32-33
Infra red rays 94-95
Intelligent design 42
Internal conditions 16
Investigations 7-10
Ions 16, 99
Iron 57
Isotopes 99
IVF 18

J

Joules (J) 86

L

Lamarck's Theory 42
LH 16
Limestone 55-56
Lipoproteins 20

M

Malnourishment 19
Margarine 71
Measurements 7, 11
Metabolic rate 19
Metals 57-61
Microwaves 94-95, 97
Minerals 57

N

Natural selection 41-42
Nervous system 14-15
Neurones 14-15
Neutrons 52, 99
Non-renewable energy sources
    89-90, 93
Nuclear fuel 89-90, 93
Nuclei 52, 99
Observations 7-8
Oestrogen 16
Optical fibres 96
Ores 57, 60
Ovaries 16

P

Pathogens 30
Periodic table 52, 59
Pituitary gland 16
Plant cuttings 38
Plant oils 70
Plastics 67-68
Pollution 44, 47-48
Polymers 65-68
Population explosion 44
Power 86, 88
Precision 10
Predation 41
Presenting data 7, 11
Protons 52, 99

R

Radiation 82-83, 94, 99-104
Radio waves 94-95
Radioactivity 99-104
Receptors 14-15
Red-shift 106
Reflection 94
Reflex action 15
Refraction 94
Reliable 7
Renewable energy sources 91-93
Reproduction 37-38

S

Salt 20
Science 7, 12-13
Semmelweiss, Ignaz 31
Sexual reproduction 37
Smart alloys 58, 61
Social issues 12
Spinal chord 14-15
Sports drinks 17
Statins 25
Steel 57-58
Stimuli 15
Sustainable development
    45-46, 49

Synapse 14

T

Tectonic plates 73-65, 78
Telescopes 105-107
Temperature (body) 16
Thalidomide 23
Thermal energy 82-83
Tissue culture 38
Titanium 59
Tobacco 24, 28-29
Transition metals 59

U

Ultraviolet rays 94-95, 98
Universe 105-107

V

Vaccination 30, 32-33
Valid 7
Variables 9
Variation 37
Vegetable oils 70, 72
Viruses 30-33
Visible light 94-95

W

Water content 16
Watts (w) 86
Wegener, Alfred 74, 78
White blood cells 30
Wood 89

X

X-rays 94-95

Periodic Table

Key

Mass number

$\uparrow$

1
H
hydrogen
1

Atomic number (Proton number)

Group	1	2											3	4	5	6	7	0
																		4 **He** helium 2
	7 **Li** lithium 3	9 **Be** beryllium 4											11 **B** boron 5	12 **C** carbon 6	14 **N** nitrogen 7	16 **O** oxygen 8	19 **F** fluorine 9	20 **Ne** neon 10
	23 **Na** sodium 11	24 **Mg** magnesium 12											27 **Al** aluminium 13	28 **Si** silicon 14	31 **P** phosphorus 15	32 **S** sulfur 16	35.5 **Cl** chlorine 17	40 **Ar** argon 18
	39 **K** potassium 19	40 **Ca** calcium 20	45 **Sc** scandium 21	48 **Ti** titanium 22	51 **V** vanadium 23	52 **Cr** chromium 24	55 **Mn** manganese 25	56 **Fe** iron 26	59 **Co** cobalt 27	59 **Ni** nickel 28	63.5 **Cu** copper 29	65 **Zn** zinc 30	70 **Ga** gallium 31	73 **Ge** germanium 32	75 **As** arsenic 33	79 **Se** selenium 34	80 **Br** bromine 35	84 **Kr** krypton 36
	85 **Rb** rubidium 37	88 **Sr** strontium 38	89 **Y** yttrium 39	91 **Zr** zirconium 40	93 **Nb** niobium 41	96 **Mo** molybdenum 42	[98] **Tc** technetium 43	101 **Ru** ruthenium 44	103 **Rh** rhodium 45	106 **Pd** palladium 46	108 **Ag** silver 47	112 **Cd** cadmium 48	115 **In** indium 49	119 **Sn** tin 50	122 **Sb** antimony 51	128 **Te** tellurium 52	127 **I** iodine 53	131 **Xe** xenon 54
	133 **Cs** caesium 55	137 **Ba** barium 56	139 **La*** lanthanum 57	178 **Hf** hafnium 72	181 **Ta** tantalum 73	184 **W** tungsten 74	186 **Re** rhenium 75	190 **Os** osmium 76	192 **Ir** iridium 77	195 **Pt** platinum 78	197 **Au** gold 79	201 **Hg** mercury 80	204 **Tl** thallium 81	207 **Pb** lead 82	209 **Bi** bismuth 83	[209] **Po** polonium 84	[210] **At** astatine 85	[222] **Rn** radon 86
	[223] **Fr** francium 87	[226] **Ra** radium 88	[227] **Ac*** actinium 89	[261] **Rf** rutherfordium 104	[262] **Db** dubnium 105	[266] **Sg** seaborgium 88	[264] **Bh** bohrium 107	[277] **Hs** hassium 108	[268] **Mt** meitnerium 109	[271] **Ds** darmstadtium 110	[272] **Rg** roentgenium 111							

Elements with atomic numbers 112–116 have been reported but not fully authenticated

*The Lanthanides (atomic numbers 58–71) and the Actinides (atomic numbers 90–103) have been omitted.

Cu and **Cl** have not been rounded to the nearest whole number.

The lines of elements going across are called periods.

The columns of elements going down are called groups.